Taking Property and Just Compensation

Recent Economic Thought Series

Editor:
Warren G. Samuels
Michigan State University
East Lansing, Michigan, U.S.A.

Other books in the series:

Feiwel, G.: Samuelson and Neoclassical Economics
Wade, L.: Polltical Economy: Modern Views
Zimbalist, A.: Comparative Economic Systems: Recent Views
Darity, W.: Labor Economics: Modern Views
Jarsulic, M.: Money and Macro Policy
Samuelson, L.: Microeconomic Theory
Bromley, D.: Natural Resource Economics: Policy Problems and Contemporary Analysis
Mirowski, P.: The Reconstruction of Economic Theory
Field, A.: The Future of Economic History
Lowry, S.: Pre-Classical Economic Thought
Officer, L.: International Economics
Asimakopulos, A.: Theories of Income Distribution
Earl, P.: Psychological Economics; Development, Tensions, Prospects
Thweatt, W.: Classical Political Economy
Peterson, W.: Market Power and the Economy
DeGregori, T.: Development Economics
Nowotny, K.: Public Utility Regulation
Horowitz, I.: Decision Theory
Mercuro, N.: Law and Economics
Hennings, K. and Samuels, W.: Neoclassical Economic Theory, 1870 to 1930
Samuels, W.: Economics as Discourse
Lutz, M.: Social Economics
Weimer, D.: Policy Analysis and Economics
Bromley, D. and Segerson, K.: The Social Response to Environmental Risk
Roberts, B. and Feiner, S.: Radical Economics

Taking Property and Just Compensation

Law and Economics Perspectives of the Takings Issue

Edited by
Nicholas Mercuro
University of New Orleans

Kluwer Academic Publishers
Boston / Dordrecht / London

Distributors for North America:
Kluwer Academic Publishers
101 Philip Drive
Assinippi Park
Norwell, Massachusetts 02061 USA

Distributors for all other countries:
Kluwer Academic Publishers Group
Distribution Centre
Post Office Box 322
3300 AH Dordrecht, THE NETHERLANDS

Library of Congress Cataloging-in-Publication Data
Taking property and just compensation: law and economics perspectives of the takings issue/edited by Nicholas Mercuro.
p. cm. — (Recent economic thought series)
Includes bibliographical references and index.
ISBN 0-7923-9233-7
1. Eminent domain—United States. 2. Compensation (Law)—United States. I. Mercuro, Nicholas. II. Series.
KF5599.A75T35 1992
343.73'0252—dc20
[347.303252] 92-6061
CIP

Printed on acid-free paper.

Printed in the United States of America

Contents

Contributors

Robin Paul Malloy
College of Law
Syracuse University
E.I. White Hall
Syracuse, NY 13244-1030

Steven G. Medema
Department of Economics
Campus Box 181
University of Colorado at Denver
P.O. Box 173364
Denver, CO 80217

Nicholas Mercuro
Department of Economics and Finance
University of New Orleans
New Orleans, LA 70148

Gary Minda
Brooklyn Law School
250 Joralemon St.
Brooklyn, NY 11201

Susan Rose-Ackerman
Yale Law School
Yale Station
New Haven, CT 06520

Charles K. Rowley
Center for Study of Public Choice
George Mason University
Fairfax, VA 22030

Thomas S. Ulen
College of Law
University of Illinois at Urbana-Champaign
504 East Pennsylvania Ave.
Champaign, IL 61820

Taking Property and Just Compensation

1 THE TAKINGS ISSUE: A CONTINUING DILEMMA IN LAW AND ECONOMICS

Nicholas Mercuro

When do regulations of property amount to a taking of that property such that under the taking clause of the Fifth Amendment we are required to compensate the individuals thus regulated? And when do regulations amount simply to an exercise of the police power, requiring no compensation to those regulated?—Pilon (1988; p. 153)

1. Introduction

Taken together, these two questions constitute the takings issue, an issue that has been raised with respect to the development of land-use regulations in the United States for more than 100 years. It is an issue that continues to attract the attention of legal scholars and economists.

The origin of the regulatory, land-use takings issue can be traced back to the early nineteenth century when the United States was attempting to develop a large-scale transportation system.[1] Much of the early development of turnpikes, canals, and railroads was accomplished under the power of eminent domain, either by public entities or by private franchises granted the power of eminent domain. Initially, compensation was broadly required for the taking of legal interests of those persons whose property was somehow injured consequent to a state appropriation of their rights. Towards the mid-1800s, with the emerging conceptualization of property as a physical object—and the attendant narrowing of the definition of compensable takings—compensation was generally denied for all but physical appropriations. Thus, state-sponsored development largely proceeded along a noncompensable tract (Reznik 1973, pp. 854–858).

In the second half of the 1800s the issue changed as the United States began to be confronted with the economic consequences of (1) urbanization and (2) the continued development of its rapidly expanding transportation system. Policy makers were searching for a means to direct and control—for the government to regulate—the forces of private economic development and urban growth. It was recognized at that time that the problems associated with urbanization and expanding transportation systems could be attacked only retrospectively if reliance were left exclusively to the legal remedy of nuisance law. Planners and regulators, not wanting to rely on a retrospective remedy, recognized that what was needed was a prospective remedy—namely, police power regulations (Reznick 1973, pp. 858–866).

By the mid-1800s, it was generally recognized in law that a legal basis for regulation existed either under (1) the concept of overruling necessity—permitting regulations without compensation under the doctrine "the welfare of the people is the supreme law"—or (2) the charter-based system of police regulation—the basis for promulgating regulations directed at traditional, narrow common-law nuisance categories.[2]

In several state cases (from 1826–1831), under the principle that "no man should use his property so as to injure that of his neighbor," government regulations were typically upheld and compensation denied.[3] However, recognition of a prospective remedy was still needed to attend to the problem of urbanization. As Reznick observed:

> The concept of overruling necessity was limited, however, to extreme situations; the concept of police regulation was still closely tied to the narrow nuisance law both in its focus on existing nuisances and in its inability to reach any activities that had not traditionally been viewed as nuisances. In its traditional form, therefore, police regulation could not meet the need for legislative authority to deal prospectively with numerous small incidents that cumulatively threatened the public interest. (Reznick 1973, p. 863)

It was in 1846 that the Supreme Judicial Court of Massachusetts handed down its decision in *Commonwealth v. Tewksbury*. In that decision the court more directly addressed the issue regarding the applicability of constitutional limitations on takings to exercises of the regulatory power. The rule annunciated by the court was that regulation of uses was not considered a taking, but rather a legitimate legislative determination to restrain uses inconsistent with or injurious to the rights of the public.

Some five years later, the same Massachusetts court, in its landmark ruling in *Commonwealth v. Alger* (1851), reaffirmed the legitimacy of police power regulation. In *Alger*, the court was careful to distinguish between compensable exercises of the eminent domain power where the taking was for public benefit versus the uncompensated police power regulations promulgated by legislative bodies intended to restrain injurious private use by the owner (Bosselman, Callies, and Banta 1973, pp. 110–114). Thus, the state courts established a police power that would enable the legislature to pass regulations to deal prospectively with the many issues arising due the economic growth and urbanization.

The U.S. Supreme Court became active in taking issue cases in 1871. In the early decisions of the Court, no clear pattern emerged (Bosselman, Callies, and Banta 1973, p. 117). However, some have argued that a series of cases adjudicated in the state courts and subsequently in the U.S. Supreme Court had the effect of dampening both the police power and the power of eminent domain. In several cases, the previous narrow doctrine of compensation was legislatively altered in an attempt to prevent overuse of the police power. At the same time, courts began to return to a broadened definition as to which government actions constituted compensable takings under eminent domain (Reznick 1973, pp. 886–887).

It was not until 1887 that the U.S. Supreme Court provided a definitive explication of the distinction between the police power and the power of eminent domain. In the case of *Mugler v. Kansas* the Court stated that "a prohibition simply upon use of property for purposes that are declared, by valid legislation, to be injurious to the health, morals, or safety of the community, cannot, in any just sense, be deemed a taking or an appropriation of property for the public benefit. . . . In the one case, the nuisance only is abated; in the other, unoffending property is taken away from an innocent owner" (*Mugler v. Kansas* 1887, pp. 668–669). The Supreme Court's analysis rested on the principle that all property in the United States was held under the implied obligation that the owner's use of its shall not to be injurious to the community. Consequently, those restrictions that were designed to protect the general public and were enacted pursuant to the state's police power could not be invalidated simply because they interfered with or even destroyed some property interests.

Subsequent to the court's ruling in *Mugler*, the police power (now conceptually distinct from eminent domain) was construed to be quite broad and was extended well beyond simple nuisance prevention. Under the doctrine annunciated in *Mugler*, little weight was given to the impact of police power regulations on property owners. The extent to which the definition of property was associated with and limited to physical objects, then police power regulations were generally, upheld notwithstanding the fact that the rights of owners were being attenuated (Reznick 1973, p. 871).

The doctrine annunciated in *Mugler* remained in place until 1922. In that year, Justice Holmes, in ruling in *Pennsylvania Coal Co. v. Mahon*, first annunciated the continuum of appropriation theme for the U.S. Supreme Court. Justice Holmes wrote:

> Government hardly could go on if to some extent values incident to property could not be diminished without paying for every such change in the general law. As long recognized, some values are enjoyed under an implied limitation and must yield to the police power. But obviously the implied limitation must have its limits, or the contract and due process clauses are gone. One fact for consideration in determining such limits is the extent of the diminution. When it reaches a certain magnitude, in most if not in all cases there must be an exercise of eminent domain and compensation to sustain the act. . . . So the question depends upon the particular facts. The general rule at least is that while property may be regulated to a certain extent, if regulation goes too far it will be recognized as a taking. (*Pennsylvania Coal Co. v. Mahon* 1922, pp. 159, 161)

In effect, the Holmes' approach put the police power on a continuum with the power of eminent domain—exceeding the former would necessarily result in an exercise of the latter.

Since 1922, Holmes' general rule has purportedly helped guide the courts in making determinations as to whether police power regulations constitute a taking in violation of the Fifth Amendment of the U.S. Constitution. As of today, the case has been cited in the state and federal courts just under 100,000 times (Freilich and Carlisle 1988, p. 9-2). However, almost 40 years after the annunciation of the Holmes' rule, in commenting on the jurisprudence of takings litigation, Allison Dunham in 1962 observed that "the judgments . . . appear to make up a crazy-quilt pattern of Supreme Court Doctrine," that "there are no specific constitutional limitations," and "that there are floundering and differences among judges and among generations of judges" (Dunham 1962, pp. 63–65, 105).

In the years since Dunham described the jurisprudence of takings litigation, three related events have taken place. First, the U.S. Supreme Court handed down several takings issue decisions initially in the late 1970s, then early in the 1980s, and then again the so-called "blockbuster cases" in the 1987 term (Freilich and Carlislie 1988). In addition, not long after the court's rulings in the 1987 cases and directly attributable to them, President Reagan issued an Executive Order entitled *Governmental Actions and Interference with Constitutionally Protected Property Rights* (Executive Order 1988).

The second event to take place could be expected. With the rise of the several Fifth Amendment takings issue cases, many legal scholars analyzed and commented on these cases from their traditional mode of doctrinal analyses and discourse. The result was a prodigious body of legal analysis of the several taking issue cases, albeit doctrinal in nature.

Finally, during these same intervening years, several schools of thought that have come to comprise the law and economics field were emerging. These schools of thought now include the new law and economics, public choice theory, institutionalist law and economics, the legal reformist school, critical legal studies, and classical-liberal, political economy.[4]

While much has been gained from the traditional legal scholars' doctrinal mode of analysis of the takings issue, we have decided to pursue the law and economics approach in a further attempt to explicate the takings issue. Given the decline of law as an autonomous discipline (Posner 1987) and given that, as a consequence, law is beginning to look outward (Minow 1987), this book is presented in the belief that contributions from scholars from the various schools of thought that comprise law and economics can compliment the traditional doctrinal approach of law and perhaps help bring about a deeper understanding of the jurisprudential questions and economic issues surrounding the takings issue.

To this end, each contributor to this book was selected as "representative" of one of the schools of thought comprising law and economics. In addition, each contributor was provided with a collection of recent U.S. Supreme Court cases (those summarized in section 2 below) along with President Reagan's Executive Order. The charge to each contributor was to conduct a legal-economic analysis of the cases (plus additional cases if so desired) and the President's Executive Order from the vantage point of their respective school of thought.

We recognize that not all law and economics scholars will agree with the schools of thought as delineated above. Nor are they necessarily likely to concur with the legal-economic analysis set forth by the "representative" of their school of thought. Nonetheless, as the discipline of law and economics continues to advance, it remains heterodox; there are several vantage points from which to describe and analyze the interrelationships between the two disciplines. It is hoped that the analyses from the several vantage points provided here will compliment the prodigious body of existing doctrinal, legal analysis of the takings issue and deepen its understanding.

As will become evident after a complete reading of the following chapters, in many respects it appears we may *not* have come a very long way from Dunham's assessment that "this area of jurisprudence appears to make up a crazy-quilt pattern of Supreme Court Doctrine." Medema, quoting Bruce Ackerman, observed that existing takings law could be labelled "a chaos of confused argument" (Medema, in this book). Furthermore, in his chapter, Minda, commenting on the Justices Holmes, Brandeis, and Stevens opinions, wrote: "When seen in the light of legal dialectic established by Holmes and Brandeis in *Mahon*, modern decisions such as *Keystone* evoke an ironic sense of *deja vu*" (Minda, in this book). On the other hand, a careful review of the Supreme Court cases used here as our vehicle of analysis suggests that perhaps the Supreme Court justices, in hearing and deciding, these cases, confronted what may be termed *vuja de*—the eerie feeling that comes over you when *none* of this looks familiar.

2. Review of the Cases[5]

Penn Central Transportation Company v. The City of New York, 1978

In 1965, New York City adopted its Landmarks Preservation Law, an act intended to protect historic landmarks and neighborhoods. Under the Act, the Landmarks Preservation Commission (an 11-member agency) was empowered to designate a building to be a landmark. Upon such designation, the owner would have to (1) maintain the building in good repair and (2) have any proposed alterations or extensions to the building be approved by the Commission in advance.

In 1967, the Grand Central Terminal, which was owned by the Penn Central Transportation Company, was designated a "landmark" and the block it occupies was designated a "landmark site." Grand Central Terminal is an eight-story structure that Penn Central uses as a railroad station and leases space to commercial interests. In early 1968, Penn Central entered into a renewable 50-year lease with UGP Properties, Inc. Under the agreement, UGP was to construct a multistory office building (a 55-story tower) above the terminal. (A 20-story office tower, part of the original building's design, was never constructed.) In return, UGP promised to pay Penn Central $1 million a year during construction and thereafter $3 million annually. Two plans were presented to the Commission for review along with applications for "certificates" for permission to go ahead with the project. Each plan was found deficient by the Commission but for different reasons, and the certificates were denied.

Under the procedures set forth under the Landmarks Law, Penn Central/UGP could have sought judicial review of the denial of the certificates. They chose not to and instead filed suit in the New York Supreme Court (Trial Term) claiming that the application of the Landmarks Preservation Law had taken their property without just compensation in violation of the Fifth and Fourteenth Amendments to the U.S. Constitution. Penn Central/UGP sought both (1) declaratory, injunctive relief barring New York City from using the Landmarks Law to prevent construction of the tower and (2) monetary damages for the "temporary taking" that occurred between the date the terminal was declared a historic landmark and the date the restrictions arising from the Landmarks Law would be voided. The trial court granted the injunctive relief but severed the question of monetary damages.

On appeal, the New York Supreme Court (Appellate Division) reversed, holding that the restrictions on the development of Penn Central Terminal were necessary to promote the public purpose of protecting landmarks. The Court ruled that while Penn Central had succeeded in showing that they had been deprived of the property's most profitable use, they had not been unconstitutionally deprived of their property. The New York Court of Appeals affirmed summarily, rejecting any claim that the Landmarks Law had taken property without just compensation.

The U.S. Supreme Court affirmed the New York Court of Appeals decision. In reaffirming that no taking had occurred, the Court rejected various arguments set forth by Penn Central/UGP. The Court concluded that while the restrictions inherent in the Landmarks Law might reduce the economic value of the property, the U.S. Supreme Court had uniformly rejected the proposition that diminution in property value, standing alone, could establish a taking. The Court also found no merit in either Penn Central/UGP's arguments that the Landmarks Law deprived them of the use of the "air rights" above the terminal, or their argument that the Landmarks Law applied only to individuals who owned "selected" properties. As to the former, the Court noted it had consistently restricted the development of air rights, and, as to the latter, it recognized that the law was comprehensive and designed to preserve all historic structures wherever they were found in the city.

The Supreme Court went on to reject two additional claims by Penn Central/UGP. The first claim was that the commission's designation of a building as a landmark was an arbitrary or subjective decision. The Court suggested that this issue should have been raised in the judicial review procedure earlier eschewed by Penn Central/UGP. The second claim argued that the Landmark Law did not impose identical restrictions on all structures in a particular physical settings. As the Supreme Court observed, such legislation often results in differential impacts on various owners—that does not constitute a taking. The U.S. Supreme Court concluded that New York City's Landmarks Preservation Law did not affect a taking of Penn Central/UGP's rights.

Keystone Bituminous Coal Association v. DeBenedictis, 1987

Throughout the 20th century, the State of Pennsylvania had passed several laws and regulations that attempted to minimize the amount of mine subsidence (the lowering of land surface caused by the extraction of underground coal) in the State of Pennsylvania. In 1966 the Pennsylvania legislature recognized that the commonwealth's existing mine subsidence legislation had failed to protect the public interest with respect to land conservation, preservation of tax bases, and land development. Consequently, in 1966 Pennsylvania passed the Bituminous Mine Subsidence and Land Conservation Act, an act designed to diminish subsidence and subsidence damage in the vicinity of certain structures and specific areas. The act authorized the Pennsylvania Department of Environmental Resources to implement and enforce a comprehensive program to prevent or minimize subsidence and to regulate its consequences. Section 4 of the act prohibited mining that caused subsidence damage to three categories of pre-existing structures: public buildings, dwellings used for human habitation, and cemeteries. Since 1966 the Department of Environmental Resources had applied a formula that generally required 50 percent of the coal beneath structures protected by Section 4 to be kept in place as a means for providing surface support.

Section 6 of the act authorized the Department of Environmental Resources to revoke a mining permit if (1) the removal of coal causes damage to a structure or area protected by Section 4, and (2) the operator has not either repaired the damage or deposited a sum of money with the Department of Environmental Resources equal to the reasonable cost of repair.

In 1982, an association of coal mine operators and four corporations filed suit in the U.S. District Court seeking to enjoin officials of the Department of Environmental Resources from enforcing the Subsidence Act and the implementation of the associated regulations. The four corporations and coal mine operators alleged that both Section 4 of the Subsidence Act as implemented by the "50 percent rule" and Section 6 of the Subsidence Act constituted taking of their private property without compensation in violation of the Fifth Amendment of the U.S. Constitution.

It should be noted that Pennsylvania's land tenure system permits the right of support (to prevent subsidence) to be separated from the ownership from surface rights and mineral rights. Consequently, most surface landowners in the state's coal mining areas did not have the right of support. Previous owners of the land either sold it to the mining companies or the mining companies did not transfer it when they sold surface rights. Thus, in effect, the Pennsylvania Act required underground coal miners to leave pillars of coal in place to support structures owned by others on the surface. Enforcement of the Pennsylvania Department of Environmental Resources' 50 percent rule would required the coal companies to leave approximately 27 million tons of coal in place. It is because they owned that coal but could no longer mine it that they contended that Pennsylvania's Subsidence Act had appropriated their rights without just compensation.

The U.S. District Court found that the restriction on the use of the coal operators' property was an exercise of the Commonwealth's police power, justified by Pennsylvania's interest in health, safety, and general welfare of the public. The coal operators alleged that Pennsylvania recognized three separate estates in land—the mineral estate, the surface estate, and the support estate—and that the support estate had been *entirely* destroyed by the act. In rejecting the petitioner's claim, the District Court concluded that the support estate consisted of a bundle of rights including some of which were not affected by the act.

On appeal, the U.S. Court of Appeals affirmed the lower court ruling, in deciding that the Subsidence Act was a legitimate means of protecting the environment of the Commonwealth, its economic future, and its wellbeing. The Court of Appeals also rejected the coal operators' argument that the support estate had been entirely destroyed. However, it did not rely on the fact that the support estate itself constitutes a bundle of many rights. Rather, the court of appeals concluded that the support estate was just one segment of a larger bundle of rights that included either the surface estate or the mineral estate.

In reviewing the Subsidence Act, the U.S. Supreme Court observed that the Pennsylvania legislature specifically found that important public interests were to be served by enforcing a policy that is designed to minimize subsidence in certain areas. It found that the Commonwealth of Pennsylvania was acting to protect the public interest in health, the environment, and the fiscal integrity of the area. With respect to these public interests, the Supreme Court noted that inasmuch as the District Court and the Court of Appeals were both convinced that the legislative purposes set forth in the statute were genuine, substantial, and legitimate, they (the Supreme Court) would have no reason to conclude otherwise.

The Supreme Court went on to restate its hesitancy to find a taking when the state merely attempts to restrain uses of property that are tantamount to public nuisances. The Court ruled that the Subsidence Act sought to advance the public interest by preventing activities similar to public nuisances.

The coal operators advanced two arguments to support their contention. First, they argued that the 27 million tons of coal that had to be left in place constituted a *separate segment of property* for takings law purposes. The Supreme Court ruled that the 27 million tons of coal that had to be left in place amounted to only 2 percent of the coal, and there was no basis for treating this 2 percent as a *separate* parcel of property. The Court concluded that there was no showing that petitioners' reasonable investment-backed expectations were materially affected by the additional duty to retain the small percentage of coal that must be used to support the structures protected by Section 4.

The coal operators' second argument was that the Subsidence Act had the consequence of destroying the entire value of their unique support estate. The Supreme Court recognized that Pennsylvania property law was unique in regarding the support estate as a separate interest in land that can be conveyed apart from either the mineral estate or the surface estate. Relying on the judgment in the court of appeals, the U.S. Supreme Court reafirmed that the support estate is always owned by either the owner of the surface or the owner of the minerals. Thus, as a practical matter, the support estate had value only insofar as it protects or enhances the value of the surface or the mineral estate with which it is associated. Its value was merely a part of the entire bundle of rights possessed by the owner of either the coal or the surface. The Court concluded by stating that because the coal operators retained the right to mine virtually all of the coal in their mineral estates, the burden the act placed on the support estate did not constitute a taking. So stated, the Supreme Court ruled the Pennsylvania Bituminus Mine Subsidence and Land Conservation Act did not constitute a taking under the Fifth Amendment.

Hodel v. Irving, 1987

In the late 19th century, the U.S. Congress, as part of a series of land acts that intended to speed the assimilation of Indians into American society, adopted a statute (the General Allotment Act, 1887) authorizing, among other things, the allotment of specific tracts of reservation land to individual Indians. In 1889, Congress passed the Sioux Allotment Act (with similar provisions) directed at the Sioux Nation. After 1910, the individual reservation landowners were permitted to dispose of their tracts in accordance with regulations set forth by the U.S. Secretary of the Interior. Within 20 years, the allotment policy of individualizing tracts of land proved disastrous. Because of cumulative acts of sale, various leasing arrangements, and the fact that, since the land was held in trust and could not be partitioned, the tracts became owned by more and more individuals with each successive generation. Land ownership became splintered with multiple, undivided interests, resulting in the extreme fractionation of the tracts of Indian lands.

Government hearings took place, and various reports were issued from 1928 through 1966 attesting to the unworkable and economically wasteful allotment policy. It was not until 1983 that the U.S. Congress passed the Indian Land Consolidation Act. At issue was Section 207 of the act which provided that small, undivided, fractional individual property interests, that were unproductive during the year preceding the owners' death, would escheat to the tribe. Congress' aim was to make the Indians' ancestral lands more productive in future years. Three members of the Oglala Sioux Tribe were heirs to four former members of the tribe who died in 1983 and collectively owned 41 fractional interests. Were it not for Section 207 of the act, the property would have passed to the three members (2 units, 26 units, and 13 units, respectively). However, under the Consolidation Act, the 41 fractional interests would revert back to the tribe.

The three members of the tribe filed suit in the U.S. District Court for the District of South Dakota arguing that Section 207 constituted a taking of their rights without just compensation in violation of the Fifth Amendment. The district court found that Section 207 was constitutional, ruling that the three tribe members had no vested interests in the property of the four descendants prior to their death. On appeal, the U.S. Court of Appeals reversed, finding that the four tribe members had the right to control the disposition of their property at death (in accordance with the Sioux Allotment Statute).

The U.S. Supreme Court recognized that the exteme fractionation of Indian lands was a serious public problem and that the act that encouraged the consolidation of Indian lands was of a public purpose of high order. However, the Supreme Court also found that the character of the government regulation here to be "extraordinary." That is, the Court found that the Consolidation Act amounted to a virtual abrogation of the right to pass on a certain type of property to one's heirs. Thus, the Court stated that the regulation "goes too far" and affirmed the judgement of the U.S. Court of Appeals which concluded that the act constituted a taking and that the four descendants had a right, derived from the original Sioux Allotment Statutes, to control disposition of their property at death.

First English Evangelical Lutheran Church of Glendale v. The County of Los Angeles, California, 1987

In two earlier cases, *Agins v. the City of Tiburon, 1980* and *San Diego Gas and Electric Company v. the City of San Diego 1981*, the U.S. Supreme Court left open the question as to the proper remedy (monetary damages or declaratory, injunctive relief) for a landowner whose property had been taken by a regulatory ordinance. This issue was resolved in 1987 in *First English Evangelical Lutheran Church of Glendale v. the County of Los Angeles, California.*

San Diego Gas and Electric Company v. the City of San Diego, 1981. San Diego Gas acquired acreage in 1966 as a possible site for a nuclear power plant (412 acres). Approximately one-half of the acreage served as a drainage basin for three river systems. When acquired, the land was zoned for industrial or agricultural use.

In 1973, the San Diego City Council rezoned parts of the property, reducing the acreage for industrial use. Not long thereafter, the city established an open-space plan as part of a long-term state conservation plan which directly impacted the property acquired by San Diego Gas. In 1974, San Diego Gas and Electric filed an action in California Superior Court against the city, alleging that the city's rezoning and open-space plan constituted a taking of property without just compensation in violation of the takings clause of the Fifth Amendment. San Diego Gas sought damages of $6,150,000. The superior court found that a taking had in fact occurred, and a jury subsequently set the value of damages at $3 million.

On appeal, the California Court of Appeal affirmed the superior court's ruling. In July of 1978, the Supreme Court of California granted the City of San Diego's petition for a hearing (previously denied by the Court of Appeal). However, before the hearing began, in June of 1979 the California Supreme Court returned the case back to the California Court of Appeal in light of the recent ruling by the California Supreme Court in the *Agins* case.

Agins v. City of Tiburon, 1980. In 1968, Donald and Bonnie Agins purchased five acres of unimproved land for the purpose of residential development in Tiburon overlooking San Francisco. Subsequently, the City of Tiburon prepared an open-space comprehensive plan and adopted a zoning ordinance that, among other things, limited housing density. The Aginses sued the city, claiming the action constituted a taking of property without just compensation in violation of the Fifth Amendment of the U.S. Constitution. They sought a declaration that the ordinances were facially unconstitutional and $2 million in monetary damages in inverse condemnation.

In 1979, the California Supreme Court held that (1) the ordinance did allow the Aginses to construct between one and five residences, and (2) an owner temporarily deprived of substantially all beneficial use of his land by a zoning regulation was *not* entitled to an award of monetary damages in an inverse condemnation proceeding but, instead, had the exclusive remedy of an action for declaratory injunctive relief or a writ of mandamus. The California Supreme Court denied the Aginses any relief ruling that the Fifth Amendment did not require compensation as a remedy of "temporary" regulatory takings. That is, compensation would not be required unless the challenged regulation had been held excessive by the courts and the government had nevertheless decided to continue the regulation in effect.

In 1980 the U.S. Supreme Court ruled that the zoning ordinances substantially advanced legitimate government goals. They observed that there was no indication that the Aginses' five-acre tract was the only property affected by the ordinance. The Aginses, like other property owners, would share the benefits and burdens of the city's exercise of its police power. The Court ruled that in assessing the fairness of the zoning ordinances, the benefits must be considered along with any diminution in market value that the Aginses might suffer. In addition, the Aginses were free to pursue their reasonable investment expectations by submitting a development plan to local officials. The Court concluded that it could not be said that the impact of general land-use regulations had denied the Aginses the "justice and fairness" guaranteed by the Fifth and

Fourteenth Amendments. As to the issue regarding whether the Aginses could recover damages in inverse condemnation, the Court ruled that because no taking had occurred, the Court did not have to consider whether a state may limit the remedies available to a person whose land has come under a "temporary" regulatory taking.

San Diego Gas (*continued*). In the light of the Agins decision, once the case was remanded back to it, the California Court of Appeal reversed the Superior Court's decision and held that San Diego Gas could *not* recover monetary damages through inverse condemnation. However, neither did the court of appeal invalidate the zoning ordinance or the open-space plan that had impacted San Diego Gas. The court of appeal held that the record presented factual disputes not covered by the superior court and noted that declaratory relief might well be available if San Diego Gas desired to retry the case. The California Supreme Court denied further review.

The U.S. Supreme Court dismissed San Diego Gas's appeal, stating that while the California Court of Appeal had decided that monetary compensation was not a remedy, since there had not been a full hearing as to the facts, it could not be determined whether a taking in fact has occurred to occasion a judgment for declaratory injunctive relief.

First English Evangelical Lutheran Church of Glendale v. County of Los Angeles, California, 1987. In 1957 First English Evangelical Lutheran Church acquired 21 acres of land in the Los Angeles National Forest. The land was a natural drainage channel for a watershed area. The church operated a retreat and recreation center—Lutherglen—for handicapped children. The camp's buildings and the church were located on the flat land which took up about one-half of the camp's acreage.

Lutherglen operated for many years, but in 1978 (about six months after a forest fire denuded the hills upstream from the camp) a flood occurred, destroying all of the buildings of Lutherglen. Within one year, the County of Los Angeles adopted an interim ordinance prohibiting the (re)construction of any building in the flood protection area—an area that included the land upon which Lutherglen had once stood. The church promptly filed a complaint in California Superior Court, alleging that the ordinance denied the church *all* use of Lutherglen for a considerable period of years and (notwithstanding the Agins decision) sought to recover monetary damages in inverse condemnation for loss of use.

The Superior Court granted a motion to strike the allegation, basing its ruling on *Agins v. Tiburon* in which the California Supreme Court previously held that suits alleging regulatory takings are limited to nonmonetary relief. Because First English alleged a regulatory taking and sought monetary damages, the superior court deemed the allegation (that the ordinance denied all use of Lutherglen) to be irrelevant, having no bearing on the cause of action. The superior court reaffirmed *Agins* that the proper challenge to the ordinances was by way of declaratory relief.

On appeal, the California Court of Appeal affirmed the trial court's decision. The court felt obligated to follow *Agins* because the U.S. Supreme Court had not yet ruled on the question of whether a state may constitutionally limit the remedy for a taking to nonmonetary relief. The Supreme Court of California denied further review.

The U.S. Supreme Court concluded that the invalidation of an ordinance without the payment of fair value for use of the property during a period of time in which a landowner was denied use of the property under a regulatory ordinance (i.e., "temporary regulatory taking") was a constitutionally insufficient remedy for a taking. The Court ruled that the Fifth Amendment to the U.S. Constitution makes clear that it is designed not to limit the governmental interference with property rights per se, but rather to secure compensation in the event of otherwise proper interference amounting to a taking. Thus, where the government's activities had already worked a taking of all use of property, no subsequent action by the government could relieve it of the duty to provide monetary compensation for the period during which the taking was effective.

The Court went on to recognize that their present holding would undoubtedly lessen, to some extent, the freedom and flexibility of land-use planners and governing bodies of municipal corporations when enacting land-use regulations. But, they stated, such consequences necessarily flowed from any decision upholding a claim of constitutional right; many of the provisions of the U.S. Constitution were designed to limit the flexibility and freedom of governmental authorities, and the just compensation clause of the Fifth Amendment was one of them. So stated, the U.S. Supreme Court ruled that government action that works a taking of property rights necessarily implicates the constitutional obligation to pay just compensation.

Nollan v. the California Coastal Commission, 1987

The Nollans owned beachfront property in Ventura County, California. Their lot was located between two oceanside public park/beaches—to the north, Faria County Park and to the south, the Cove. The Nollans had a small bungalow on the property that fell into disrepair; they decided to demolish the building and replace it.

In order to do so, the California Public Resources Code required that they first get a permit from the California Coastal Commission. In February 1982, the Nollans submitted a permit application to the commission stating their said purpose. The commission recommended that the permit be granted subject to the condition that the Nollans provide lateral access to the public beaches in the form of an easement across their property (the beachfront portion). The lateral access would make it easier for the public to get to and from Faria County Park and the Cove.

The Nollans protested, but the commission overruled and granted the permit with the lateral access condition. The Ventura County Superior Court remanded the case to the commission for a full hearing. At the conclusion of the hearing, the commission subsequently reaffirmed its decision.

In the California Superior Court, the Nollans argued that the lateral access condition constituted a violation of the takings clause of the Fifth Amendment of the U.S. Consitution. The Superior Court ruled on the Nollans' behalf, finding that since there was nothing in the record to show that there would be an adverse impact on the public's access to the sea, the court directed the commission to strike the access condition from the permit. On appeal, the California Court of Appeal reversed the superior court's ruling, arguing that (1) the California Coastal Law requires the permit for construction to include the access condition and (2) although the access condition diminished the value of the Nollans' lot, it did not deprive them of all reasonable use of their property.

The case was appealed to the U.S. Supreme Court where the court found that when individuals are given a permanent and continuous right to pass to and from, so that the real property may continuously be traversed, even though no particular individual is permitted to station himself permanently upon the premisses, a permanent physical occupation has occurred. The Supreme Court took note that the commission believed that the public interest would have been served by a continuous strip of publicly accessible beach along the coast and that the commission may well have been right that it was a good idea. However, the Court concluded that, be that as it may, the Nollans (and other coastal residents) along could not be compelled to contribute to its realization. The U.S. Supreme Court stated that California was free to advance its comprehensive program if it wished by using its power of eminent domain for this public purpose. If it wants an easement across the Nollans' property, the court stated that "it must pay for it." The U.S. Supreme Court upheld the Nollans' claim, ruling that the California Coastal Commission could not, without paying compensation in eminent domain, impose the lateral access condition as part of the permission to rebuild.

Pennell v. City of San Jose, 1988

In 1979 the City of San Jose, California, enacted a rent control ordinance. Under the ordinance, the city may annually set a "reasonable rent" comprised of (1) an increase by as much as eight percent, plus (2) an increment based on seven factors that are reviewed by the Mediation Hearing Officer. If a tenant objects to a greater than eight percent increase in rent, a hearing is required before the hearing officer to determine whether the landlord's proposed increase is reasonable under the circumstances.

Of the seven factors to be considered, the first six factors were taken to be objective in that they were derived from (1) the history of the premises, (2) the landlord's costs of providing an adequate rental unit, and (3) the prevailing status of the rental market for comparable housing. Application of the first six factors resulted in an objective determination of a reasonable rent increase. The seventh factor included in the ordinance was termed "hardship to tenants." The law stated that, with respect to the incremental rent increase (beyond the eight percent statutory minimum), any tenant whose household income and monthly housing expenses met certain income requirements, would be deemed to be suffering from financial and economic hardship; such hardship must be considered in the hearing officer's determination of the incremental rate request. It was the potential denial of the incremental rent increase on grounds of the tenant's financial hardship that was at issue in this case. That is, the potential reduction of the rent increase below that which would otherwise be a reasonable rent (under the mechanism set up under the ordinance), was alleged to be a taking of property in violation of the Fifth and Fourteenth Amendments to the U.S. Constitution.

Richard Pennell (owner of 109 rental units) and the Tri-County, California, Apartment House Owner's Association sued in Superior Court of Santa Clara County seeking a declaration that the ordinance was, on its face, constitutionally invalid inasmuch as application of the tenant hardship clause violated the Fourteenth and Fifth Amendment's takings clause. They argued that the potential reduction (solely attributable to the application of the provision regarding the tenant's hardship), from what otherwise would have been a reasonable rent increase based on the other six specified factors, constituted a taking in that it transferred the landlord's property to individual hardship tenants.

The Superior Court of California entered a judgment on behalf of Pennell and the association. The California Court of Appeal affirmed the lower court's ruling. However, the Court of Appeal's decision was subsequently reversed by the Supreme Court of California which found the ordinance was not in violation the takings clause.

The U.S. Supreme Court noted that the ordinance made it mandatory to consider the hardship to the tenant. That is, under conditions specified in the ordinance and when requested by an aggrieved party, the hearing officer was required to consider the economic hardship imposed on the present tenant. If the proposed increase constituted an unreasonably severe financial or economic hardship, then the officer could order that the excess of the increase to be disallowed. However, the U.S. Supreme Court noted that there was no evidence that this provision had ever been used. Thus, the U.S. Supreme Court found the two lower courts' ruling to be premature.

However, the U.S. Supreme Court went on to consider the substantive merits of the case. In doing so, the Court recognized the legitimate goal of price regulation within the context of the police powers of the state. Specifically, it found the purpose of the ordinance—that of preventing unreasonable rent increases caused by the city's housing shortage—to be legitimate. And, the Court found the ordinance to represent a rational attempt to accommodate the conflicting interests of protecting tenants from burdensome rent increases while at the same time ensuring that landlords were guaranteed a fair return on their investment. The Court went on to find that the ordinance, which so carefully considered both the individual circumstances of the landlord and the tenant before determining whether to allow an additional increase in rent over and above certain amounts that are deemed reasonable, did not, on its face, violate the U.S. Constitution's Fifth and Fourteenth Amendments' prohibition against taking of private property for public use without just compensation.

Executive Order 12630—*Governmental Actions and Interference with Constitutionally Protected Property Rights*

The purpose of the President's Executive Order was to insure that future government actions were to be undertaken on a well-reasoned basis with due regard to the financial impact of the obligations imposed on the federal government by the just compensation clause of the Fifth Amendment of the U.S. Constitution. The Executive Order, in light of the recent Supreme Court decisions, made clear that governmental actions that did not formally invoke the condemnation power, including regulations, may result in a taking for which compensation is required. Under the Executive Order executive departments and agencies were called on to review their actions carefully to prevent unnecessary takings. The order also assisted federal department and agencies in undertaking such reviews by calling on the U.S. Attorney General to promulgate guidelines so that government decision makers could evaluate carefully the effect of their administrative, regulatory, and legislative actions. The order required government officials to be sensitive to anticipate and account for the obligations imposed by the just compensation clause of the Fifth Amendment and to plan and carry out governmental actions so that they did not result in the imposition of unanticipated or undue additional financial burdens on the public.

3. A Preview

Susan Rose-Ackerman finds that there is a lack of consistent, formal principals in takings law. She argues that the Supreme Court should move to articulate an orderly doctrinal jurisprudence: "This is one legal area in which almost any consistent, publicly articulated approach is better than none." From the legal reformist perspective, Rose-Ackerman provides a unique vantage point to frame the takings question and analyze the Supreme Court cases—a perspective that unifies physical and regulatory takings. In the tradition of the legal reformist approach to law and economics, Rose-Ackerman advocates the use of policy analytic tools to help resolve legal-economic issues based on the concepts of efficiency, equity, and political legitimacy.

Steven G. Medema approaches the takings issue cases from the vantage point of institutionalist law and economics. He provides a brief characterization of the institutionalist approach to law and economics that incorporates the concepts of power, ideology, selective perception, the necessity of choice, and mutual interdependence. Medema provides a predominantly positive description of the several Supreme Court cases in analyzing factors and forces at work in takings issue jurisprudence. His detailed analysis of the cases suggests that law is made, not discovered, and that, given the radical indeterminacy of rights, society, through its legal institutions, is constantly confronted with the inevitable necessity of choice in making law.

Charles K. Rowley reviews the nature of scope of constitutionalism, judicial review, and explored the public choice pressures on the Supreme Court justices. After a detailed discussion of the takings clause, Rowley argues that there is an inherent tendency (particularly with respect to the takings issue) for the federal and state governments to grow and to invade the economic rights of U.S. citizens. He argues that as a result of judicial deference to the legislature and of unprincipled judicial activism marked by undistinguished contributions to jurisprudence from high court incumbents, there has occurred a serious erosion of the economic liberties of U.S. citizens.

Rowley concludes that the U.S. Supreme Court has failed repeatedly to uphold the vision of the Founding Fathers and the wording of the Constitution by the continued deference to the legislative branch of government with respect to the interpretations of the takings clause of the Fifth Amendment. In addition, he finds that liberal democratic justices have allowed their individual political agendas to subvert the Constitution in its intended protection of economic property rights.

From the heterodox world of critical legal studies, Gary Minda analyzes the jurisprudence of takings law from the perspective of Jean-Francois Lyotard's idea of postmodernism. In the tradition of the postmodern legal critics' emphasis on the ideas of contradiction, contingency, and interpretive reversals, Minda explores the dialectic structure of takings law.

Using the Supreme Court cases as his vehicle of analysis, Minda describes the doctrinal shifts, the emerging dialectic patterns, and the turn to postmodernism. In the latter context, while advancing an indeterminacy thesis about takings doctrine, Minda shows that postmoderns still argue that a meaning and coherence can be discovered in takings law in terms of the socially constructed understandings that judges have adopted in fashioning takings doctrine. In this sense, Minda's chapter helps to explain both the doctrinal confusion of takings case laws and the predictable pattern of the outcome of the cases.

From the vantage point of the new law and economics, Thomas S. Ulen offers a theoretical justification for the taking power as well as workable definition of its limits. Ulen argues that if the only meaningful constraint on the taking power is the requirement that the government pay the private property owner just compensation, then the taking power is likely to be exercised inefficiently. Consequently, to promote efficiency, he proposes the addition of a second constraint on this government activity—"the public-good constraint." Once having laid out the dual-constraint theory, Ulen then discusses the Supreme Court cases and concludes that the taking power will be efficiently exercised only under the dual constraints—the just compensation constraint and the public-good constraint.

Robin Paul Malloy adopts the classical-liberal theory as his vantage point to critically analyze the takings issue cases. Malloy traces the origins of the classical-liberal theory to Adam Smith with a commitment steeped in individualist philosophy and a commitment to natural rights. Malloy clearly differentiates the classical-liberal theory from critical legal studies, liberalism, conservativism, and also differentiates it from the libertarian tradition. In his unique analysis of the takings issue cases, Malloy traces an evolutionary trend in takings law jurisprudence. Malloy's evolutionary critique of the several taking issue cases uses a three-stage approach that includes (1) the laissez-faire approach, (2) the general rules approach, and (3) the discretionary approach. From the vantage point of the classical-liberal approach to law and economics, Malloy concludes that current takings law jurisprudence reflects a trend toward a communitarian framework while rejecting individualist philosophy.

Notes

1. The brief history of the regulatory takings issue presented here is largely drawn from Bosselman, Callies, and Banta (1973) and Reznick (1973). See also Treanor (1985).

2. Most of the takings issue cases were decided in the state courts prior to the Civil War. It was in the latter third of 19th century that the U.S. Supreme Court began handing down decisions (Bosselman, Callies, and Banta 1973, pp. 105–106).

3. See, for example, *Brick Presbyterian Church v. Mayor of New York*, 5 Cow. 538 (N.Y., Sup. Ct. 1826); *Coates v. Mayor of New York*, 7 Cow. 585 (N.Y., Sup. Ct. 1827); *Baker v. Boston*, 29 Mass. 183 (1831).

4. A very brief but suggestive list of contributions to these respective schools of thought includes: new law and economics (Posner, 1986; Cooter and Ulen, 1988); public choice theory (Mueller, 1989; Johnson, 1991); institutionalist law and economics (Samuels and Schmid, 1981; Schmid, 1987); the legal reformist school (Rose-Ackerman, 1989; Sunstein, 1990; see also Minda, 1989; pp. 111–112 and Fiss, 1986, pp. 7–8); critical legal studies (Kelman, 1987; Minda, 1989); and classical, liberal, political economy (Malloy, 1990). For an overall review of these schools of thought, see Mercuro (1989).

5. Section 2 is intended to provide a brief review of the majority opinions of the U.S. Supreme Court as reported in the *U.S. Supreme Court Reporter*. I have summarized and presented the facts of each case in this section and edited each respective chapter so as to reduce the potential for repeated restatement of the facts. I have drawn directly from the case materials as reported in an attempt to provide an accurate restatement of what actually transpired in each case. My purpose in stating this here is to avoid what otherwise would be excessive citations within the brief review of cases.

References

Bosselman, F., Callies, D., and Banta, J. 1973. *The Taking Issue: An Analysis of the Constitutional Limits of Land Use Control*. Washington, DC: U.S. Government Printing Office.

Cooter, R., and Ulen, T. 1988. *Law and Economics*. Glenview: Scott, Foresman & Co.

Dunham, A. 1962. "*Griggs v. Allegheny County* in Perspective: Thirty Years of Supreme Court Expropriation Law." In *Supreme Court Review*, P.B. Kurkland, ed., 63–106. Chicago: University of Chicago Press.

Johnson, D.B. 1991. *Public Choice: An Introduction to the New Political Economy*. Mountainview, CA: Mayfield Public Co.

Fiss, O.M. 1986. "The Death of the Law?" *Cornell Law Review* 72:1–16.

Freilich, R.H., and Carlisle, R.G. 1988. "The U.S. Supreme Court Blockbuster Cases of 1986–1987: Analyzing Inverse Condemnation and Regulatory Taking Cases." In *Planning, Zoning, and Eminent Domain*, J.R. Moss, ed., 9-1–9-26. New York: Matthew Bender & Co.

Kelman, M. 1987. *A Guide to Critical Legal Studies*. Cambridge, MA: Harvard University Press.

Malloy, R.P. 1990. *Law and Economics: A Comparative Approach to Theory and Practice*. St. Paul: West Publishing Co.

Mercuro, N., ed. 1989. *Law and Economics*. Boston: Kluwer Academic Publishers.

Minda, G. 1989. "The Law and Economics and Critical Legal Studies Movements in American Law." In *Law and Economics*, N. Mercuro, ed., 87–122. Boston: Kluwer Academic Publishers.

Minow, M. 1987. "Law Turning Outward." *Telos: A Quarterly Journal of Critical Thought* 73:79–100.

Mueller, D.C. 1989. *Public Choice II*. Cambridge: Cambridge University Press.

Pilon, R. 1988. "Property Rights, Takings, and a Free Society." In *Public Choice and Constitutional Economics*, J.D. Gwartney and R.E. Wagner, eds., 151–179. Greenwich: JAI Press.

Posner. R. 1986. *Economic Analysis of Law* 3rd ed. Boston: Little, Brown and Co.

———. 1987. "The Decline of Law as an Autonomous Disipline: 1962–1987." *Harvard Law Review* 100:761–780.

Reznick, S.M. 1973. "Land Use Regulation and the Concept of Takings in Nineteenth Century America." *University of Chicago Law Review* 40:854–872.

Rose-Ackerman, S. 1989. "Law and Economics: Paradigm, Politics, or Philosophy. In *Law and Economics*, N. Mercuro, ed., 233–258. Boston: Kluwer Academic Publishers.

Samuels, W.J., and Schmid, A.A., eds. 1981. *Law and Economics*. Boston: Martinus Nijhoff Publishing Co.

Schmid, A.A. 1987. *Property, Power and Public Choice*. New York: Praeger Publishing.

Sunstein, C. 1990. "Paradoxes of the Regulatory State." *University of Chicago Law Review* 57:407–441.

Treanor, W.M. 1985. "The Origins and Original Significance of the Just Compensation Clause of the Fifth Amendment." *Yale Law Journal* 94: 694–716.

U.S. Executive Office of the President. 1988. Executive Order 12632, "Government Actions and Interference with Constitutionally Protected Rights" (March 15, 1988).

CASES

Agins v. City of Tiburon, 100 S. Ct. 2138 (1980).

Baker v. Boston, 29 Mass. 183 (1831).

Brick Presbyterian Church v. Mayor of New York, 5 Cow. 538 (N.Y. Sup. Ct. 1826).

Coates v. Mayor of New York, 7 Cow. 585 (N.Y. Sup. Ct. 1827).

Commonwealth v. Tewksbury, 52 Mass. (11 Met.) 55 (1846).

Commonwealth v. Alger, 61 Mass. (7 Cush.) 53 (1851).

First English Evangelical Church v. County of Los Angeles, 107 S. Ct. 2378 (1987).

Hodel v. Irving, 107 S. Ct. 2076 (1987).

Keystone Bituminous Coal Association v. DeBenedictis, 107 S. Ct. 1232 (1987).

Mugler v. Kansas, 123 U.S. 623 (1887).

Nollan v. California Coastal Commission, 107 S. Ct. 3141 (1987).

Penn Central Transportation Co. v. New York City, 98 S. Ct. 2646 (1978).

Pennell v. City of San Jose, 108 S. Ct. 849 (1988).

Pennsylvania Coal Co. v. Mahon, 43 S. Ct. 158 (1922).

San Diego Gas and Electric Co. v. City of San Diego, 101 S. Ct. 1278 (1981).

2 REGULATORY TAKINGS: POLICY ANALYSIS AND DEMOCRATIC PRINCIPLES

Susan Rose-Ackerman

1. Introduction

The Fifth Amendment to the U.S. Constitution provides that no private property shall be taken for public use without just compensation (U.S. Constitution, Fifth Amendment). To the policy analyst this phrase seems, at first, compatible with the view that government should balance benefits against costs. Recall, however, that a cost-benefit test does not require that compensation actually *be* paid, only that the gainers *could* do so. Cost-benefit analysis is agnostic about questions of distributive justice. The central policy analytic issues are, then, the efficiency consequences of takings doctrine for private investors and public officials and the fairness of alternative rules. An economic analysis of takings law does not imply that everyone harmed by government actions should be compensated. Such a conclusion would only result from a strong normative commitment to the status quo distribution of property rights.

The Supreme Court has not adopted a policy analytic approach in resolving takings questions. Instead, it has required compensation when tangible things are actually taken directly by the government and refused compensation when the citizen "merely" suffers a diminution in value of his/her property. Easy cases requiring compensation occur when the government physically invades your property by building a highway through your cornfield or condemning your house site for use as a public swimming pool. Hard cases, which do not usually generate compensation, arise when the state builds a highway which keeps your gas station intact but provides no exit ramp nearby or constructs a sports stadium next to your house (Ackerman 1977; Peterson 1989).

In recent years, as the regulatory impact of the government has grown, a festering issue of takings law has achieved new importance. If a public regulation limits the value of your property, can you sue for compensation? The Supreme Court appears to be reexamining this issue. Thus it seems appropriate to bring a policy analytic perspective to bear on this constitutional question.

Section 2 demonstrates that the Court does not appear to be articulating consistent formal principles in the takings area. Section 3 argues that it should try to do just that. Whatever the merits of ad hoc balancing in other areas of law, it has special difficulties in the takings area because of the important role of investment-backed expectations. Section 4 suggests a legal-reformist perspective on the takings question that unifies physical and regulatory takings and provides a way to distinguish between government actions that require compensation and those that do not. The reformist approach seeks to bring policy analytic tools to bear on the study of legal problems without ignoring distributive justice concerns. It argues that judges themselves should apply social science reasoning, especially in legal fields such as takings law where judicial opinions have consequences for substantive policy.[1]

2. The State of Takings Law

Four regulatory takings cases were decided in the 1987 term: *Nollan v. California Coastal Commission*, 107 S. Ct. 3141 (1987); *First English Evangelical Church v. County of Los Angeles*, 107 S. Ct. 2378 (1987); *Hodel v. Irving*, 107 S. Ct. 2076 (1987); and *Keystone Bituminous Coal Association v. DeBenedictis*, 107 S. Ct. 1232 (1987). Although some commentators purport to find a pattern (e.g., Michelman 1988), these cases do not appear to represent orderly doctrinal development. Contrary to the usual result in regulatory takings cases, the plaintiffs won in three of the four cases, and in the fourth, *Keystone v. DeBenedictis*, the decision was five to four. Furthermore, *Keystone* involved a statute very similar to the one that was invalidated in *Pennsylvania Coal Company v.*

Mahon, the one early case in which a regulatory taking *was* found. All four cases produced multiple opinions, and all but *Hodel v. Irving* produced sharp dissents. Only Justice White was with the majority in all four cases although in *Hodel* he joined another justice's concurrence. In short, the court does not seem to have united behind a single view of the takings clause. The future direction of takings law is very much in doubt.[2] The court has left itself free to move in any number of directions in the future without having explicitly to overrule any of these cases.

This conclusion is confirmed by examining the one regulatory takings case decided in the 1988 term, *Pennell v. City of San Jose*. The seven-justice majority was achieved by refusing to rule on whether a taking had occurred in the absence of a concrete example of harm (*Pennell*, pp. 856–857). The two justices writing in partial dissent would have reached the merits and found a taking.[3]

The Supreme Court seems to be inordinately proud of the ad hoc nature of its takings opinions and has reiterated its support of case-by-case balancing in the current crop of opinions. Thus, Justice Stevens in *Keystone* cites with approval the statement in *Kaiser Aetna* that:

> . . . this court has generally "been unable to develop any 'set formula' for determining when 'justice and fairness' require that economic injuries caused by public action be compensated by the government, rather than remain disproportinately concentrated on a few persons." Rather, it has examined the "taking" question by engaging in essentially ad hoc, factual inquires that have identified several factors—such as the economic impact of the regulation, its interference with reasonable investment backed expectations, and the character of the government action—that have particular significance.[4]

Justice Rehnquist, dissenting in *Keystone*, found nothing to disagree with here: "Admittedly, questions arising under the Just Compensation Clause rest on ad hoc factual inquiries, and must be decided on the facts and circumstances on each case."[5] The only exception occurs in the partial dissent in *Pennell* written by Justice Scalia and joined by Justice O'Connor (*Pennell*, p. 860).

In short, the recent cases represent a continuation of the trend toward ad hoc balancing.[6] This result is unfortunate. What takings law needs is a good dose of formalization.

3. The Perils of Case-by-Case Analysis

The court's glorification of ad hoc balancing is impossible to reconcile with a belief in the importance of preserving "investment-backed expectations." Takings law should be predictable, on this view, so that private individuals can confidently commit resources to capital projects.[7] Nevertheless, as many economically oriented writers have argued, no taking can legitimately be claimed if the property owner correctly anticipated that an uncompensated state action was possible and if this belief affected the price paid for the asset. Some property values "are enjoyed under an implied limitation and must yield to the police power," according to Justice Holmes (*Pennsylvania Coal Company v. Mahon*, p. 413).

If, however, takings jurisprudence is both ad hoc and ex post, investors may have a very difficult time knowing whether a particular predictable state action will or will not be judged to be a taking. Therefore, even if the menu of possible state actions is known and probabilities can be assigned to each policy, investors will not be able to make informed choices because the court has not given them clear standards to determine when compensation will be paid.[8] The shifting doctrines of takings law introduce an element of uncertainty into investors' choices that has nothing to do with the underlying economics of the situation. This uncertainty creates two problems. First, investors do not know whether damages will be paid. Second, in the event that damages are not paid, investors will be left bearing the costs of an uninsurable risk. Thus, the justices need to recognize that the "investment-backed" expectations they discuss are themselves affected by the nature of takings law. To the extent that investors are risk averse, the very incoherence of the doctrine produces inefficient choices. When legal rules affect behavior, clarity is a value in itself, independent of the actual content of the rule.

The problem of judicially created uncertainty is exacerbated by the ex post nature of court decisions. Judges are reluctant to decide cases until someone has "actually" been harmed. Not only are they reluctant to articulate general principles of takings law, judges are also unwilling to make general rulings on the status of state actions under individual statutes. Thus, in *Keystone* (at p. 1241) Justice Stevens, in discussing *Pennsylvania Coal Company v. Mahon*, dismisses Justice Holmes' analysis of the general validity of the act as an uncharacteristic "advisory opinion." Stevens then goes on to argue that no taking has occurred under the similar Pennsylvania law at issue in *Keystone* because at the time of the lawsuit no company could actually demonstrate that it had been harmed. The companies were asking the court to pass on the general legitimacy of the statute, and this the majority declined to do.[9] Similarly, in *Pennell* an association of landlords was given standing to challenge a portion of San Jose's rent control ordinance, but their claim that a taking had occurred was dismissed as "premature" because no landlord had actually sufferend harm from the disputed provision.[10] Thus, in the field of regulatory takings, where the future direction of the law is unclear, economic actors cannot obtain a prospective ruling from the court on whether a particular law will effect a taking. They must wait until a concrete harm has occurred before the statute can be tested. In the face of this uncertainty investors may forego otherwise profitable activities, and thus, the current state of the law may produce an inefficiently low level of investment.

Investors are not the only ones adversely affected by the incoherence and unpredictability of takings law. Government officials may be affected as well since the vagueness of the doctrine may act as a force for conservatism among public officials. Risk-averse officials facing the possibility of damage suits against their jurisdictions may restrict their activities simply because they dislike uncertainty.[11] As Stevens notes in his dissent in *First English* (at p. 2399, n. 17): "It is no answer to say that '[a]fter all, if a policeman must know the Constitution, then why not a planner?' To begin with, the Court has repeatedly recognized that it, itself cannot establish any objective rules to assess when a regulation becomes a taking. How then can it demand that land planners do any better?"

As the court moves to reconsider the regulatory takings area, it appears to be developing a jurisprudence that is working against the fundamental goal of the takings clause. The clause is basically an attempt to reconcile an unpredictable, democratically responsible polity with the existence of a capitalist economy based on private property and individual initiative.[12] The ad hoc nature of the law could introduce an element of uncertainty into private investment decisions that could make the coexistence of democracy and private property more, rather than less, difficult.

4. Toward a Takings Jurisprudence

Let us move now from criticism to prescription. If the courts did try to make sense of the takings issue as a general matter, what should they say? The answer has both an efficiency and an equity component. Section 4.1 outlines an efficiency analysis of the takings issue that stresses its impact on both private and public investment and on the distribution of risk in society. Section 4.2 considers the role of takings law in enhancing political legitimacy and contributing to the fairness of the distribution of wealth.

As economists have long argued, the distinction between physical and regulatory takings is not meaningful in efficiency terms, and it also has little to recommend it under most ethical theories. Although this distinction retains a hold on the legal mind,[13] the takings jurisprudence outlined below does not begin with that dichotomy as a first principle. The analysis instead provides a general overview of the takings issue.

4.1 Efficiency

To begin, one must distinguish between efficient and inefficient compensated takings. The efficiency question has three prongs: (1) the possibility of over- or underinvestment by private individuals (the "private investment" issue); (2) the problem of government-created uncertainty (the "insurance" issue); and (3) the impact of takings doctrine on the decisions of public officials (the "public investment" issue).

The private-investment issue concentrates on the use that the government intends to make of the property. The fundamental distinction is between improvements to property that the government will use and improvements that it will destroy. On this first efficiency ground only the former should be completely compensated. Full compensation in other cases generally will be inefficient because it will produce overinvestment. If you expect to be fully compensated for a public policy that destroys your property, you will invest too much in the property.[14] Thus, a homeowner should be compensated both when the state takes his home to turn it into a tourist attraction and when the state passes a regulation requiring the homeowner to permit public access to his garden one month a year. On this first rationale, however, he should not be fully compensated for the value of a house that is destroyed to make way for a highway. Under such a compensation system, when the state destroys existing investments, homeowners will behave efficiently when compensation is set between zero and the level of investment that would be efficient in the absence of any compensation for the taking. Leaving aside the insurance issues discussed below, a level of compensation above zero would only be required on efficiency grounds if courts wanted to force governments to take into account the opportunity costs of their actions.[15] In such cases the court would need to judge the efficient level of homeowner investment ex ante given the possibility of future governmental use.

Notice that in this case the compensation decision would depend only on the government's use of the property. This compensation policy is designed solely to produce optimal investment decisions by private owners and government bodies. Both the economic status of the owner and the magnitude of the loss would be irrelevant. Therefore, owners should be compensated for any land-use regulation, such as an historical preservation ordinance, when public benefits flow from past investment spending by individuals. Unfortunately, in practice, the probability of compensation is highest in just those areas where overreliance is most likely. If the state destroys your "thing," it usually will be required to pay you for it.[16] In contrast, if it merely uses your assets without taking title to them by, for example, requiring you to comply with historical preservation standards, the state generally will not be required to compensate you.[17] This gives owners of buildings that might in the future be declared landmarks an incentive to tear them down quickly so that the issue will not arise (cf. Fischel 1985, p. 174). Thus, legal doctrine in this area illustrates clearly the conflict between "scientific policymaking" and "ordinary observing" isolated in Bruce Ackerman's study of takings doctrine (Ackerman 1977). Economic analysis suggests a rule that is directly opposed to the idea that government should only pay for things that it physically appropriates.

A compensation rule designed to limit overreliance would only have the hypothesized behavioral consequences, however, if government actions are reasonably predictable so that investors can base their decisions on informed predictions about what the government will do in the future. Thus, the compensation rule proposed above should, in principle, be supplemented with a public policy of announcing public actions in advance and by stating at the same time that compensation will be paid only to those in possession of the property at the time of the announcement. Subsequent sales contracts would be required to include clauses explaining the future government action.

A requirement that governments announce their actions in advance, however, while fine in principle, misconceives the nature of most political processes.[18] At any point in time a wide range of public policies is possible. Some may be enacted this year, some next year, and others never. Thus, few policies will be wholly unexpected, and none will be completely certain. Nevertheless, takings law should require property owners to make informed guesses and should encourage governments to be as specific as possible about their plans. A rule tying compensation to the date a project is announced would advance this goal.

Given the uncertainty that is, I believe, an inherent feature of representative democratic government, the insurance branch of the efficiency analysis becomes of critical importance. The problem of risk spreading, unlike the issue of overinvestment, is tied to the situation of the private owner, independent of the government's use of the property. Because of its contrasting focus, this second efficiency concern produces results that will sometimes conflict with the first. Conflicts can be resolved by deciding whether government is best viewed as a well-organized process with known probabilities attached to possible future actions or as an essentially random and unpredictable enterprise, at least in its impact on particular persons. When the latter view is closest to being correct, compensation may be justified because it acts as a form of insurance. Even if the state is certain to carry out a particular policy, such as building a highway, no one may be able to predict who will be affected adversely, that is, what route will be chosen. If the ex ante probability of being harmed is distributed broadly across the population and if *no* compensation is paid, two different results are possible. On the one hand, if people are risk neutral, they all rationally cut back their investment just enough to compensate for the risk of expropriation. On the other hand, if people are risk averse, the uncertainty created by the threat of harm may lead them to underinvest and to hold their assets in a form that is unlikely to be afffected by the public program.

Underinvestment would not occur if insurance were available, but the risks discussed here are generally uninsurable in the private market both because of the arbitrary incidence of harm and the problems of moral hazard and adverse selection. Moral hazard occurs when the existence of insurance leads the insured person to take actions that increase the probability or the magnitude of the loss. In this context, it occurs if property owners secretly lobby to have their property taken or at least do not actively oppose a policy that will produce that result. While such lobbying is possible when the government pays compensation itself, the obvious budgetary consequences of such behavior will help to check abuses. Adverse selection occurs if insurance companies cannot adequately sort property owners into risk classes. Then high-risk and low-risk owners are charged the same rate so that very low-risk owners may decide to self-insure. The remaining pool of insured owners is now riskier and premiums must rise. Now the remaining low-risk owners may opt out of the pool. If the insurance companies have less information about risks than property owners, profitable insurance contracts may be impossible to write (Blume and Rubinfeld 1984, pp. 584–599; Fischel 1988, p. 50).

Therefore, when government creates risks for which private insurance is unavailable, efficient risk distribution provides an economically oriented reason for basing the compensation decision on the magnitude of the harm suffered. In considering the degree of harm, courts must decide what standard of comparison to use. For example, should they define the plaintiff's property as the coal that cannot be mined because of the regulatory statute, so that 100 percent of it has been taken, or as the firm's entire mining operation, so that only a small share has been lost?[19] A generally accepted rule of thumb is that individuals behave in a risk-averse way when a major portion of their total wealth is threatened. Since owner-occupied housing represents a large proportion of most owners' personal wealth, government should compensate homeowners when it takes their houses either through physical confiscation or through a regulation that makes them uninhabitable (Blume and Rubinfeld 1984). Conversely, if it confiscates their toasters or passes an ordinance making them unusable, no compensation would need to be paid on risk-spreading grounds. In short, the standard of comparison should be the individual's total wealth, not just the property "affected" by the taking. In contrast, broadly held corporations should be viewed as risk neutral, even toward large losses, because shareholders and other investors can insure by holding a diversified portfolio of investments. Compensation might, however, be provided to employees and owners of specialized assets if either group will suffer large declines in permanent income or wealth relative to their expectations in the absence of the public program. The courts should develop some simple rules of thumb that, while not perfectly adapted to all the individual situations that arise, will nevertheless provide insurance protection to most of those who would demand it.

The final element in an efficiency analysis concerns the impact of takings law on the calculations of public officials. The compensation requirement can be understood as a way to force public policymakers to consider the opportunity costs of their proposed actions. Policies that "take" private property would then have concrete budgetary impacts that would be immediately reflected in tax bills or borrowing capacity. The efficiency consequences of a comprehensive compensation requirement depend on one's view of the way government policy is made. If cost-benefit tests are used, actual compensation is not required since the analyst can be expected to take into account all costs and benefits, not just those that show up in the budget. Efficient takings rules can depend entirely upon the impact of compensation on the behavior of private individuals. Conversely, if decisionmakers are imperfect agents of the public, compensation requirements may have little impact on their choices because the required payments come from taxpayers, not from the decisionmakers' own pockets. Once again, but for very different reasons, takings rules can depend on their impact on private individuals. In contrast, if public choices are the result of the competition of various groups for political benefits, powerful groups will not need a constitutionally mandated takings doctrine in order to preserve their interests. They will be able to insist that the overall legislative package be beneficial to them. Left out of this account, however, are politically ineffective individuals severely harmed by some public policy. Efficiency requires that their costs be taken into account; yet the operation of the political process may not incorporate these costs. Under this view of the political system, compensation should be paid for these losses to force politicians to recognize their existence (Levmore 1988).

Therefore, since government policymaking can, at least, sometimes be characterized as a struggle between organized groups (Peltzman 1976; Schlozman and Tierney 1986; Stigler 1971), takings law should consider whether the affected individuals suffer special difficulties in having their interests taken seriously by the political process. The takings clause, however, is unlikely to be an effective means of equalizing the power of various population groups. It can be most effective as a way to protect the property interests of unorganized individuals with nothing in common except that they would otherwise bear the costs of some public policy.

Thus, an efficient takings doctrine should not be primarily concerned with the impact of the doctrine on the calculations of public officials. Instead, except for special claims advanced by the politically weak, the emphasis should be on encouraging efficient actions by private property owners. This perspective produces the following rough guide to deciding cases. Always compensate for property that will be used by government in the form in which it is provided by the owner. In other cases, compensate when the asset represents a major proportion of the owner's wealth so that a hypothesis of risk aversion is plausible. Employ a presumption in favor of risk aversion for individuals and risk neutrality for publicly held corporations. In addition, compensate even risk-neutral individuals whose loss represents a large proportion of their wealth if these individuals are politically ineffective.

To counteract the moral hazard created by compensation, courts should develop a notion close to the requirement to mitigate damages in contract law.[20] When government appropriation becomes likely, owners should be reimbursed only for new investments that either can be used by the government or would be rational if no compensation were to be paid. To minimize the private burden of this last provision, employ a presumption in favor of the private property owner with burden of proof on the government to show both that it has given notice and that the investment was excessive.

4.2 Political Legitimacy and Fairness

Efficiency is not the whole story in analyzing the takings doctrine. When public policies are uncertain and have unpredictable impacts on small groups in the population, the legitimacy of the state may depend on the payment of compensation to mitigate the arbitrary distributive consequences of many public policies (Ackerman 1977, pp. 52–53, 68, 79–80; Ely 1980, pp. 97–99; Michelman 1968; Sax 1964, pp. 64–65, 75–76; Tribe 1988, pp. 605–607). Citizens whose assets have been taken are unlikely to be satisfied with the argument that the system is fair ex ante. Compensation is then a substitute for imposing severe restrictions on the substance of public policies or the degree of consent required. Thus, the court has interpreted the fifth amendment as designed to prevent

> . . . the public from loading upon one individual more than his just share of the burdens of government, and says that when he surrenders to the public something more and different from that which is exacted from other members of the public, a full and just equivalent shall be returned to him.[21]

Similarly, Justice Scalia, in finding that a taking had occurred in *Nollan*, argues that even if the California Coastal Commission's policy is sound, it does not follow that coastal residents "can be compelled to contribute to its realization . . . if [the Commission] wants an easement across [their] property, it must pay for it" (*Nollan v. California Coastal Commission*, p. 3150).

However, the U.S. Constitution, in permitting policies to be adopted by majority votes in representative assemblies and approved by the president, did not contemplate that all statutes would meet with unanimous approval. Some people would suffer losses while others benefitted. The status quo is not given the deeply privileged position that it would have under an unanimity rule. Therefore, since some losses can be imposed constitutionally, the problem for takings jurisprudence is to decide when an individual has borne more than his or her "just share of the burdens of government."[22] This is a question that should be taken up in a self-conscious way by the court.[23] While a full-fledged theory of the takings clause cannot be developed here, I can nevertheless isolate three situations in which compensation should *not* be paid.

The first issue is the specification of the property entitlement itself.[24] Compensation should not be paid when the complainant cannot legitimately claim to be entitled to the benefits that are lost when the government acts.[25] For example, courts have found that individuals do not have the right to create a nuisance. Thus, if the state imposes regulations or confiscates a nuisance, the owner has no right to claim compensation. Nothing has been taken that the individual had a right to claim as his own. The classic statement is in *Mugler v. Kansas*: "All property in this country is held under the implied obligation that the owner's use of it shall not be injurious to the community."[26] Citing *Mugler* with approval, Justice Stevens in *Keystone* states that the court hesitates "to find a taking when the state merely restrains uses of property that are tantamount to public nuisances."[27]

The difficulty with this doctrine is twofold. First, Ronald Coase has shown that in a two-sided controversy it is not straightforward to decide who "caused" the harm (Coase 1960; Tribe 1988, p. 594). Second, this doctrine may tie the regulatory state too closely to doctrines of the common law that may be obsolete in particular regulatory situations. This compensation rule makes some types of regulatory programs much more expensive than others. In practice, however, courts do not seem to have limited themselves to common-law nuisances. The *Mugler* case itself dealt with brewery property made valueless by a Kansas constitutional amendment prohibiting the manufacture and sale of intoxicating liquors, and the opinion's language is quite broad:

> The power which the States have of prohibiting such use by individuals of their property as will be prejudicial to the health, the morals, or the safety of the public is not—and, consistently with the existence and safety of organized society cannot be—burdened with the condition that the State must compensate such individual owners for pecuniary losses they may sustain, by reason of their not being permitted, by a noxious use of their property, to inflict injury upon the community. (*Mugler v. Kansas*, pp. 668–669)

Justice Stevens quotes this statement both in his opinion in *Keystone* and in his dissent in *First English*. Justice Rehnquist, however, would read the nuisance exception quite narrowly to accord more closely with common-law doctrine. He argues that "the nuisance exception to the taking guarantee is not coterminous with the police power itself (*Penn Central Transportation Company v. City of New York*, p. 145 (Rehnquist J., dissenting))." It is instead a "narrow exception allowing the government to prevent 'a misuse or illegal use.' (*Keystone*, p. 1256, 107 S. Ct. at 1256 (Rehnquist J., dissenting) (quoting *Curtin v. Benson*, 222 U.S. 78, 86 (1911))." A similar contrast in views is evident in *Nollan*. Justice Scalia argues that the state has taken an "essential stick in the bundle of rights" while Justice Brennan finds that the owners have no legitimate claim (*Nollan v. California Coastal Commission*, pp. 3145, 3159). These different views of the content of legitimate property entitlements imply that prior to any resolution of the takings issue the court must resolve fundamental questions concerning the nature of property.[28] These questions should be resolved without giving a canonical status to common-law jurisprudence.

Second, the state should be authorized to appropriate excess profits. This principle, implicit in antitrust law,[29] provides a justification for the Supreme Court's refusal to find a taking in *Keystone*. The court found that all mines would continue to operate and that the losses would not be severe.[30] This finding, if correct, implies that the companies were earning excess profits that could be used to pay for the regulation without causing anyone to go out of business. This standard also supports Brennan's dissent in *Nollan*. He argues that the Nollans "can make no tenable claim that either their enjoyment of their property or its value is diminished by the public's ability merely to pass and re-pass a few feet closer to the seawall beyond which appellants' house is located" (*Nollan v. California Coastal Commission*, p. 3157). Thus, the appellants' claim could be viewed as an attempt to extract rents from their exclusive control of a piece of beach needed for convenient access between two public beaches. Under this view, they do not deserve compensation because they had no right to these economic rents. Finally, in *Pennell*, the court reiterates previous decisions finding that the monopoly power of private business provides a justification for public action that lowers these returns (*Pennell v. City of San Jose*, pp. 857–859).[31]

Third, compensation should not be paid if the government action is analogous to a private action that is seen as one of the risks of economic life. For example, if the government competes with a private business, this should not produce a takings claim because competitive losses do not give rise to damage claims in the private sector. These losses, labeled pecuniary externalities by economists, do not have the adverse efficiency consequences of externalities that arise when individuals use scarce resources for which they do not pay. The distributive consequences produced by market pressures are a cost of maintaining the incentives needed to make markets work efficiently. Thus, if the government sells surplus military supplies, it should not compensate private firms selling competing products. Similarly, the Tennessee Valley Authority should not have to compensate competing power companies for lost business. Finally, a regulation that is cheaper for one firm to comply with than another should not give rise to a compensation claim from the disadvantaged firm.

5. Conclusions

In this chapter I have not tried to develop a comprehensive answer to the takings question. My main message, however, is that such an effort is sorely needed. While the court can try for a principled resolution, this is one legal area in which almost any consistent, publicly articulated approach is better than none. Clear statement, even if not backed by clear thinking, will do much to preserve the investment-backed expectations the court talks about so much. Clear thinking would be even better, and here I have provided only a rough guide. The suggestions based on efficiency, equity, and political legitimacy outlined above must be supplemented with an understanding of just what it is that people can be said to own.[32] In attempting to answer that question, historically generated expectations may need to be preserved for the sake of fairness, but they should not straitjacket our thinking about the future.

Notes

1. See Rose-Ackerman (1988b, 1992). For related discussions see Edley (1990) and Sunstein (1990). This chapter is a revision of "Against Ad Hocery: A Comment on Michelman" (Rose-Ackerman, 1988a). Frank Michelman's position is stated in "Takings 1987," *Columbia Law Review*, 88:1600–1629 (1988), and "A Reply to Susan Rose-Ackerman," *Columbia Law Review*, 88:1712–1713 (1988).

2. Contrast this claim with Executive Order 12630, March 15, 1988, "Governmental Actions and Interference with Constitutionally Protected Property Rights." While the order uses qualifying language, it is a willful overreading of the likelihood that regulatory actions will produce a successful takings claim. It states that "recent Supreme Court decisions . . . have . . . reaffirmed that government actions that do not formally invoke the condemnation power, including regulations, may result in a taking for which just compensation is required" (Sect. 1a). Federal policies, including regulations, are to be examined for the possibility of a successful takings claim. At the same time as the order was issued, the Justice Department urged private individuals to bring takings claims (*Legal Times*, May 16, 1988). This creates the possibility of noncontested settlements in which the government pays compensation on claims that would not be upheld in a court challenge.

3. The takings cases decided in the 1990 term did not clarify Supreme Court jurisprudence on the regulatory takings issue. One, *Preseault v. I.C.C.*, 110 S. Ct. 914 (1990), dealing with the status of private landholders' claims when a railbed is used as a hiking trail, was judged not ripe for decision. Plaintiffs were required first to pursue their suit in the Court of Claims. A concurrence by three justices, including O'Connor and Scalia who dissented in *Pennell*, argued that in determining whether a taking has occurred state law should determine the character of the property entitlement (*id.*, p. 926–928). The second, *United States v. Sperry Corporation*, 110 S. Ct. 387 (1989), concerning a fee charged by the government for use of the Iran-United States Claims Tribunal was judged a user fee, not a taking.

4. *Kaiser Aetna v. United States*, 444 U.S. 164, 175 (1979) (quoted at 107 S. Ct., pp. 1232, 1247; citations omitted). Actually, Stevens is quoting from *Hodel v. Virginia Surface Mining and Reclamation Association, Inc.*, 452 U.S. 264, p. 294 (1981), which quotes *Kaiser*. The internal quotation in *Kaiser* is from *Penn Central Transportation Company v. New York City*, 438 U.S. 104, p. 124 (1978). The Court repeats this language in *Pennell v. City of San Jose*, 108 S. Ct. 849, p. 856.

5. 107 S. Ct. at 1254. Similar language is found in Brennan's majority opinion in *Andrus v. Allard*, 444 U.S. 51, p. 65 (1979): "There is no abstract or fixed point at which judicial intervention under the Takings Clause becomes appropriate. Formulas and factors have been developed in a variety of settings. Resolution of each case, however, ultimately calls as much for the exercise of judgment as for the application of logic."

6. For a fuller treatment of this issue that reaches the same conclusion see Peterson (1989). However, in Peterson (1990), she argues that "takings decisions can best be explained by saying that a compensible taking occurs whenever the government intentionally forces A to give up her property, unless the government is seeking to prevent or punish wrongdoing by A" (p. 59). She argues that the federal courts define wrongdoing by looking to "societal judgments" (p. 86). The courts themselves have failed to supply a consistent rationale for their decisions, but she is able to infer one from an evaluation of the outcomes. Peterson's analysis is purely positive. Even if she is correct as a descriptive matter, however, I would still argue for the reformed approach outlined below.

7. Michelman (1968). Michelman's position has been employed by the Supreme Court in *Kaiser Aetna v. United States*, 444 U.S. 164, p. 175; *Keystone Bituminous Coal Association* v. *DeBenedictis*, 480 U.S. 470, pp. 493, 499.

8. See Epstein (1988). Epstein's own proposed reformulation of takings doctrine is, I believe, unsatisfactory. See *infra* note 32.

9. Rehnquist in dissent would have been willing to do this. He argues that in *Pennsylvania Coal* the general validity of the act "was properly drawn into question." 107 S. Ct. at 1254.

10. *Pennell v. City of San Jose*, 108 S. Ct. 849, pp. 854–856. The partial dissent, in contrast, would have reached the merits of the takings claim. (pp. 860–861).

11. An expansive regulatory takings doctrine may also discourage government regulation. That result is likely and may or may not be desirable depending on one's view of the costs imposed on property owners by regulations.

12. Compare the similar position of Ackerman (1977, pp. 52–53, 68, 79–80); Ely (1980, pp. 97–98); Michelman (1968); Sax (1964, pp. 64–65, 75–76); Tribe (1988, pp. 605–607). Levmore (1988, p. 308) puts the point well: "[P]olitics works least well when it affects citizens who have difficulty influencing political bargains and . . . it is just when politics is least perfect that our legal system insists upon the use of markets . . . Thus, the requirement of explicit compensation (in imitation of market transactions) for some takings might be understood as protective of individuals who can not easily make politics part of their business."

13. *Loretto v. Teleprompter Corporation*, 458 U.S. 419 (1982). This decision found that the use of a few square inches of property on the outside of a building for a cable television cable connection constituted a taking. For a discussion of courts' emphasis on physical occupation see Ackerman (1977).

Since Loretto makes clear that even the slightest physical invasion must be compensated, lawyers have tried to extend the definition of physical invasion to include, for example, monetary exactions and a regulation that required landlords to keep single room occupancy (SRO) buildings fully rented or pay a penalty. The Supreme Court refused to accept the former claim. It pointed out that if the government's fee was viewed as a physical occupation, then "So would be any fee for services, including a filing fee that must be paid in advance" (*United States v. Sperry Corporation*, 110 S. Ct. 387, p. 395, n. 9). To the court the fungibility of money is central. They claim that: "Unlike real or personal property, money is fungible." The court does not tell us why fungibility is the touchstone or how it should be defined in a market economy.

The latter claim concerning SROs was accepted by the highest court in New York State. The majority saw the New York City law as requiring forced occupancy of one's property by strangers and therefore as being such an extreme measure as to constitute a physical occupation. They reached this conclusion in spite of the fact that the law was a regulatory statute that did not literally involve state officials in occupying SROs. See *Seawall Associates v. City of New York*, 542 N.E. 2d 1059, pp. 1062–1065 (N.Y. 1989).

14. For a fuller discussion of the issue of overinvestment, see Blume and Rubinfeld (1984) and Blume, Rubinfeld, and Shapiro (1984). As Blume and Rubinfeld argue: "Whatever the exact determination of compensation, it is important that the measure be one that cannot be directly affected by the behavior of the individual investors, since any compensation measure which can be affected by private behavior will create the possibility of inefficiency due to moral hazard" (Blume and Rubinfeld 1984, p. 618, n. 144).

15. Cf. Fischel and Shapiro (1988) who analyze situations in which government actions produce demoralization costs.

16. See the critical analysis of this doctrine in Ackerman (1977, pp. 130–136).

17. See *Penn Central Transportation Company v. City of New York*, 438 U.S. 104 (1978). But see the New York State Court of Appeals decision in *Seawall Associates v. City of New York*, 542 N.E. 2d 1059 (N.Y. 1989). The New York high court found that both a physical and a regulatory taking had occurred when New York City attempted to aid the homeless by requiring owners of SRO facilities to keep them fully rented. Exemptions and buyout provisions in the law did not overcome this finding. While the court did not use my reasoning, the result is consistent with my framework because the city law was designed to make use of existing buildings to advance a public purpose.

18. Of course, there are exceptions. In *Chang v. United States*, the Claims Court denied compensation to engineers whose employment contracts in Libya had been voided by an Executive Order issued by President Reagan. The court argued that "the risk that employment in Libya might be interrupted by tension in the relations between that government and the United States can hardly be said to have been outside the reasonable contemplation of plaintiffs at the time they entered into their employment contracts." Furthermore, the engineers should have reasonably supposed that economic sanctions against Libya were possible.

19. See *Keystone Bituminous Coal Association v. DeBenedictis*, 107 S. Ct. 1232 (1987).

20. See *Merced Irrigation District v. Woolstenhulme*, 4 Cal. 3d 478, 483 P. 2d 1, 93 Cal. Rptr. 833 (1971).

21. *Monongahela Navigation Company v. United States*, 148 U.S. 312, 325 (1893) (quoted in *Keystone Bituminous Coal Association v. DeBenedictis*, 107 S. Ct. 1232, p. 1256 (1987) (Rehnquist, C.J., dissenting)). See also *Armstrong v. United States*, 364 U.S. 40, p. 49: "The Fifth Amendment's guarentee that private property shall not be taken for a public use without just compensation was designed to bar Government from forcing some people alone to bear public burdens which, in all fairness and justice, should be borne by the public as a whole."

22. Richard Epstein takes a contrary position, reading the taking clause as imposing severe restrictions on the ability of the government to redistribute wealth. See Epstein (1985). But see Gray (1986), who criticizes Epstein's position.

23. Cf. Tribe (1988, pp. 607–613) who discusses the problematic nature of property in Supreme Court jurisprudence.

24. An instructive recent example is the attempt by the Corp of Engineers to use the Clear Water Act of 1972 to limit farmers' use of land protected from flooding by levees. The Corps argued that such farmland falls within the 1989 definition of wetlands and hence is under the jurisdiction of the Corps. In one such case the Corps wanted to require a farmer to cede 25 percent of his land as a permanent wildlife easement. The farmer, who is suing the Corps in federal court, argued:

> If my country needs my land for a public purpose, let them have it, but if they are going to take it for a public purpose, let them do it in a legal way and let the public pay for it, not send individual farmers into bankruptcy by taking away what they have spent much of their lives working for. (Quoted in William Robbins, "For Farmers, Wetlands Mean a Legal Quagmire," *New York Times*, April 24, 1990).

The farmer's pre-enforcement complaint was dismissed for lack of subject matter jurisdiction in an opinion which did not rule on the takings issue since it was judged not ripe for decision (*McGown v. United States*).

25. In upholding a fee charged to Sperry Corporation for use of the Iran-United States Claims Tribunal, the Supreme Court found that "Sperry has not identified any of its property that was taken without just compensation" [*United States v. Sperry Corporation*, 110 S. Ct. 387, p. 393 (1989)].

26. *Mugler v. Kansas*, 123 U.S. 623, 665 (1887) [quoted by Justice Stevens in his opinion in *Keystone Bituminous Coal Association v. DeBenedictis*, 107 S. Ct. 1232, p. 1245 (1987), and in his dissent in *First English Evangelical Church v. County of Los Angeles*, 107 S. Ct. 2378, p. 2391 (1987)].

27. *Keystone Bituminous Coal Association v. DeBenedictis*, 107 S. Ct. 1232, p. 1245 (1987); see also p. 1246, n. 22 (citing cases holding that compensation is not required when the public action abates a public nuisance or stops illegal activity).

28. At least three current justices, Kennedy, O'Connor, and Scalia, want to duck this question by simply upholding whatever determinations have been made by the states. In articulating this position, however, they have accepted the basic proposition that property rights are determined by law, not given a priori. See *Presault v. I.C.C.*, 110 S. Ct. 914, p. 926 (1990).

29. For another application of this principle, see Rose-Ackerman (1982).

30. "We do know, however, that petitioners have never claimed that their mining operations, or even any specific mines, have been unprofitable since the Subsidence Act was passed. Nor is there evidence that mining in any specific location . . . has been unprofitable." [*Keystone Bituminous Coal Association v. DeBenedictis*, 107 S. Ct. 1232, p. 1248 (1987)].

31. The partial dissent is even clearer on this point. Scalia argues that "when excessive rents are forbidden . . . landlords as a class become poorer and tenants as a class (or at least incumbent tenants as a class) become richer. Singling out landlords to be the transferors may be within our traditional constitutional notions of fairness, because they can plausibly be regarded as the source or the beneficiary of the high-rent problem." (*Pennell v. City of San Jose*, p. 863). See also Levmore (1988, p. 313 and the cases cited at n. 61 therein).

32. Epstein claims to present just this kind of clear rule, but he has begged many of the most important questions. He does this by taking as relatively unproblematic the issue of how private property should be defined and using a definition that does not permit concerns with distributive justice to help determine the outlines of property claims. See Epstein (1985, p. 306–329, 331–350; 1988, pp. 40–41, 44–45).

References

Ackerman, B. 1977. *Private Property and the Constitution*. New Haven: Yale University Press.

Blume, L., and Rubinfeld, D. 1984. "Compensation for Takings: An Economic Analysis." *California Law Review* 72:569–628.

Blume, L., Rubinfeld, D., and Shapiro, P. 1984. "The Taking of Land: When Should Compensation Be Paid?" *Quarterly Journal of Economics* 77:71–92.

Coase, R. 1960. "The Problem of Social Cost." *Journal of Law & Economics* 3:1–44.

Edley, C. 1990. *Administrative Law: Rethinking Judicial Control of Bureaucracy*. New Haven: Yale University Press.

Ely, J. 1980. *Democracy and Distrust*. Cambridge, MA: Harvard University Press.

Epstein, R. 1985. *Takings*. Cambridge, MA: Harvard University Press.

———. 1988. "Takings: Descent and Resurrection." *The Supreme Court Review* 1987:1–45.

Fischel, W. 1985. *The Economics of Zoning Laws*. Baltimore: Johns Hopkins.

———. 1988. "Property Rights and the Takings Clause." In *Significant Business Decisions of the Supreme Court. 1986–1987 Term*, H. Butler, W. Fischel, and W. Kovacic, eds. Washington, DC: Washington Legal Foundation.

Fischel, W., and Shapiro, P. 1988. "Takings, Insurance, and Michelman: Comments of Economic Interpretations of Just Compensation. *Journal of Legal Studies* 17:269–293.

Gray, T. 1986. "The Malthusian Constitution." *University of Miami Law Review*, 41:21–48.

Levmore, S. 1988. "Just Compensation and Just Politics." *Connecticut Law Review* 22:285–322.

Michelman, F. 1968. "Property, Utility, and Fairness: Comments on the Ethical Foundations of 'Just Compensation' Law." *Harvard Law Review* 80:1165–1258.

———. 1988. "Takings 1987." *Columbia Law Review* 88:1600–1629.

Peltzman, S. 1976. Toward a More General Theory of Regulation. *Journal of Law and Economics* 19:211–240.

Peterson, A. 1989. "The Takings Clause: In Search of Underlying Principles. Part I—A Critique of Current Takings Clause Doctrine." *California Law Review* 77:1299–1364.

———. 1990. "The Takings Clause: In Search of Underlying Principles. Part II—Takings as Intentional Deprivations of Property Without Moral Justification." *California Law Review* 78:55–162.

Rose-Ackerman, S. 1982. Unfair Competition and Corporate Income Taxation. *Stanford Law Review* 34:1017–1039.

———. 1988a. "Against Ad Hocery: A Comment on Michelman." *Columbia Law Review* 88:1697–1711.

————. 1988b. "Progressive Law and Economics—and the New Administrative Law." *Yale Law Journal* 98:341–368.

————. 1992. *Rethinking the Progressive Agenda: The Reform of the American Regulatory State*. New York: Free Press.

Sax, J. 1964. "Takings and the Police Power." *Yale Law Journal* 74:36–76.

Schlozman, K.L., and Tierney, V. 1986. *Organized Interests and American Democracy*. New York: Harper & Row.

Stigler, G. 1971. "The Theory of Economic Regulation." *Bell Journal of Economics* 2:3–21.

Sunstein, C. 1990. *After the Rights Revolution: Reconceiving the Regulatory State*. Cambridge, MA: Harvard University Press.

Tribe, L. 1988. *American Constitutional Law*, 2nd ed. Mineola, NY: Foundation Press.

U.S. Executive Office of the President. 1988. Executive Order #12632, "Government Actions and Interference with Constitutionally Protected Property Rights (March 15)." *Federal Register* 53 (March 1988):8859–8862.

CASES

Andrus v. Allard, 444 U.S. 51 (1979), 100 S. Ct. 318, 62 L. Ed. 2d. 210.

Armstrong v. United States, 364 U.S. 40 (1960), 80 S. Ct. 1563, 4 L. Ed. 2d. 1554.

Chang v. United States, 13 Cl. Ct. 555 (1987).

Curtin v. Benson, 222 U.S. 78 (1911), 32 S. Ct. 31, 56 L. Ed. 102.

First English Evangelical Church v. County of Los Angeles, 482 U.S. 304 (1987), 107 S. Ct. 2378, 96 L. Ed. 2d. 250.

Hodel v. Irving, 481 U.S. 704 (1987), 107 S. Ct. 2076, 95 L. Ed. 2d. 668.

Hodel v. Virginia Surface Mining and Reclamation Association, Inc., 452 U.S. 264 (1981), 101 S. Ct. 2352, 69 L. Ed. 2d. 1.

Kaiser Aetna v. United States, 444 U.S. 164 (1979), 100 S. Ct. 383, 62 L. Ed. 2d. 232.

Keystone Bituminous Coal Association v. DeBenedictis, 480 U.S. 470 (1987), 107 S. Ct. 1232, 94 L. Ed. 2d. 472.

Loretto v. Teleprompter Corp., 458 U.S. 419 (1982), 102 S. Ct. 3164, 73 L. Ed. 2d. 868.

McGown v. United States, 1990 U.S. Dist LEXIS 13402 (Oct 5, 1990, U.S.D.C. for the Eastern Dist. of Missouri Northern Div.).

Merced Irrigation Dist. v. Woolstenhulme, 4 Cal. 3d 478, 483 P. 2d 1, 93 Cal. Rptr. 833 (1971).

Monongahela Navigation Co. v. United States, 148 U.S. 312 (1893), 13 S. Ct. 622, 37 L. Ed. 463.

Mugler v. Kansas, 123 U.S. 623, 665 (1887), 8 S. Ct. 273, 31 L. Ed. 205.

Nollan v. California Coastal Commission, 107 S. Ct. 3141 (1987).

Penn Central Transportation Co. v. City of New York, 438 U.S. 104, 124 (1978), 98 S. Ct. 2646, 57 L. Ed. 2d. 631.

Pennell v. City of San Jose, 485 U.S. 1 (1988), 108 S. Ct. 849, 99 L. Ed. 1.
Pennsylvania Coal Co. v. Mahon, 260 U.S. 393, 413–414 (1922), 43 S. Ct. 158, 67 L. Ed. 322.
Preseault v. I.C.C., 110 S.Ct. 914 (1990), 108 L. Ed. 2d. 1.
Rochester Gas and Electric Corp. v. Public Service Commission, 71 N.Y. 2d 313 (1988).
San Diego Gas and Electric Co. v. San Diego, 450 U.S. 621 (1981), 101 S. Ct. 1287, 67 L. Ed. 2d. 551.
Seawall Associates v. City of New York, 542 N.E. 2d 1059 (N.Y. 1989).
United States v. Sperry Corp., 110 S. Ct. 387 (1989), 107 L. Ed. 2d 290.

3 MAKING CHOICES AND MAKING LAW: AN INSTITUTIONAL PERSPECTIVE ON THE TAKINGS ISSUE

Steven G. Medema

In every opinion a court not only resolves a particular dispute one way or another, it validates or authorizes one form of life—one kind of reasoning, one kind of response to argument, one way of looking at the world and at its own authority—or another.—James Boyd White[1]

Five votes. Five votes can do anything around here.—Justice William J. Brennan, Jr.[2]

1. Introduction

The institutional approach to law and economics has its roots in the work of Henry Carter Adams (1954), Robert Lee Hale (1923), and John R. Commons (1924); it is currently reflected in the work of such scholars as Warren J. Samuels, A. Allan Schmid, Nicholas Mercuro, Steven G. Medema, and H. H. Liebhafsky.[3] The approach taken here is predominately positive—to identify and analyze the fundamental factors and forces at work in the legal-economic process and to assess their implications for future performance. Law is seen as a function of a multiplicity of factors and forces, including power, ideology, time (including the evolution of the economic system), selective perception, and mutual interdependence. Law reflects an inevitable choice process, and outcomes are seen as a function of these choices.

This chapter presents an institutional analysis of the takings issue.

In the next section, we will lay out an institutional perspective on the takings issue. In subsequent sections, several recent takings cases, as well as an Executive Order of the President of the United States regarding the takings issue, will be examined from this perspective. The final section contains some concluding remarks regarding the state of takings jurisprudence.

2. An Institutional Perspective on the Takings Issue

The takings clause of the Fifth Amendment to the U.S. Constitution states: ". . . nor shall private property be taken for public use, without just compensation." The resolution of the takings issue thus requires definitions of the concepts of "private property," "taken," "public use," and "just compensation." The history of judicial opinions and academic literature[4] in this area, as well as the chapters contained in this book, suggest very strongly that these matters are by no means settled or clear, that "Truth" has not yet been discovered. Indeed, one of the most basic points that will be made here is that there is no Truth to be found in these matters. Any particular resolution of the takings issue is the outcome of a variety of complex factors and forces, some readily apparent and some less so, which, while rendering ex post determinate solutions, do not in any conclusive sense render solutions that are "correct."

The starting point for our analysis here is the dual nature of all rights. Rights function to expand the opportunity sets of those who have them and restrict the opportunity sets of those exposed to the exercise of those rights (Samuels 1981, p. 197). Legal change functions to expand the opportunity sets of some and restrict the opportunity sets of others in the process of altering rights and exposures. What is fundamental here is that *losses* are *ubiquitous*: any legal change restricts someone's opportunity set, that is, engenders losses. The question that remains is whether the losers will be compensated for their losses. This is the matter at the heart of the resolution of the takings issue.

One consequence of the ubiquitous nature of these losses is that not all losses can be compensated. The issue then becomes whether the loss is in fact a "taking" for which "just compensation" is owed. The resolution of this issue is the process of rights creation and recreation. If the action which led to Alpha's loss is said to be a taking for which compensation is due, then what is being said is that Alpha had a right and that right was taken away. If it is determined that no taking occurred, and hence that no compensation is due, then Alpha is treated as not having possessed a right. The result, then, is that some losers are treated as having rights while others are not (Samuels 1981, p. 192). What remains is the determination of when losses are said to be compensable takings and when they are not. There is an *inevitable necessity of choice* here: a choice as to whose losses are compensated, which in turn reflects the choice of what factors and forces are to govern whether a taking has occurred. Ex post, solutions are determinate; ex ante, society is radically indeterminate, necessitating choice.

The necessity of choice in the face of radical indeterminacy mandates that some valuational process is involved in the resolution of the takings issue. If we accept the premise that not all losses can be compensated, the valuational process must operate to distinguish between equivalent (in the sense of agents with losses) situations so that some are seen as requiring compensation while others are not. In the takings area, this valuational process has led to the formulation of rules for resolving disputes. While it is typical to contrast a "rules" approach with a "discretion" approach, this is, at the deep level, a false dichotomy. The necessity of choice in the formulation of legal rules—the adoption of one rule rather than others—is fundamentally a discretionary choice. As we will see, moreover, the determination of how the facts of a given case fit the rule is a highly discretionary process.

The recognition of the essential valuational and discretionary element at work here leads us to the most fundamental force at work in the resolution of the takings issue, that of *selective perception* (Samuels and Mercuro 1981, p. 216). Selective perception is operative at several levels. At the most basic level, it is operative in the formulation of legal rules. Since not all losses can or will be compensated, the chosen rule selectively elevates some interests to protected status (rights) while other interests are left unprotected (nonrights). The fact that certain classes of interests are deemed more worthy of protection than others is purely normative and subjective; there is no a priori reason why any one set of interests should be protected over others. All of this is a function of one's view of the world, including ideology, reflecting the world one wants to see made and remade through law.

Selective perception is also operative in the application of a rule in resolving a particular case. Especially important here are the definition of what constitutes the relevant unit of property, the evaluation of benefits and costs (including injuries and losses), the invocation and interpretation of precedents, and the juxtaposition of the rule with the perceived facts of the case. This selectivity is inherent in the resolution of takings disputes and becomes readily apparent in the differential resolutions of seemingly identical cases, as well as in the arguments put forth in the majority and minority opinions of individual cases.

The choice of a particular rule serves several functions, the most important of which are the resolution of the problem of order, the obfuscation of loss, legitimation, and psychic balm. In the face of radical indeterminacy, the law establishes order, or social control. The process here is one of "making" rather than "discovering"; not "order," but rather "order on whose terms." The choice of a certain rule (selectively done), where many are possible, gives rise to a certain order (selectively arrived at), where many are possible. The choice of a particular rule also serves to obscure losses. Certain interests become rights and the destruction of these interests becomes loss. At the same time, however, certain interests are deemed nonrights and the destruction of these interests nonlosses. In fact, losses are ubiquitous, and the fact that certain losses are not perceived as such (or at least are not seen as worthy of compensation) reflects the inevitable selectivity element operative here.

The adoption of a particular takings rule also serves a legitimation function. Decisions are seen as in some sense correct or legitimate due to their grounding in a rule:

> What is legitimized here includes specific substantive legal changes (for example, changes in the differential legal protection given to interests or rights), the existing decisional system or structure, and the mode of thought (the legal style of thinking, definition of reality, and the normative structure of social reality). (Samuels and Mercuro 1981, p. 233)

Acceptance and legitimacy flow from legal rules and redound upon the decisions that result from their application.

In a related vein, the use of rules serves as a psychic balm in a world of radical indeterminacy (Samuels and Mercuro 1981, p. 233). The rule provides a comfortable sensation that decisions are anchored in "high principle" (Samuels and Mercuro 1981, p. 233) rather than being the product of the whimsy of the moment. This facet of legal rules ". . . functions to obscure the necessity of choice, [and] to absorb the reality of loss . . ." (Samuels and Mercuro 1981, p. 233).

What is key, in all of this, is that a particular takings rule or test is chosen where many are possible:

> The use of these tests is essentially selective and arbitrary. Their use in any particular case is a matter of decision, of ultimate pure choice. They are not deducible by deductive logic or by inference from the facts. There is no automatic litmus test by which the tests themselves can be selected for applicability. They are categories (empty boxes) with variable selective

> contents whose adoption is almost if not wholly subjective. They neither individually nor collectively provide a formula or calculus by which Fifth Amendment takings can be distinguished from unprotected police power actions. Each test represents a relevant, however imprecise, consideration or basis for differentiation but collectively they both permit and require the exercise of choice for their selection and application. The very use of these tests functions to legitimize takings which escape their use while also functioning to obscure the inevitable choice and specificity of application involved. (Samuels and Mercuro 1981, p. 230)

Any result is a function of the rule, selectively chosen, which underlies it, as well as the selective application of the rule, and hence will be "clear" and "determinate" only in a very limited and ex post sense.

In the following sections, several recent takings cases will be evaluated in light of the foregoing analysis. The decisions will be seen to hinge crucially not only on the specific rule chosen but also on the way in which that rule is applied. Often, different components of the rule will point in opposite directions—some toward finding a taking and others toward finding no taking. In such instances, certain components of the rule are given privileged status over other components, but yet this ordering is not always consistent across cases. All of this will serve to illustrate the inevitable selectivity element operative here, and the inherently tentative and ad hoc nature of the resolution of the taking issue.

3. Setting the Stage: *Penn Central v. City of New York*

Subsequent to New York City's enactment of its Landmark Preservation Law Penn Central entered into a lease agreement with UGP Properties under which UGP would construct a 50-story office building over the terminal. The Landmarks Commission refused to approve this alteration, and Penn Central filed suit, claiming that their property had been taken in violation of the Fifth Amendment. Appellants maintained that the satisfaction of the law's goals could not proceed without just compensation to those whose property has been designated an historic landmark (*Penn Central*, p. 2662). In an opinion that was to pave the way for the next decade of takings jurisprudence, the U.S. Supreme Court denied Penn Central's takings claim (*Penn Central*, p. 2666).

In this opinion for the Court, Justice Brennan stated the issue at hand as

> . . . whether a city may, as part of a comprehensive program to preserve historic landmarks and historic districts, place restrictions on the development

> of individual historic landmarks . . . without effecting a "taking" requiring the payment of "just compensation." [*Penn Central*, p. 2650]

Justice Brennan then proceeds to make the case for the preservation of historic buildings an districts, and how the N.Y.C. Landmarks Preservation Law fits in with this (*Penn Central*, p. 2651).[5] The Grand Central Terminal is worthy of designation as an historic landmark, according to Brennan, because "it is regarded not only as providing an ingenious engineering solution to the problems presented by urban railroad stations, but also as a magnificent example of the French beauxarts style" (*Penn Central*, p. 2654). Having determined that the Grand Central Terminal is indeed worthy of preservation, it remains for the Court to determine if the law works a taking for which compensation is owed.

While recognizing the past inability of the Court "to develop any 'set formula' for determining when 'justice and fairness' require [compensation]" (*Penn Central*, p. 2659) for government-caused economic injuries, Justice Brennan identifies three factors "that have particular significance" (*Penn Central*, p. 2659). First, there is the general economic impact of the regulation on the claimant, and more specifically, "the extent to which the regulation has interfered with distinct investment-backed expectations" (*Penn Central*, p. 2659). Second, "the character of the government action" is relevant (*Penn Central*, p. 2659).[6] Finally, it is relevant to consider the extent to which the government action promotes "'the health, safety, morals, or general welfare'" of the citizenry (*Penn Central*, p. 2659). In each instance, Justice Brennan cites cases in which these criteria have been used, as authority for their use in the present case. It bears noting, however, that in naming these three factors as important ones for the issue at hand, he has implicitly excluded others, such as first possession and economic efficiency, as relevant considerations. His decision, then, will be reflective of this selective perception as to the appropriate factors in determining a taking.

Penn Central makes several claims as to how the Landmarks Law, as applied to their parcel, effects a compensable taking of private property. First, appellants claim that the application of the law "deprived them of any gainful use of their 'air rights' above the Terminal and that irrespective of the value of the remainder of their parcel, the city has 'taken' their right to this superadjacent airspace, thus entitling them to 'just compensation' measured by the fair market value of these air rights" (*Penn Central*, p. 2662). Thus, appellants are invoking what Margaret Jane Radin (1988) has called a "conceptual severance" view of property, that a right inheres in each stick of a property interest bundle, and that the removal of any stick from the bundle constitutes a taking for which compensation is owed. The Court, however, rejects this argument, stating that it is not enough to "establish a 'taking' simply by showing that they have been denied the ability to exploit a property interest that they heretofore had believed was available for development" (*Penn Central*, p. 2662). Indeed, the Court's rejection of the conceptual severance view of property could hardly be more clear:

> "Taking" jurisprudence does not divide a single parcel into discrete segments and attempt to determine whether rights in a particular segment have been entirely abrogated. . . . this Court focuses rather both on the character of the action and on the nature and extent of the interference with rights in *the parcel as a whole*—here, . . . the landmark site. (*Penn Central*, p. 2662; emphasis added)

In making this assertion, moreover, Justice Brennan cites several precedents in which the conceptual severance view has been rejected.

Of interest is that Justice Rehnquist, in his dissenting opinion (joined by Chief Justice Burger and Justice Stevens), argues the opposite on this point. He cites several cases in which the Court *has* adhered to the conceptual severance view of property and maintains that this is the view of property that inheres in the Constitution (*Penn Central*, pp. 2668–2669). The definition of property chosen has substantial implications for takings jurisprudence. The rejection of the conceptual severance definition leads to a far narrower definition of what constitutes a taking than would obtain if the conceptual severance view were adopted. The Court's decision in this case can thus be seen as resting on the rejection of the conceptual severance view of property, and is in this sense selective, as adherence to the conceptual severance view would likely lead to the opposite result.

The second claim made by appellants is that the application of the Landmark Law effects a taking because it "has significantly diminished the value of the Terminal site" (*Penn Central*, p. 2662), and does so in a manner inconsistent with the Constitution because it is discriminatory in that it applies only to individuals who own historically designated properties (*Penn Central*, p. 2663). The Court's rejection of this discrimination claim rests on their interpretation of the ordinance as "embodying a *comprehensive* plan to preserve structures of historic or aesthetic interest wherever they might be found in the city" (*Penn Central*, p. 2663; emphasis added), as evidenced by the fact that over 400 landmarks and 31 historic districts have been designated under this law. Thus, its "comprehensive" nature makes the law nondiscriminatory—the lines of discrimination being the treatment of *one historic structure versus another historic structure*, rather than between *one structure and another structure.* The Court rejects the claim that a taking occurs because the law has a more severe impact on some owners than on others on the grounds that much legislation designed to promote the general welfare has such disparate impacts, and in prior cases this has not been sufficient grounds to constitute a taking (*Penn Central*, p. 2664). The Court also rejects the claim that appellants do not benefit from the law since the general application of the law "benefits all New York citizens and all structures, both economically and by improving the quality of life in the city as a whole" (*Penn Central*, p. 2664), that there is some reciprocity of advantage.

That all of the foregoing reflects selective perception can be seen by looking to the dissenting opinion of Justice Rehnquist. First, there is the selective perception as to what constitutes discriminatory government action. Recall that the Court's line of demarcation regarding discrimination here is that various historic landmarks are treated equally, in that its application to 400 buildings makes it "comprehensive." Rehnquist views this very differently: "Of the over one million buildings and structures in the city of New York, appellees have *singled out* 400 for designation as official landmarks" (*Penn Central*, p. 2666; emphasis added). Rehnquist, then, draws the line of demarcation between one structure and another, and views 400 out of one million as a "discriminatory," or "singled out," as opposed to a "comprehensive" number (he calls it "relatively few") (*Penn Central*, p. 2667). Thus, we have selective perception as to what constitutes discrimination. Justice Rehnquist also disputes the Court's claim that the impact of the law on appellants is not severe, claiming that the costs of keeping the exterior features of the structure in good repair are substantial, and that there is "little or no offsetting benefit" (*Penn Central*, p. 2667). Here, then, we have selective perception as to the evaluation of benefits and costs. What is severe to one justice is small, or even not recognized, by another.

The third claim that is made by the appellants is that the government has appropriated a portion of their property for a strictly governmental use, that government is acting in its enterprise capacity, such as occurred in *U.S. v. Causby* (1946) (*Penn Central*, p. 2665). The Court rejects this claim, stating that this case "is not remotely like that in *Causby*" (*Penn Central*, p. 2665), and that "the Landmarks Law neither exploits the appellants parcel for city purposes nor facilitates nor arises from any entrepreneurial operations of the city" (*Penn Central*, p. 2665). Rather, "[t]he Landmarks Law's effect is simply to prohibit appellants or anyone else from occupying the space above the Terminal, while permitting appellants to use the remainder of the parcel in gainful fashion" (*Penn Central*, p. 2665), and hence no compensable taking has occurred.

Contrast this with Justice Rehnquist's dissent: "While Penn Central may continue to use the terminal site as it is presently designated, appellees otherwise 'exercise complete dominion and control over the surface of the land' . . . and must compensate the owner for his loss" (*Penn Central*, p. 2670). Again, we see the element of selective perception here as to whether the government action constitutes entrepreneurial use and hence whether the case fits the precedent set in *Causby*.

To this point, the Court has established that the failure of the Landmark Law to provide "just compensation" does not render the law invalid. Next, the Court turns to the issue of whether the law, as applied to Penn Central, has an impact so severe that it must be deemed a taking for which compensation is owed (*Penn Central*, p. 2665).

Here, the Court begins with the "reasonable expectations" issue. The application of the Landmarks Law to the terminal does not interfere with the present use of the terminal. Moreover,

> [i]ts designation as a landmark not only permits but contemplates that appellants may continue to use the property precisely as it has been used in for the past 65 years: as a railroad terminal containing office space and concessions. *So the law does not interfere with what must be regarded as Penn Central's primary expectation concerning the use of the parcel.* [*Penn Central*, p. 2665; emphasis added]

Furthermore, says the Court, the law does not keep Penn Central from earning a reasonable return on its investment (*Penn Central*, p. 2665). The Court also finds no merit in the appellants' claim that the effect of the law upon their air rights is "substantial." The appellant have not been denied *all* use of the air space above the terminal. Rather, they have been denied permission to build a 50-story office tower. The Landmarks Commission has left open the possibility that other types of alterations that would better harmonize with the terminal may be approved (*Penn Central*, p. 2666). Furthermore, Penn Central still retains the ability to transfer their air rights to several parcels in the area and hence could profit from them in that way (*Penn Central*, p. 2666). The Court does allow that the value of these rights may not constitute "just compensation" if a taking were found to have occurred, but it does "mitigate whatever financial burdens the law has imposed on the appellants" (*Penn Central*, p. 2666), and hence it cannot be said that the burden on the appellants is "substantial."

Justice Rehnquist's dissenting responses to these arguments further illuminates the selective perception at work in resolving these issues. With regard to the reasonable return argument, Rehnquist states that while the destruction of reasonable return is grounds for establishing a taking, the fact that one is still able to make a reasonable return does not mean that no taking has occurred. Rather, "[i]t is the character of the invasion, not the amount of damage resulting from it, so long as the damage is substantial, that determines the question whether it is a taking" (*Penn Central*, p. 2672).

Several important issues present themselves here. First, we have differing opinions, as between the majority and the dissent, as to how the "reasonable return" issue is to be handled. Both the majority and the dissent seem to grant that Penn Central is earning a reasonable return, but each reaches a different conclusion regarding the relevance of this for determining a taking. Second, while the majority seems to find the reasonable return issue to be dispositive of the issue, it is the character of the government action that seems to be dispositive for the dissent.[7] The selectivity element is operative here both between the rules and within the rules themselves as applied to this case. To begin with, there is no reason for elevating either the reasonable return rule or the character of the government action rule above the other, or above any other possible rule, for that matter. Any given rule is selected out of a wide range of possible rules, no one of which has any prior claim to legitimacy over any other. As regards the application of the rules themselves, the Court equates past use with "reasonable expectations" where there is no basis for doing so. The fact that the terminal has operated in a particular way in the past does not mean that it is unreasonable to expect that they could construct on the existing structure, especially since the original plans for the building included a 20-story tower (which was never built).[8] The selectivity element operative in analyzing the character of the government action has been discussed above and will not be repeated here.

The Court's decision in *Penn Central* set the stage for the next decade of takings jurisprudence. Justice Brennan's opinion gave rise to what has come to be known as the *Penn Central* test, embodying the criteria of economic impact, the character of the government action, and the protection of health, safety, morals, and general welfare. As the analysis of the majority and dissenting opinions in this case has shown, however, the application of a specific rule, the substance of which seems to be accepted by the majority and dissent, does not necessarily lead to a conclusive result. Here, the majority saw a small economic impact while the dissent saw a large one. Furthermore, there was not only disagreement over the character of the government action, whether the Landmarks

Law "goes too far," there was also the claim, in the dissent, that this criterion is dispositive of the issue. These themes, or variants on them, will continue to arise in the cases discussed below.

4. A HINT OF TEMPORARY TAKINGS: *San Diego Gas and Electric Co. v. City of San Diego*

What is perhaps most unique about *San Diego Gas and Electric Co. v. City of San Diego* (1981) is that the implications for the takings issue lie in the dissent rather than in the majority opinion. While the Court finds that the case must be left undecided because the Court lacks jurisdiction, the dissent claims that the Court does indeed have jurisdiction and proceeds to analyze the case on the merits. In writing for the dissent, Justice Brennan establishes a rule regarding "temporary" regulatory takings which laid the groundwork for the Court's decision in *First English Evangelical Lutheran Church v. City of Glendale* (1987), the result being a dramatic expansion of the scope of the compensation principle.

In 1966, appellant acquired a tract of land for possible use as a site for a nuclear power plant to be built in the 1980s. In 1973, the City of San Diego rezoned an area which included appellant's property to agricultural uses and adopted an open-space plan, placing appellant's property among the open-space areas (*San Diego Gas and Electric Co.*, p. 1290). In 1974, appellants sued the city, claiming that the rezoning and the adoption of the open-space plan effected a taking in that it deprived the them of "the entire beneficial use of the property" (*San Diego Gas and Electric Co.*, p. 1290). The city disputed this claim, since they had never denied any development plan for the property and were not necessarily bound by the open-space plan in considering development (*San Diego Gas and Electric Co.*, p. 1291).

The California Supreme Court determined, based on *Agins v. Tiburon* (1980), that the only available remedy where a zoning regulation has the effect of depriving a person of all use of his land is invalidation, that monetary damages are not available (*San Diego Gas and Electric Co.*, pp. 1292–1294). Appellant appealed to the U.S. Supreme Court, which determined that it did not have jurisdiction in the case because no final judgment had been rendered as to whether a taking had occurred (*San Diego Gas and Electric Co.*, p. 1294).

Writing for the dissent, Justice Brennan (joined by Justices Stewart, Marshall, and Powell) disputes the Court's claim that no final judgment has been rendered. Brennan cites the opinion of the California Court of Appeal, which says that

> [u]nlike the person whose property is *taken* in eminent domain, the individual who is *deprived* of his property due to the state's exercise of its police power is not entitled to compensation. . . . rather, the party's remedy is administrative mandamus. (*San Diego Gas and Electric Co.*, p. 1298; emphasis in original)

Thus, based on *Agins*, California Courts are prohibited from finding that a police power regulation constitutes a compensable taking, and hence we do indeed have a final judgment, one that says that no taking has occurred here and hence no compensation is required (*San Diego Gas and Electric Co.*, pp. 1299–1301). We have, says Brennan, "a classic final judgment" (*San Diego Gas and Electric Co.*, p. 1301).

Having resolved that we do have a final judgment, Justice Brennan next turns to an analysis of the merits of the appellant's claim. The question at issue is:

> . . . whether a government entity must pay just compensation when a police power regulation has effected a "taking" of "private property" for "public use" within the meaning of [the Just Compensation Clause of the Fifth Amendment]. Implicit in this question is the corollary issue whether a government entity's exercise of its regulatory police power can ever effect a taking within the meaning of the Just Compensation Clause. (*San Diego Gas and Electric Co.*, p. 1301; footnotes omitted)

Justice Brennan's answer to these questions is an emphatic "Yes," that the California Supreme Court "flatly contradicts clear precedents of this Court" (*San Diego Gas and Electric Co.*, p. 1302) in holding that the exercise of the police power can never go so far as to constitute a compensable taking.[9]

The fatal flaw in the analysis of the California Court is its "failure to recognize the essential similarity of regulatory 'takings' and other 'takings' " (*San Diego Gas and Electric Co.*, pp. 1303–1304): "From the property owner's point of view, it may not matter whether his land is condemned or flooded or whether it is restricted by regulation to use in its natural state, if the effect in both cases is to deprive him of all beneficial use of it" (*San Diego Gas and Electric Co.*, p. 1304). Thus,

> [i]t is only logical, then, that government action other than acquisition of title, occupancy, or physical invasion can be a "taking," and therefore a de facto exercise of the power of eminent domain, when the effects completely deprive the owner of all or most of his interest in the property. (*San Diego Gas and Electric Co.*, p. 1304).

Thus, Justice Brennan has reaffirmed that government regulatory actions may constitute takings (regarding the character of government action criteria in *Penn Central*) if there is substantial economic impact (regarding the economic impact criterion in *Penn Central*).

What remains, then, is to resolve the issue as to whether a regulation that is found to be a taking must be accompanied by monetary compensation or whether, alternatively, invalidation of the regulation is sufficient. It is here that Brennan's dissent has the most potentially wide-ranging impact if it is applied in future cases.[10] In Brennan's view, mere invalidation of the contested regulation is not sufficient. The rule he proposes here is that

> . . . once a court finds that a police power regulation has effected a "taking," the government entity must pay compensation for the period commencing on the date the regulation first effected the "taking," and ending on the date the government entity chooses to rescind or otherwise amend the regulation. (*San Diego Gas and Electric Co.*, p. 1307)

While invalidation does keep the owner from suffering future losses, it does not make the owner whole for losses suffered up to the time of invalidation. Since the just compensation provision is meant to leave the harmed party as well off as before the regulation, compensation is owed for this "temporary taking" (*San Diego Gas and Electric Co.*, pp. 1305–1306).

What Justice Brennan has done in the foregoing is in part to acknowledge the ubiquitous nature of takings. Here, Brennan does this both in equating regulatory takings and physical invasion, and in equating "temporary" and "permanent" takings for purposes of compensation. From a consistency standpoint, this is, of course, a good thing. Government actors occasion losses in regulatory and physical invasion cases, and losses are losses whether they are permanent or temporary. In the latter case, the same analysis that is applied to permanent irreversible takings should also be applied to temporary reversible ones (*San Diego Gas and Electric Co.*, p. 1307). Of course, there is no reason for stopping here. The same line of analysis could be used to hold that market-determined losses should be subject to the analysis of the takings clause, since it is government that gives effect to the market system. Eventually, we get to the point of impracticability, that takings are ubiquitous and to compensate all of them would be economically impossible. The line, then, must be drawn somewhere. Brennan's rule moves that line out a bit, but there is no necessary reason why it should not be moved farther, or even moved at all.

5. *Keystone*: *Penn Central* AFFIRMED

The Court's decision in *Keystone Bituminous Coal Association v. DeBenedictis* (1987) may best be seen as an affirmation of its decision in *Penn Central.* In this case, appellants claim that the Pennsylvania Bituminous Mine Subsidence Act, which requires that 50 percent of the coal beneath pre-existing public buildings, dwellings, and cemeteries be left unmined, constitutes a taking of their property rights in such coal. In *Pennsylvania Coal v. Mahon* (1922), the Court found that a subsidence act similar in many respects to the one in question here effected a taking.

In his opinion for the Court, Justice Stevens states, citing *Agins and Penn Central*, that the relevant considerations in resolving a challenge to a land-use regulation are whether the regulation substantially advances legitimate state interests and whether it denies the owner economically viable use of her land, including the violation of reasonable investment-backed expectations (*Keystone*, p. 1242). Appellants' challenge fails on both counts.

While the Kohler Act, the act challenged in *Pennsylvania Coal v. Mahon*, was rejected as serving private rather than public interests, the Subsidence Act does serve "important public interests . . . by enforcing a policy that is designed to minimize subsidence in certain areas" (*Keystone*, p. 1242). Its goals, says the Court, are "genuine, substantial, and legitimate" (*Keystone*, p. 1242), "acting to protect the public interest in health, the environment, and the fiscal integrity of the area" (*Keystone*, p. 1243). The Court goes so far as to say that the state is "exercising its police power to abate activity *akin to a public nuisance*" (*Keystone*, p. 1243; emphasis added). Thus, by defining subsidence as a nuisance, the Court is able to substantiate its claim that the Subsidence Act protects health and safety, since it has long been recognized that use of the police power to resolve nuisance disputes does not constitute a taking.

Writing in a dissent that is strikingly similar to his dissent in *Penn Central*, Chief Justice Rehnquist disputes the distinction that the Court draws between this case and *Pennsylvania Coal v. Mahon*, stating that the differences "verge on the trivial" (*Keystone*, p. 1254). The Kohler Act was, he says, intended to serve public, not private, interests, but "the mere existence of a public purpose was insufficient to release the government from the compensation requirement" (*Keystone*, p. 1255). "Public purpose" should not, according to Rehnquist, be viewed as a sufficient condition for finding no taking, but rather as a necessary condition for the government exercise of its takings power—the "public use" requirement of the Fifth Amendment (*Keystone*, p. 1256). What is important for resolving takings issues, says Rehnquist, is the *nature* of the government action (*Keystone*, p. 1256). The question then becomes whether the nuisance criterion applies here, since prevention of a nuisance falls within the bounds of the police power. The nuisance exception, according to Rehnquist, is "a narrow exception allowing the government to prevent a 'misuse or illegal use,'" rather than "[a] broad exception" to protect "health, welfare, and safety" (*Keystone*, p. 1256). Furthermore, the central purposes of the Subsidence Act are not the protection of health, welfare, and safety, but rather the "preservation of buildings, economic development, and maintenance of property values to sustain the Commonwealth's tax base" (*Keystone*, p. 1257). That is, this is essentially an economic measure. Thus, says Rehnquist, the facts here do not support the Court's contention that the Subsidence Act is a nuisance regulation.

What we have here, then, are two very different views of the issues at hand. We have two different readings of the Subsidence Act, one saying it promotes health, safety, and welfare, and the other saying that it promotes certain economic interests. We also have competing views as to what constitutes a nuisance: for the Court it is any activity that impinges on health, safety, or welfare, and for the dissent it is only those activities that constitute misuse or illegal use—something far narrower, according to Rehnquist, than protecting health, safety, and welfare. All of this illustrates the selective nature of perception, identification, and definition of the issues surrounding these disputes.

Having decided that the act does indeed advance legitimate state interests, the Court turns to an examination of the economic impact of the regulation. Citing *Agins v. Tiburon* (1980), Justice Stevens states that "[t]he test to be applied . . . is fairly straightforward. A statute regulating the uses that can be made of property effects a taking if it 'denies an owner economically viable use of his land . . .'" (*Keystone*, p. 1247). Appellants fail to satisfy this requirement.

In making their claim of substantial economic impact, appellants invoke a conceptual severance view of property, arguing that the coal under these protected structures constitutes a distinct property interest, the support estate, and that the state has taken their rights in this distinct interest, depriving them of all economically viable use of this property (*Keystone*, pp. 1247–1248). Citing Michelman (1967), the Court rejects the conceptual severance view of property; the relevant unit is the entire parcel, not individual segments within the parcel (*Keystone*, p. 1248). The coal that must be left unmined under the act constitutes only a small portion of the total amount of coal available for mining. Furthermore, only about 75 percent of the coal can be profitably mined. Since appellants are still able to mine nearly all of the coal in their mineral estates, and since they are able to do so profitably, there is no substantial economic impact and their reasonable expectations have not been violated. Thus, the Court is unable to find a taking on these grounds (*Keystone*, pp. 1249–1250).

Following the line taken in his dissent in *Penn Central*, Chief Justice Rehnquist disputes the Court's rejection of the conceptual severance view of property, claiming that "'"the right to coal consists in the right to mine it"'" (*Keystone*, p. 1257), and that the effect of the act is not merely "to forbid one 'particular use' of property with many uses but to extinguish *all* beneficial use of petitioners' property" (*Keystone*, p. 1257; emphasis in original). Having adopted the conceptual severance view, Justice Rehnquist's conclusion that a taking has occurred logically follows, since if a right inheres in each strand of coal owned by appellants, the prohibition from mining that coal deprives appellants of all economically viable use of that coal, "destroy[ing] completely any interest in a segment of property" (*Keystone*, p. 1259).

The resolution of the economic impact claim, then, turns entirely on the definition of property. If one rejects the conceptual severance view, then it is fairly straightforward to conclude that there is no taking (although we still have the fuzzy lines, selectively drawn, of what constitutes a "substantial" economic impact on the entire parcel). Acceptance of the conceptual severance view, in contrast, leads directly to the conclusion that a taking has occurred here, since the entire segment of the bundle has been destroyed from appellants' point of view. While neither of these definitions has any prior claim to legitimacy, we see here an affirmation of the decision made in *Penn Central*, that the relevant unit of property is the parcel as a whole, rather than the discrete segments.

In *Keystone* we see striking parallels to *Penn Central*. The *Penn Central* test is affirmed, and the conceptual severance view of property is again rejected. We also see conflicting perceptions of the *Penn Central* test as applied: large versus small economic impact, acceptable versus extreme character of government action, and broad and narrow definitions of health, safety, morals, and general welfare. Justice Rehnquist again claims that the character of the government action is dispositive. The Court's view of the legitimacy of this claim is difficult to ascertain, both in *Keystone* and in *Penn Central*, since the Court rejects the contention that the government action goes too far. The next case we will analyze, *Hodel v. Irving* (1987), sheds some light on this question.

6. *Hodel v. Irving*

In response to the increasingly extreme fractionation of Indian lands, Congress enacted Section 207 of the Indian Land Consolidation Act of 1983, which provided that

> No undivided fractional interest in any tract of trust or restricted land within a tribe's reservation or otherwise subjected to a tribe's jurisdiction shall descendent [*sic*] by intestacy or devise but shall escheat to that tribe if such interest represents 2 per centum or less of the total acreage in such tract and has earned to its owner less than $100 in the preceding year before it is due to escheat. (*Hodel v. Irving*, p. 2079)

In addition, Congress made no provision for compensation to owners whose property interests are removed under Section 207 [*Hodel v. Irving*, p. 2080]. Appellants claim that this act worked a taking of the property of their decedents.

In writing for the Court, Justice O'Connor first sets out a series of facts which would lead the Court to find that no taking has occurred. First, discouraging fractionation does serve a legitimate public purpose, and the extreme nature of the fractionation problem "may call for dramatic action" (*Hodel v. Irving*, p. 2081) such as that of Section 207.[11] Second, since this property is usually leased rather than improved upon and used by the owners, there is no reason to conclude that any investment-backed expectations have been violated (*Hodel v. Irving*, p. 2083). Third, there seems to be some reciprocity of advantage at work here since consolidation of lands in the tribe benefits the members of the tribe (*Hodel v. Irving*, p. 2083). In fact, according to the Court, "the whole benefit gained is greater than the sum of the burdens imposed since consolidated lands are more productive than fractionated lands" (*Hodel v. Irving*, p. 2083). From an efficiency perspective, then, a finding of no taking would be appropriate.

Despite the fact that the public interest, investment-backed expectations, and economic efficiency criteria point toward finding no taking in this case, the Court asserts that these factors are outweighed by the fact that "*the character of the government action here is extraordinary*" (*Hodel v. Irving*, p. 2083; emphasis added). The extraordinary character of the government action here comes from the virtual

> . . . abrogation of the right to pass on a certain type of property—the small undivided interest—to one's heirs. In one form or another, the right to pass on property—to one's family in particular—has been part of the Anglo-American legal system since feudal times. (*Hodel v. Irving*, p. 2083)

While some adjustments of the rules governing descent and devise are legitimate, what we have here is a case where "descent and devise are completely abolished" (*Hodel v. Irving*, p. 2084), a result so extreme that it triggers the just compensation clause of the Fifth Amendment. Furthermore, this law abolishes descent and devise even in cases where there may be some consolidation, rather than increasing fractionation (*Hodel v. Irving*, p. 2084).

Appellants claim that the compensation clause should not be triggered here because the value of the affected interests is small, but the Court rejects this argument since while the income generated by these property interests is usually small, the same is not always true of the *value* of these interests (*Hodel v. Irving*, pp. 2082, 2084). Justice Stevens, in his concurring opinion, goes even further:

> The Sovereign has no license to take private property without paying for it and without providing its owner with any opportunity to avoid or mitigate the consequences of the deprivation simply because the property is relatively inexpensive. The Fifth Amendment makes no distinction between grand larceny and petty larceny. (*Hodel v. Irving*, p. 2089; citations omitted)

But Justice Steven's reasoning here flatly contradicts the Court's opinions in *Penn Central* and *Keystone*, the latter of which he himself wrote. In each of these cases, one of the grounds for holding that no taking has occurred was the Court's perception that the economic impact was small. The Court was indeed, in those cases, drawing a "distinction between grand larceny and petty larceny." There seems to be no way of reconciling these disparate claims other than as selective application of rules to justify the result that comports with the judge's view of the world.

There are two additional issues that deserve mention here. The first is the selective elevation of the "character of government action" criterion over the public interest, investment-backed expectations, and reciprocity of advantage criteria, especially given that the latter were all invoked in the process of finding no taking in the *Penn Central* case. Thus, Justice Rehnquist's claim, made in *Penn Central* and *Keystone*, that the character of the government action criterion should outweigh the others, is affirmed. Second, one could make a strong case for finding that no taking has occurred here based on the Court's previous resolutions of the conceptual severance versus parcel-as-a-whole definition of property. If one adopts the conceptual severance view, then one stick in the bundle, descent and devise, has been taken and hence compensation is owed. From the parcel-as-a-whole view, however, descent and devise may be seen as only one part of the bundle of rights and could easily be viewed as sufficiently small as to preclude the triggering of the just compensation clause. Given that the Court has come down on the side of the parcel-as-a-whole view in the past, it is surprising that this discussion does not come up here.

We see here, then, that the application of a given rule will not lead to a conclusive result. Different facets of a rule may point in different directions, and hence the decision will depend on which aspects of the rule are allowed to take precedence. The selective elevation of certain facets of a rule over others brings to the fore the necessity of choice involved at all levels of the taking issue.

7. First English v. County of Los Angeles

In response to a 1978 flood of the Mill Creek Canyon, the County of Los Angeles enacted an ordinance that prohibited any construction or reconstruction of buildings or structures in an interim flood protection area on the grounds that "it was 'required for the immediate preservation of the public health and safety . . .' " (*First English*, p. 2382). This interim flood protection area included Lutherglen, a camp owned by appellant which was destroyed by the flood. Appellant filed an inverse condemnation claim, stating that the ordinance denied them all use of this Lutherglen property (*First English*, p. 2382). The Superior Court of California and, on appeal, the California Court of Appeal denied appellant's inverse condemnation claim based on *Agins v. Tiburon* (1980), which held that suits alleging regulatory takings are limited to nonmonetary relief (*First English*, pp. 2382–2383). The issue before the Court was whether the decision of the Supreme Court of California in *Agins*, that the Fifth Amendment does not require compensation for "temporary" regulatory takings, was constitutional (*First English*, p. 2383).

In his opinion for the Court, Chief Justice Rehnquist begins his analysis of this issue by pointing to the equivalence under the Fifth Amendment of physical invasions and regulations which have the effect of destroying an owner's property interest. From here, Chief Justice Rehnquist goes on to analyze cases of temporary physical invasion takings, from which he concludes that "[t]hese cases reflect the fact that 'temporary' takings which, as here, deny a landowner all use of his property, are not different in kind from permanent takings, for which the Constitution clearly requires compensation" (First English, p. 2388). Thus, since temporary physical invasions constitute takings, and since regulatory takings are equivalent to physical invasion takings, the Court has no problem arriving at the conclusion that "[i]nvalidation of the ordinance or its successor ordinance after this period of time, though converting the taking into a temporary one, is not a sufficient remedy to meet the demands of the Just Compensation Clause" (*First English*, p. 2388).

Appellee claims that requiring compensation for damages incurred prior to invalidation is inconsistent with the Court's decisions in *Danforth v. United States* (1939) and *Agins v. Tiburon* (1980). In each case, appellants claimed that the activities of the government preliminary to condemnation constituted takings. The Supreme Court rejected these claims on the grounds that such fluctuations in the value of property are "'incidents of ownership'" (*First English*, p. 2388; see citations in case) and that "the valuation of property which has been taken must be calculated at the time of the taking and that depreciation in the value of the property by reason of preliminary activity is not chargeable to the government" (*First English*, p. 2388). This, according to the Court, is something entirely different than damages that occur over the period between enactment of an ordinance and its ultimate invalidation (*First English*, p. 2389). Thus,

> where the government's activities have already worked a taking of all use of property, no subsequent action by the government can relieve it of the duty to provide compensation for the period during which the taking was effective. (*First English*, p. 2389)

Invalidation, then, is "a constitutionally insufficient remedy" (*First English*, p. 2389).

In his dissenting opinion, Justice Stevens rejects the Court's asserted symmetry between temporary physical and temporary regulatory takings. In making this distinction, Stevens points to the Court's rulings that regulations do not constitute takings unless they substantially diminish the value of the property (*First English*, p. 2393). While the regulation may destroy most or all of the value of appellants' property, it does so only up to the time at which the regulation is invalidated, after which point appellants again have full use of their property. Thus, for Stevens, what the Court calls a "temporary regulatory taking" is in fact a small diminution of value:

> Why should there be a distinction between a permanent restriction that only reduces the economic value of property by a fraction—perhaps one-third—and a restriction that merely postpones development of a property for a fraction of its useful life—presumably far less than a third? (*First English*, p. 2395)

These are, says Stevens, "irreconcilable results" (*First English*, p. 2395). What we have here are static and dynamic views of property. The Court's view is static in that it looks at property at a point in time and sees total deprivation of use. Justice Stevens, in adopting a dynamic view, sees only a small deprivation since only a few years out of the property's total useful life have been removed. Neither of these referential time frames has a prior claim to legitimacy over the other, and the choice of one or the other is necessarily selective. Interestingly, Stevens' comments here contradict his concurring opinion in *Hodel v. Irving* where he states that "[t]he Fifth Amendment draws no distinction between grand larceny and petty larceny" (*Hodel v. Irving*, p. 2089). His own inconsistency seems far more "irreconcilable" than the results of the Court that he is criticizing.

Stevens also rejects the Court's "artificial distinction" (*First English*, p. 2396) between what the Court calls noncompensable "incidents of ownership" and temporary losses of the type at issue here. Since the former is not classified as a taking, the latter should not be either. Stevens is correct in his assertion that there is no a priori distinction between those losses classified as incidents of ownership and those classified as temporary takings. However, he is not correct, in an a priori sense, in saying that neither of these instances should constitute takings. Rather, we could easily reach the opposite result: since there are losses in both instances, both could be said to constitute takings. The fact that one instance is classified as an "incident of ownership" and the other as a "temporary regulatory taking" points to the selectivity element operative in the resolution of the takings issue.

First English, then, establishes a class of temporary regulatory takings, reflecting an acceptance of Justice Brennan's reasoning in his dissent in *San Diego Gas and Electric Co.* (1981). In establishing this class of temporary takings, the Court also refines the economic impact criterion to encompass a fairly short-run view of losses, or, alternatively, a very high social rate of discount. Furthermore, the public health and safety claims made as justification for the Interim Ordinance made by the County of Los Angeles seem to be substantially discounted in the Court's analysis here, in contrast to the prominence that such considerations are given in the process of finding no taking in *Keystone*. One is left to wonder whether the term "temporary taking" applies to the taking itself or to the rationale the Court chooses to use in a particular case.

8. Nollan v. California Coastal Commission

In *Nollan v. California Coastal Commission* (1987), the Nollans applied to the California Coastal Commission for a permit to demolish the existing bungalow on their property and replace it with a three-bedroom house. The commission granted their request, "subject to the condition that they allow the public an easement to pass across a portion of their property bounded by the mean high tide line on the one side, and their seawall on the other side" (*Nollan*, p. 3143). The reasons given by the commission for requiring this easement were that

> . . . the new house would increase blockage of the view of the ocean, thus contributing to the development of "a 'wall' of residential structures" that would prevent the public "psychologically . . . from realizing a stretch of coastline exists nearby that they have every right to visit" [,] . . . increase private use of the shorefront . . . [, and] "burden the public's ability to traverse to and along the shorefront." (*Nollan*, pp. 3143–3144)

Appellants claim that the condition should be invalidated because it violates the takings clause (*Nollan*, p. 3144).

Writing for the Court, Justice Scalia begins with the assertion that had the commission required the Nollans to provide an easement to increase public access, rather than making the easement a condition of the building permit, "we have no doubt that there would have been a taking" (*Nollan*, p. 3145). Scalia bases this claim on previous Court holdings regarding the fundamental right to exclude others from one's property and the assertion that requiring an easement to allow people to continually traverse one's property is equivalent to a "permanent physical occupation" (*Nollan*, p. 3145). The issue then becomes, for the Court, "whether requiring [the easement] to be conveyed as a condition for issuing a land use permit alters the outcome" (*Nollan*, p. 3146).

In his dissenting opinion, Justice Brennan disputes the Court's assertion that requiring an easement would be a taking here. The right of exclusion here is, he says, limited by the provision of the California Constitution that prohibits denial of access to navigable waters when such access is required for public purposes (*Nollan*, pp. 3153–3154). The Court rejects Brennan's claim on the grounds that the easement provides access "along" the water rather than "to" the water (*Nollan*, p. 3145). Yet, this easement would provide access between two public beaches, thus enhancing access "to" water. All of this turns on the scope of one's definition of access "to" water as well as what constitutes valid public purpose, all of which is subject to selective perception and identification.

Relying on the tests set forth in *Agins* and *Penn Central*, the Court states that "land use regulation does not effect a taking if it 'substantially advance[s] legitimate state interests' and does not 'den[y] an owner economically viable use of his land'" (*Nollan*, p. 3146, citing *Agins*). The Court assumes that the commission's goals here satisfy the public use requirement (*Nollan*, pp. 3146–3147).[12] In spite of this, however, the court concludes that the permit condition does indeed work a taking because, in its words, "the condition . . . utterly fails to further the end advanced as the justification for the [permit condition]" (*Nollan*, p. 3148). In making this assertion, the Court says that

> . . . .[i]t is quite impossible to understand how a requirement that people already on the public beaches be able to walk across the Nollans' property reduces any obstacles to viewing the beach created by the new house. It is also impossible to understand how it lowers any "psychological barrier" to using the public beaches, or how it helps to remedy any additional congestion on them caused by construction of the Nollans' new house. We therefore find that the Commission's imposition of the permit condition cannot be treated as an exercise of its land use power for any of these purposes. Our conclusion on this point is consistent with the approach taken by every other court that has considered the question, with the exception of the California state courts. (*Nollan*, p. 3149; footnote omitted)[13]

Thus, "the building restriction is not a valid regulation of land use, but 'an out-and-out plan of extortion'" (*Nollan*, p. 3148). Hence, while the goals set forth by the commission are both valid and legitimate, the conveyance of an easement along the shoreline does not accomplish these goals, and if the commission wants an easement across the Nollans' property, "it must pay for it" (*Nollan*, p. 3150). Thus, to the economic impact, legitimate state interest, and character of government action criteria of *Penn Central* and *Agins*, we have the additional criterion of the relation of the regulation to the announced goals that underlie it.

Justice Brennan takes issue with this finding in his dissent, claiming that it goes against the grain of a large number of previous cases that mandate only that the state could reasonably assume that the regulation would meet the goals set forth by the state (*Nollan*, p. 3151). Here, that is accomplished by virtue of the fact that the lateral easement will offset the reduction in visual access by leaving an equal net amount of access (*Nollan*, pp. 3152–3153). Such decisions on correspondence, says Brennan, are best left to state and local officials who are most familiar with the issues, unless the outcomes are "clearly arbitrary and unreasonable" (*Nollan*, p. 3153). Of course, this is exactly what the Court has done; the difference in the majority and dissenting opinions here is due to differing perceptions as to what constitutes "arbitrary and unreasonable." For the Court, the divergence between the goals and effects was "arbitrary and unreasonable," as evidenced by their language that the permit condition "utterly fails to further the end advanced as the justification for the prohibition" (*Nollan*, p. 3148). For Brennan, the opposite holds. Here we again have a situation where different justices view the set of facts and precedents and arrive at opposite conclusions.

Finally, Justice Brennan deals with the issue of whether the regulation "goes too far." He points to what he sees as a "minimal" physical interference (*Nollan*, p. 3156) (in contrast with the Court viewing this as a physical invasion), and the lack of any economic disadvantage in rejecting the idea that this condition goes too far. Furthermore, he says, there is some reciprocity of advantage here in that similar restrictions on other owners in the area allow the Nollans to walk along near their property. What we have, according to Brennan, is not a taking, but rather a regulation "that represents a reasonable adjustment of the burdens and benefits of development along the California coast" (*Nollan*, p. 3160).

9. Pennell v. City of San Jose

Pennell v. City of San Jose (1988) involves a challenge to a rent-control ordinance enacted in 1979 by the City of San Jose, California. This ordinance allowed tenants to challenge any rent increase in excess of 8 percent before a "Mediation Hearing Officer" (*Pennell*, p. 854). In assessing the "reasonableness" of the rent increase, the hearing officer was to consider seven factors, including hardship to the tenant (*Pennell*, p. 862). This rent-control ordinance was enacted for the purpose of

> . . . alleviat[ing] some of the more immediate needs created by San Jose's housing situation. These needs include but are not limited to the prevention of excessive and unreasonable rent increases, the alleviation of undue hardships upon individual tenants, and the assurance to landlords of a fair and reasonable return on the value of their property. (*Pennell*, p. 854)

Appellants, an apartment-house owners association, allege that the ordinance, and especially the "tenant hardship" provision, constitutes a taking under the Fifth and Fourteenth Amendments and also violates the equal protection and due process clauses of the Fourteenth Amendment.

Appellants contend that the tenant hardship provision of the ordinance does not serve the purpose of eliminating excessive rents. The determination of what is "excessive" versus what is "reasonable" is to be found in the other six criteria, which are essentially cost- or market-based. By requiring the hearing officer to take tenant hardship into account, the city is, according to appellants, establishing a transfer program from landlords to hardship tenants. In doing so, "the Ordinance forces private individuals to shoulder the 'public' burden of subsidizing the poor tenants housing" (*Pennell*, p. 856), and thus works a taking.

In addressing this claim, the Court determined that "it would be premature to consider this claim on the present record" (*Pennell*, p. 856). The Court's rationale here is that the tenant hardship provision has never been used to reduce a proposed rent increase, nor does the provision *require* the hearing officer to make a reduction in the proposed rent increase in the presence of hardship. The takings claim cannot be resolved without a "concrete factual setting in which the hardship provision has actually been applied" (*Pennell*, p. 857). The Court also rejected appellants' claims that the ordinance violated the due process and equal protection clauses of the Fourteenth Amendment.

Justice Scalia, joined by Justice O'Connor, concurred with the Court's decision regarding the due process and equal protection challenges, but dissented in the resolution of the takings claim. Scalia maintains that appellants' claim was not premature and that, in fact, the tenant hardship provision constitutes an uncompensated taking of private property. Justice Scalia accepts appellants' claim that the determination of excessive versus reasonable rent increases lies in the six cost- and market-based criteria alone:

> Once the other six factors of the ordinance have been applied to a landlord's property, so that he is receiving only a reasonable return, he can no longer be regarded as a "cause" of exorbitantly priced housing; nor is he any longer reaping distinctively high profits from the housing shortage. The seventh factor, the "hardship" provision, is invoked to meet a quite different social problem: the existence of some renters who are too poor to afford even reasonably priced housing. (*Pennell*, p. 862).

The poverty problem, according to Scalia, is not attributable to landlords but to society at large, and the traditional method of dealing with this problem is through social welfare programs. While social programs allow the public to bear the burden of reducing poverty, the tenant hardship provision puts this burden (as it applies to affordable housing) on a few private individuals. What we have here, says Scalia,

> . . . is not "regulating" rents in the relevant sense of preventing rents that are excessive; rather, it is using the occasion of rent regulation (accomplished by the rest of the Ordinance) to establish a welfare program privately funded by those landlords who happen to have "hardship" tenants. (*Pennell*, p. 863)

Since landlords cannot be regarded as the source of tenant poverty, such regulation constitutes a taking.

Looking at Justice Scalia's reasoning in the light of the *Penn Central* test, we see the implicit assertion that the character of the government's action may be so extreme as to outweigh considerations of economic impact and public purpose. As in *Hodel v. Irving*, we have a situation where the economic impact may well be small in many instances. Furthermore, there is the recognition that availability affordable housing for the poor, like the prevention of fractionation of Indian lands, is a valid public purpose. In light of *Hodel v. Irving*, one wonders what the Court is waiting for. The Court acknowledges the legitimacy of the public purpose in its decision, which leaves only economic impact and the character of the government action. The character question is present in the existence of the tenant hardship provision itself, as illustrated in the dissent of Justice Scalia. The fact that the Court did not accept this view suggests that it does not view the character issue is dispositive. What we are left with, then, is the economic impact, and the implication that massive reductions in rent increases on the grounds of tenant hardship may be takings while small reductions would not be. Of course, this is all speculative. If correct, however, it suggests a sharp break with the decision in *Hodel v. Irving* and leads one to wonder why the ability to pass on property at death is more important than the ability to charge the market price for use of one's property.

10. RULES ENTRENCHED: Executive Order 12630

On March 15, 1988, President Ronald Reagan issued Executive Order 12630 for the purpose of assisting

> . . . Federal departments and agencies in undertaking [reviews of their actions] and in proposing, planning, and implementing actions with due regard for the constitutional protections provided by the Fifth Amendment and to reduce the risk of undue or inadvertent burdens on the public fisc resulting from lawful government action. (Executive Order, p. 8859)

This order arose largely from the impact of the recent Supreme Court decisions on the takings issue, and represents an attempt to internalize to government decisionmakers some of the information as to what may or may not constitute a taking.

If one reads the order after having read the important taking cases of the previous decade or so, one will be struck by the extent to which the decisions in these cases are reflected in the order. At the most basic level, the order reflects the Court's willingness to find takings in the impacts of certain types of regulations. Thus, the references to "actions" in the passage from the order quoted above reflect actions that include proposed federal regulations and legislation and applications of these regulations to specific parcels of property, as well as the federal actions constituting physical invasions of property (Executive Order, p. 8860). In the process of evaluating these actions, federal officials are charged with anticipating their potential takings impact and, where there is the possibility that a taking may occur, to include the costs of providing "just compensation" in the analysis. In mandating this benefit-cost analysis, the order internalizes the costs of potential losers from a regulation or from legislation into the government's decisionmaking calculus.[14]

In *First English*, the Court distinguished between losses which are what it calls "incidents of ownership", those activities preliminary to a regulation that may engender losses but do not constitute takings and temporary regulatory takings. The order reflects this distinction in its description of policies and actions that *do not* have takings implications. This list includes "[s]tudies or similar efforts or planning activities" (Executive Order, p. 8860) as well as "[c]ommunications between Federal agencies or departments and State or local planning agencies regarding planned or proposed State or local actions regulating private property . . ." (Executive Order, p. 8860). Federal officials need not worry that such activities would in and of themselves constitute takings, even though such activities may result in losses for those whose property would be affected if the actions under discussion are put into law. Furthermore, the order acknowledges the Court's establishment of class of temporary regulatory takings in *First English*: ". . . governmental action may amount to a taking . . . even if the action constituting a taking is temporary in nature" (Executive Order, p. 8861). Moreover, reflecting the Court's decision in *San Diego Gas and Electric Co.*, "[w]hen a proposed action involves a permitting process or any other decision-making process that will interfere with, or otherwise prohibit, the use of private property pending the completion of the process, the duration of the process shall be kept to the minimum necessary" (Executive Order, p. 8861).

The *Penn Central* test, which sets forth the criteria of economic impact (including the effect on reasonable expectations), the character of government action, and public purpose (including the effect on health, safety, morals, and general welfare) in evaluating takings cases, is also given prominent play in the order. With respect to economic impact, the order specifies that government officials should be aware that "[a]ctions . . . that substantially affect . . . value or use . . . may constitute a taking of property . . . even though the action results in less than a complete deprivation of all use or value, or of all separate and distinct property interests in the same private property . . ."(Executive Order, pp. 8860–8861). With respect to the character of the government action, a criterion reaffirmed in *Hodel v. Irving*, the order holds that ". . . the restriction imposed on the use shall not be disproportionate to the extent to which the use contributes to the overall problem that the restriction is imposed to redress" (Executive Order, p. 8861). Finally, with respect to public purpose, the order says that

> . . . the mere assertion of a public health or safety purpose is insufficient to avoid a taking. Actions to which this Order applies asserted to be for the protection of public health and safety, therefore, should be undertaken only in response to real and substantial threats to public health and safety, be designed to advance significantly the health and safety purpose, and be no greater than is necessary to achieve the health and safety purpose. (Executive Order, p. 8861)

The controversial requirement of matching the goals of a regulation with its effects, set out in *Nollan*, is also prominent here. In fact, the order reflects *Nollan* so far as to specify the guidelines as to the establishment of permit conditions:

> . . . any conditions imposed on the granting of a permit shall:
> [1] Serve the same purpose that would have been served by a prohibition of the use or action; and
> [2] Substantially advance that purpose. (Executive Order, p. 8861)

In his dissent in *Nollan*, Justice Brennan maintains that insistence on a precise fit between goals and effects is

> . . . insensitive to the fact that increasing intensity of development in many areas calls for far-sighted, comprehensive planning that takes into account both the interdependence of land uses and the cumulative impact on development. (*Nollan*, pp. 3161–3162)

He goes on to express the hope that the decision in *Nollan* "is an aberration, and that a broader vision ultimately prevails" (Nollan, p. 3162; footnote omitted). Alas, the Executive Order seems to point to the fact that the decision is already becoming entrenched.

Thus far, our discussion of this order has concentrated on the reflection in the order of recent case law in the takings area. The discussion of the specific cases, above, has pointed to some of the problems inherent in all of this, and will not be repeated here. There is, however, an additional part of this order that merits special attention, as it illustrates in vivid fashion the crux of the issues raised in the analysis in this chapter.

In setting out the list of "'[p]olicies that do not have takings implications'" (Executive Order, p. 8859), the first one put forth is "[a]ctions abolishing regulations, discontinuing governmental programs, or modifying regulations in a manner that lessens interference with the use of private property" (Executive Order, p. 8860). What we have here is a total failure to recognize the dual nature of rights. There simply is no such thing as "more" or "less" government interference; rather, there is simply the choice as to whose interests government will give effect. This is fundamental. Just as the imposition of regulations results in gainers and losers, so, too, the abolition or regulations results in gainers and losers. There is no a priori basis for the claim that the former may go so far as to constitute a taking while that latter may not. The failure to recognize this, be it in an Executive Order or in the judicial resolution of cases, is glaring evidence of the selective and ideological processes at work in the resolution of the taking issue.

11. Conclusion

The analysis of these cases, as well as of the Executive Order, demonstrates very clearly the entrenchment of the takings tests set forth in *Penn Central* and *Agins*. The criteria put forth in these tests—economic impact, the character of the government action, and protection of health, safety, morals, and general welfare—reflect the outcome of the process that Donald Schon has called "naming and framing":

> Each story conveys a very different view of reality and represents a special way of seeing. From a situation that is vague, ambiguous, and indeterminate . . . , each story selects and names different features and relations which become the "things" of the story . . . Each story places the features it has selected within the frame of a particular context . . .
>
> Each story constucts its view of social reality through a complementary process of naming and framing. (Schon 1979, p. 264; emphasis in original)

While this naming and framing process is present at the point of formulating rules, it is also present at a second level, that of applying the rule. In a decision rule with multiple criteria, such as the *Penn Central* test, different criteria may point in different directions. The resolution of such a case, then, necessitates the elevation of one or more of these criteria over the others, the "naming" of certain criteria as dispositive for the issue at hand. The selectivity of this choice process becomes especially apparent when we see majority and dissenting opinions elevating different criteria to prominence, and in the process reaching different conclusions. What we see, in such a case, is that "[a] description which seems neutral reveals itself as one-sided when brought up against a different description, the selective character of which is indicated by [the qualities] to which one chooses to give prominence" (Perelman 1982, p. 45).

Law is made, not discovered, and hence the search for a Holy Grail must inevitably come up empty. We confront a necessity of choice in the face of radical indeterminacy, and the use of rules in such a context results in what Frederick Schauer calls "the vice of formalism":

> One view of the vice of formalism takes that vice to be one of deception, either of oneself or of others. To disguise a choice in the language of definitional inexorability obscures that choice and thus obstructs questions of how it was made and whether it could have been made differently. The use of the word "formalism" in this sense hinges on the existence of a term . . . whose contested application generates the choice. Some terms, like "liberty" and "equality," [including the terms relevant to the taking clause,] are *pervasively indeterminate*. It is not that such terms have no content whatsoever; it is that *every* application, every concretization, every instantiation requires the addition of supplementary premises to apply the general term to specific cases. Therefore, any application of that term that denies the choice made among various eligible supplementary premises is formalistic in this sense. (Schauer 1988, pp. 513–514; footnotes omitted)

While the invocation of these rules, as well as the resolution of cases under their aegis, serves to obfuscate this necessity of choice, the juxtaposition of these majority and dissenting opinions illuminates some of this choice.

In 1977, Bruce Ackerman labelled the existing case law in the takings area "a chaos of confused argument" (Ackerman 1977, p. 8). It is not clear that we have moved beyond this. The rules are perhaps more specific, but the applications are no more clear. And even if they were, we would still be left with one set of results where many are possible. What we see is a reflection of five votes, by five human beings, each of whom views the world in a particular way. And law marches on.

Notes

1. Taken from White (1990, p. 101).
2. Quoted in Hentoff (1990, p. 60).
3. See, for example, Samuels (1981, 1989), Samuels and Mercuro (1980, 1981), Samuels and Schmid (1981), Schmid (1987, 1989), Medema (1989), and Liebhafsky (1987).

4. See, for example, Michelman (1967), Sax (1971), Berger (1974), Ackerman (1977), and Epstein (1985).

5. New York City's justification for its law stated that it would benefit the citizens by

> . . . fostering "civic pride in the beauty and noble accomplishments of the past"; protecting and enhancing "the city's attractions to tourists and visitors"; "support[ing] and stumul[ating] business and industry"; "strengthen[ing] the economy of the city"; and promoting "the use of historic districts, landmarks, interior landmarks and scenic landmarks for the education, pleasure and welfare of the people of the city." (*Penn Central*, p. 2651)

6. Physical invasions are almost always found to constitute takings, but many regulations are not—there must be some room for adjusting the benefits and burdens of life to facilitate the common good without triggering the takings issue.

7. As seen above, the character of the government action is, for the dissent, such that a taking has occurred.

8. For example, the fact that I have had apple pie for dessert every night for the past 10 years does not mean that it is unreasonable to expect that I can have cherry pie some night.

9. Justice Brennan cites *Penn Central* (1978) and *Goldblatt v. Town of Hempstead* (1962) for support here, the foundation for all of this being the opinion of Justice Holmes in *Pennsylvania Coal v. Mahon* (1922), where Holmes stated that " 'while property may be regulated to a certain extent, if regulation goes too far it will be recognized as a taking' " (*San Diego Gas and Electric Co.*, p. 1302).

10. As we will see, Justice Brennan's analysis here was applied in the establishment of a class of temporary takings in *First English* (1987).

11. For an example of the extreme nature of the problem, see *Hodel v. Irving* (1987, p. 2081).

12. Of interest is that the court does not deal with the economically viable use part of the *Agins* test.

13. Justice Scalia goes on to cite numerous cases here for support, which is interesting in light of Justice Brennan's dissenting comments discussed below.

14. This internalization process is not comprehensive, however. Rather, it reflects only the losses of the type that have been declared takings according to the Court's rules.

References

Adams, H.C. 1954. *Relation of the State to Industrial Action and Economics of Jurisprudence*. New York: Columbia University Press.

Ackerman, B.A. 1977. *Private Property and the Constitution*. New Haven: Yale University Press.

Berger, Lawrence. 1974. "A Policy Analysis of the Taking Problem. "*New York University Law Review* 49 (2&3):165–226.

Commons, J.R. 1924. *Legal Foundations of Capitalism*. New York: Macmillan.

Epstein, R.A. 1985. *Takings: Private Property and the Power of Eminent Domain*. Cambridge, MA: Harvard University Press.

Hale, R.L. 1923. "Coercion and Distribution in a Supposedly Noncoercive State." *Political Science Quarterly* 38 (September):470–494.

Hentoff, N. 1990. "The Constitutionalist." *The New Yorker* 66 (May 12):45–70.

Liebhafsky, H.H. 1987. "Law and Economics from Different Perspectives." *Journal of Economic Issues* 21 (December):1809–1836.

Medema, S.G. 1989. "Discourse and the Institutional Approach to Law and Economics: Factors That Separate the Institutional Approach to Law and Economics from Alternative Approaches." *Journal of Economic Issues* 23 (June):417–423.

Mercuro, N., and Ryan, T.P. 1984. *Law, Economics and Public Policy*. Greenwich, CT: JAI Press.

Michelman, F.I. 1967. "Property, Utility, and Fairness: Comments on the Ethical Foundations of 'Just Compensation' Law." *Harvard Law Review* 27(2): 1165–1258.

Perelman, C. 1982. *The Realm of Rhetoric*. Notre Dame, IN: University of Notre Dame Press.

Radin, M.J. 1988. "The Liberal Conception of Property: Cross Currents in the Jurisprudence of Takings." *Columbia Law Review* 88(8):1667–1696.

Samuels, W.J. 1981. "Commentary: An Economic Perspective on the Compensation Problem." In *Law and Economics: An Institutional Perpective*, eds. W.J. Samuels and A.A. Schmid, 188–209. Boston: Martinus Nijhoff Publishing.

——————. 1989. "The Legal-Economic Nexus." *George Washington Law Review* 57(6):1556–1578.

Samuels, W.J., and Mercuro, N. 1980. "The Role and Resolution of the Compensation Principle in Society: Part Two—The Resolution. *Research in Law and Economics* 2:103–128.

——————. 1981. "The Role of the Compensation Principle in Society." In *Law and Economics: An Institutional Perspective*, eds. W.J. Samuels and A.A. Schmid, 210–247. Boston: Martinus Nijhoff Publishing.

Samuels, W.J., and Schmid, A.A. 1981. *Law and Economics: An Institutional Perspective*. Boston: Martinus Nijhoff Publishing.

Sax, J.L. 1971. "Takings, Private Property and Public Rights." *The Yale Law Journal* 81(2):148–186.

Schauer, F. 1988. "Formalism." *The Yale Law Journal* 97(4):509–548.

Schmid, A.A. 1987. *Property, Power, and Public Choice: An Inquiry into Law and Economics*, 2nd ed. New York: Praeger Publishers.

——————. 1989. "Law and Economics: An Institutional Perspective." In *Law and Economics*, ed. N. Mercuro, 57–85. Boston: Kluwer Academic Publishers.

Schon, D.A. 1979. "Generative Metaphor: A Perspective on Problem-Setting in Social Policy. In *Metaphor and Thought*, ed. A. Ortony, 254–283. Cambridge: Cambridge University Press.

U.S. Executive Order of the President. 1988. Executive Order #12630, "Governmental Actions and Interference with Constitutionally Protected Property Rights." *Federal Register* 53 (March):8859–8862.

White, J.B. 1990. *Justice as Translation: An Essay in Cultural and Legal Criticism*. Chicago: University of Chicago Press.

CASES

Agins v. Tiburon, 100 S. Ct. 2138 (1980).
Danforth v. United States, 60 S. Ct. 231 (1939).
First English Evangelical Lutheran Church v. County of Los Angeles, 107 S. Ct. 2378 (1987).
Goldblatt v. Town of Hempstead, 82 S. Ct. 987 (1962).
Hodel v. Irving, 107 S. Ct. 2076 (1987).
Keystone Bituminous Coal Association v. DeBenedictis, 107 S. Ct. 1232 (1987).
Nollan v. California Coastal Commission, 107 S. Ct. 3141 (1987).
Penn Central Transportation Company v. City of New York, 98 S. Ct. 2646 (1978).
Pennell v. City of San Jose, 108 S. Ct. 849 (1988).
Pennsylvania Coal v. Mahon, 43 S. Ct. 158 (1922).
San Diego Gas and Electric Co. v. City of San Diego, 101 S. Ct. 1232 (1987).
United States v. Causby, 66 S. Ct. 1062 (1946).

4 THE SUPREME COURT AND TAKINGS JUDGMENTS: CONSTITUTIONAL POLITICAL ECONOMY VERSUS PUBLIC CHOICE

Charles K. Rowley

1. Introduction

It is my contention that, first, the U.S. Supreme Court failed repeatedly throughout the period 1937–1985 to uphold the vision of the Founding Fathers and the wording of the Constitution by its deference to the legislative branch of government with respect to interpretations of the takings clause of the Fifth Amendment; and, second, that idelogically motivated justices allowed their individual political agendas to subvert the Constitution in its intended protection of economic property rights, especially following the threat by President Roosevelt in 1937 to pack the court by expanding its size from 9 to 15 members.

This abrogation of judicial responsibility was a consequence, at least in part, of the appointment to the court for reasons of ideology and/or political patronage, of justices who too often were second-rate legal scholars. Rational ignorance among the general population concerning

The author gratefully acknowledges financial support from the Lynde and Harry Bradley Foundation judicial expertise unjustifiably protected the prestige of their offices. Inevitably, the judgments recorded by such justices not infrequently were of such poor quality as to merit the skepticism of top-flight lawyers in private practice who either had been denied appointment to the court by dominant special interests fearful of the restoration of constitutional constraints or who had avoided the federal branch because of its low remuneration and associated low esteem by successful members of the legal profession. In the absence of effective judicial oversight, the Constitution itself became vulnerable to the pressures predictably placed on it by the various factions that stalked the political marketplace in search of wealth transfers.

In this atmosphere of judicial deference to the legislature and of unprincipled judicial activism marked by undistinguished contributions to jurisprudence from High Court incumbents, there occurred a serious erosion of the economic liberties of U.S. citizens as the predictable tendency for the federal and state governments to grow and to facilitate the invasion of the economic rights of U.S. citizens, first confronted and then overwhelmed the constraint provided by the Constitution. This tendency, particularly noticeable with regard to the takings clause provisions of the Fifth Amendment, has only been aborted since justices appointed by Presidents Reagan and Bush have gained ascendancy and have turned their own artillery against the guns of the special interests in defense of the parchment of the U.S. Constitution.

2. Constitutionalism in Historical Perspective

It is important to appreciate that constitutional law is not concerned solely with the process of judicial review as directed ultimately by the U.S. Supreme Court (Stone, Seidman, Sunstein, and Tushnet 1986, p. 1). The Constitution binds not only the Supreme Court justices but also members of the Congress, of the executive government, and of state governments. It imposes on each one the responsibility of obeying constitutional requirements regardless of whether a litigated case deals with the question. Nevertheless, the Supreme Court was established arguably as the preeminent interpreter of the Constitution and, for this purpose, was vested with a unique responsibility for upholding the integrity of the carefully drafted words of that document, as subsequently amended. Its role as a creator of laws was expressly and sharply constrained to issues concerning which the parchment of the Constitution either had nothing to say or was ambiguous in its wording.

A brief historical review offers strong support for this interpretation of the Supreme Court's responsibilities, focusing on the events that led to the collapse of the Confederacy and its supplementation by the federalists at the 1787 Philadelphia convention. Hostilities with England substantially had ended in 1781 after the successful Yorktown campaign by the Revolutionaries, although the American Revolution formally was not completed until 1783 when the final peace treaty was signed with England. In the meantime, in 1781, the 13 colonies ratified the Articles of Confederation under which they lived for seven years. The Constitution replacing these articles was written in 1787 and ratified in 1788. In 1790, the Bill of Rights was added by a process of constitutional amendment. Why were the sovereign states thus persuaded to abrogate their independence?

The Articles of Confederation were adopted in order to ensure some unification between the states in dealing with common foreign and domestic problems, but with an overriding understanding that the individual states would remain sovereign. Indeed, the first substantive provision of the articles announced that "each state retains its sovereignty, freedom, and independence, and every Power, Jurisdiction, and right, which is not by this confederation expressly delegated to the United States in Congress assembled." Nevertheless, a number of powers were conferred on the "united states in Congress assembled" most notably including "the sole and exclusive right and power of determining on peace and war," the authority to resolve disputes between the states, and the power to regulate the money supply.

The Articles of Confederation left conspicuous gaps in the powers usually vested in a national government, most notably an absence of any power to tax and to regulate commerce. In addition, two of the three branches of any national government were absent. There was no executive authority. There was no general judicial authority save for a provision authorizing the Congress to establish a national appellate tribunal to decide maritime cases.

In such circumstances, it is not at all surprising that a weak central government would encounter increasing difficulty in preserving the union, once the general euphoria of victory by the rebels had subsided and as interstate rivalries manifested themselves. Inevitably, the Confederation encountered major problems in raising the revenues necessary to meet the expenses of confederation, indeed even in attracting representatives of the states to come to Congress and attend to its designated business. In the absence of a judicial branch, Congress was powerless to maintain any rule of law for the union as a whole and to intercede judicially on interstate disputes to protect the weaker states from the pressures of the more powerful, especially those with the advantages provided at that time by access to commodious harbors.

By 1786, the Confederacy was in a state of crisis, and it appeared likely to unravel into an independent set of nation states in the absence of a new centralizing initivative. Meeting in Annapolis, state representatives approved a resolution to hold a convention in Philadelphia to review the Articles of Confederation and to propose remedies for the evident problems of the Confederacy. The unanticipated consequence of that convention was to be the arguably illegal overthrow of the Confederacy and its replacement by a Constitution which provided the foundation for a strong federal government empowered to forge a lasting union among the states subscribing to its laws. It is noteworthy that the new Constitution did not find universal consent but rather was a victory for the federalists following a major debate between those who favored and those who abhorred the notion of federalism. By no means was this outcome any reflection of some widespread calculus of consent. Even some of the states' representatives in Philadelphia conspicuously absented themselves from the convention when the final votes were registered. Ultimately, of course, the federalist government was to force by arms a union which many states grew to abhor, thus imposing an imperial autocracy on recalcitrant states.

The Constitution changed the framework established by the Articles of Confederation in a number of ways. Among the most important changes were the creation of an executive branch, the grant to Congress of the powers to tax and to regulate commerce, and the creation of a federal judiciary, including the Supreme Court, and, if Congress so determined, lower federal courts. These innovations represented an outright defeat for the antifederalists and a harbinger of the kind of centralized government that was anathema to the decentralized town meeting model that imbued the antifederalist vision of politics. They also reflected a sophisticated understanding of the strength of self-interest as the motivating force for political actors and ingenuity in the design of constraints to deter the ability of self-interested politicians and bureaucrats to create an over-powerful federal government that might crush the freedoms of individual citizens.

In *The Federalist* No. 10, James Madison addressed the problems posed by factions in the marketplace of politics and the alternative methods available for curing their mischiefs. Recognizing that the causes of faction could be removed only by suppressing liberty in a society characterized by differences in wealth and other interests, Madison urged that relief from potential damage was to be sought only in the means of controlling its effects. From this perspective, it was vain to rely on enlightened statesmen to stand against a mischievous faction and to protect the broader interests of citizens.

If a faction consisted of less than a majority, Madison supposed (incorrectly, as public choice since has demonstrated) that relief was supplied by the republican principle itself, which enabled the majority to defeat "its sinister views" by regular vote. The facility of log-rolling and/or vote trading as an avenue of escape from this constraint simply was not recognized in the late 18th century. When a majority was included in a faction, however, the form of popular government enabled it to sacrifice to its ruling passion or interest both the public good and the rights of other citizens. To secure the public good against the danger of such a faction, and at the same time to preserve the spirit and the form of popular government, then became the great object to which the inquiries of the federalists were directed.

To this end, the Constitution was designed to provide safeguards that representative government alone could not offer. Bicameralism—the division of the Congress into the House and the Senate, with two-year and six-year terms, respectively—thus was intended to ensure that some representatives would be relatively close to the people and others relatively isolated from them. Different bases of election also implied that legislation could proceed only on the basis of a supra-majority support within the population at large. Indeed, only the House of Representatives was to be elected directly. In the case of the Senate, the electoral college was to be a deliberative body standing at some distance from constituent pressures.

In *The Federalist* No. 51, Hamilton and/or Madison directed attention to separating the different powers of government as an essential prerequisite for the preservation of liberty, arguing that "each department should have a will of its own; and consequently should be so constituted that the members of each should have as little agency as possible in the appointment of the members of the others." Recognizing the high cost of maintaining such a complete separation, the authors retreated from rigorous insistence on this principle, particularly with respect to the constitution of the judicial department of government.

They argued first that primary consideration ought to be directed to securing the peculiar qualifications required for a high-quality judiciary and second that the permanent tenure by which the appointments would be held in that department must soon destroy all sense of dependence on the authority conferring individuals into office, especially if the emoluments annexed to their offices were secured against encroachment by the other departments of government. Judicial independence from the legislature was seen to be especially important, given the necessary predominance of the legislative authority in republican government.

The system of checks and balances within the federal structure thus was intended to operate as a check against self-interested representation and as a defense against tyranny, including the tyranny of the majority. The Constitution itself, enforced by disinterested judges, would prevent majorities or minorities from usurping government power to redistribute wealth or opportunities in their particular direction. The federal system also would provide additional safeguards since the jealousy of state governments and the attachment of individuals to local interests would also weaken the tendency toward the aggrandizement of power within the national institutions.

Central to the discussion over constitutional checks and balances was a deep-rooted concern among the framers of the Constitution to protect private property from the threat of seizure posed by factions in an untrammelled majoritarian system of democracy. For the framers, the problem of faction lay in large part in the danger that a self-interested group would obtain governmental power in order to put property rights at risk (Stone, Seidman, Sunstein, and Tushnet 1986, p. 16). Experience under the Articles of Confederation, where popular majorities had operated as factions in state legislatures, confirmed the existence of this danger, as did the weaker concern for private property evidenced by antifederalist opponents of the Philadelphia initiative.

Thus, the various safeguards urged in *The Federalist* and adopted in the Constitution, such as representation by officials able to take a longer term and broader view of the relevant issues, may be understood as having the protection of property rights from theft by majoritarian factions as a principal purpose. Indeed, the federalists' favorable view of lengthy deliberation and government inaction may also be associated with a desire to protect private property since inaction itself preserves the existing distribution of income and wealth. In these respects, the federalists were able to synthesize the republican conception with the emerging principles of pluralism, endorsing the essential elements of democracy while protecting private property to the extent possible from an inevitably self-interested struggle among competing groups.

The arrangements established for judicial review nestled precisely within this framework. To a considerable extent, the Supreme Court was intended to enforce the lines of division laid down in the Constitution and to ensure that the areas marked off from politics would not be subject to political revision. Boundaries marked out in the Constitution thus were to be protected from the revision of electoral majorities—a safeguard that would reinforce the other institutional checks. In the view of Stone, Seidman, Sunstein, and Tushnet (1986, p. 17), this role responded to the distinction drawn by the framers between "law" as the realm of judgment and "politics" as the realm of will or personal preference (*The Federalist* No. 78). The existence of a "realm of law" immune from politics fits securely within a system intended to protect both the public good and private rights from anticipated excesses of the majority vote.

The issue of judicial review by the Supreme Court over acts of Congress was reviewed in *Marbury v. Madison* in 1803. The most important finding in that case was that the Supreme Court was empowered to declare acts of Congress unconstitutional. Chief Justice Marshall's arguments in reaching that judgment relied not on the text of the Constitution but rather on its structure and on the evident consequences of any judgment that such judicial review was unattainable:

> The distinction between a government with limited and unlimited power is abolished, if those limits do not confine the persons on whom they are imposed, and if acts prohibited and acts allowed, are of equal obligation.

The supremacy clause itself, which provides that the "Constitution, and the Laws of the United States which shall be made in Pursuance thereof—shall be the supreme Law of the Land" would seem to establish the existence of judicial review and lend credence to Chief Justice Marshall's judgment, as does the fact that judges take an oath to uphold the Constitution. *The Federalist* No. 78 (Hamilton) further supports the interpretation that judicial review of the Congress was intended by those who formed the Constitution:

> It is far more rational to suppose, that the courts were designed to be an intermediate body between the people and the legislature, in order, among other things, to keep the latter within the limits assigned to their authority.

And:

> . . . whenever a particular statute contravenes the Constitution, it will be the duty of the judicial tribunals to adhere to the latter and disregard the former.

There is a fundamental tension in American constitutional law between the basic principle that the Constitution reposes sovereign authority in the people, who elect their representatives, and the competing principle that, in interpreting the Constitution under the doctrine of judicial review, the courts wield the ultimate judgment over the political process. There is strong evidence in *The Federalist* that this tension was not only recognized by the framers but indeed deliberately engineered.

Those who are opposed to the doctrine of judicial review question why current legislators, who are the representatives of the people, should be forced to conform to the will of those who formed the Constitution more than two centuries ago. They also claim that the institution of judicial review tends to remove questions of principle from the political process and to impact adversely on the public's sense of moral responsibility. Even among those who consider themselves to be constitutionalists are those who express concern lest the judges, in supposedly enforcing the judgments of the framers, will instead be influenced by their own views about how society should be ordered.

Those who support the doctrine claim that judicial review, by preventing normal politics from overcoming constitutional politics, is a means of ensuring that "the ignorance, apathy and selfishness of normal politics is not permitted to overcome decisions made by the public during a period of heightened mobilization and public-spiritedness" (Ackerman 1984, p. 1013). This justification is reinforced by the view that judges are better at interpretation precisely because of their insulation from political pressures that permits them to follow the ways of the scholar. Consider, for example, it is argued, the difference between a judge and a legislator in determining the meaning of freedom of speech in a climate of popular hostility to a particular point of view (Stone, Seidman, Sunstein, and Tushnet 1986, p. 32).

The tension between these two views of the nature of constitutional democracy becomes most acute concerning issues where the Constitution's provisions are vague and/or ambiguous, or indeed do not reach at all. Interpretation, in such circumstances, inevitably involves the exercise of discretion by the justices, whether overtly political or not, and presents an overwhelming temptation for each of them to indulge strictly personal preferences. Whether such discretion is, or even should be, constrained in practice by such sources as the intent of the framers, the text of the Constitution, or the prevailing conception of justice is hotly debated among scholars of constitutional law as well as by others concerned with the functioning of constitutional democracy.

3. The Nature and Scope of Judicial Review

The institution of judicial review separates the power to make laws between legislatures and the courts in a simple but effective manner.

The legislature has the exclusive power to initiate legislation. The court cannot legislate but can strike down legislation on constitutional grounds. The eminent domain clause fits perfectly into this plan, commanding courts to strike down legislation where property is taken for public use but where just compensation is not paid. Judicial discretion is (or should be) constrained by the wording of the clause, although each term—"private property," "taken," "just compensation," and "public use"—is open to a range of alternative interpretations.

There are constitutional scholars who create skepticism by claiming that words such as private property have no uniform meaning in private discourse and that they should be withdrawn from constitutional documents. Thomas Grey (1980) has argued thus, claiming that in some instances property refers to real estate while in other contexts it refers to rights good against the world; that property can refer to a remedy of restoration or injunction, as opposed to damages; that it can be regarded as a means to promote allocative efficiency or to protect individual security and independence. He has claimed that "meanings of 'property' in the law that cling to their origin in the thing-ownership conceptions are integrated least successfully into the general doctrinal framework of law, legal theory, and economics" (Grey 1980, p. 163).

Pitkin (1967) earlier had argued against such skepticism, claiming that there is no reason to give up on language at the first sign of difficulty; that although property can be used in various senses in different connections, it does not follow that the word can be used correctly in various senses in any given connection; that a varied usage is not the same thing as a vague usage; and that the problem before the courts is to specify the varieties of its application to various contexts.

Epstein (1985, p. 22) seized upon Pitkin's defense of representation to defend the use of the term "private property" in the eminent domain clause of the Constitution. He referred in particular to Blackstone's (1766, p. 2) elaboration of the rights implicit in the ownership of property: "[T]he third absolute right, inherent in every Englishman, is that of property, which consists in the free use, enjoyment, and disposal of all his acquisitions, without any control or diminution, save only by the laws of the land." This ordinary word definition, in Epstein's view, overcomes all of Grey's skepticism precisely in the manner indicated by Pitkin. Indeed, Blackstone's account of property explains what the term means in the eminent domain clause. A constitution that wishes to protect private property must take the meaning of private property from ordinary usage.

Linguistic skepticism lends currency to the notion that constitutional provisions necessarily change in meaning over time, so that each new generation must reinterpret them afresh (Ackerman 1984). This view has been forcefully expressed by advocates of the "living Constitution" with notable success during the middle and late 20th century as relativist philosophy swept through the U.S. judiciary. Once again Epstein (1985, p. 24) is critical, arguing that such a view is an invitation to destroy the rule of law; that social organizations indeed must be dynamic and change over time; but that this does not imply that legal institutions must change in fundamental ways.

The fact that words indeed do have regular, disciplined meanings, within the specific contexts in which they are used, calls into question the argument that the meaning of legal propositions can be determined only in terms of the ends that such propositions are seen to serve. There may indeed be a debate, for example, as to whether the framers introduced the eminent domain clause to protect markets, or autonomy, or both. But, as Epstein (1985, p. 26) notes, "In the end, greater progress will be made by assuming that the clause is designed to do what it says, namely to ensure that private property is not taken for public use without just compensation." Such an interpretation follows clearly from any reading of the constitutional text. It is also entirely compatible with the affection for private property repeatedly emphasized by Locke and Blackstone and shared by the framers of the U.S. Constitution.

The issue must be confronted as to what presumption, if any, should be brought to any statute challenged under the eminent domain clause, namely whether it should take the form of judicial activism, judicial pragmactivism, or judicial restraint, terms which themselves require a clear definition.

The arguments conventionally employed in favor of judicial activism—the notion that the courts actively should police the enactments of the legislature to seek out and to strike down constitutional contraventions—rest on the judgment that the democratic process may fail to protect individual rights, including property rights. The federalists themselves were skeptical of the protection available to individuals in a pluralistic legislature beset by factions. Public choice more recently has confirmed the sound sense in such skepticism and has reinforced the importance of carefully selected constitutional costraints (Buchanan 1989). Whether the federal courts can be trusted to police the constitutional parchment effectively and to uphold its integrity against factional attacks is an important unsolved issue of constitutional political economy (Rowley 1989). Unbridled judicial activism predictably will move along paths directed by the dominant special interest factions, flavored by the personal political agendas of the Supreme Court justices.

The argument in favor of judicial pragmactivism—the notion that there should be no general presumption in favor of either the judiciary or the legislature as the ultimate source of constitutional authority but that the choice between them should rest in specific circumstances on the pragmatic judgment as to which more likely would achieve principled objectives—clearly shifts discussion from process to ends-related criteria. To a judicial pragmactivist, neither judicial activism nor judicial restraint is correct all the time. Sometimes activism is justified; at other times, restraint is justified. Which stance is appropriate in what instance must be determined by reference to the likely consequences of that judgment. Different pragmactivists will be distinguished from each other by the criteria that they use to distinguish good consequences from bad consequences (Barnett 1987, p. 207).

Those who promote judicial pragmactivism would expose the U.S. polity to all the weaknesses that permeate the European parliamentary democracies. Ultimately, and despite protestations to the contrary, they lend their voices to those who more openly and less circumspectly would employ the federal courts to achieve objectives that the legislature has failed to achieve, and vice versa, in the particular circumstances of the time (Dworkin 1985; Tribe 1985). Predictably, principled activism disintegrates into the pursuit of special interest agendas where a polity is diverse in membership and disparate with respect to social goals. It is a fundamental misreading of human nature to suppose that judges have no personal policy agendas that they will pursue and attempt to impose should constitutional constraints be loosened on pragmatic grounds (Rowley 1987, p. 223).

The argument in favor of judicial restraint—the notion that the federal courts should always defer to the legislature on matters of serious political importance—is that choices concerning such matters are best left to representatives of the people, chosen by democratic procedures. The weakness in this argument, even for the most fervent disciples of the majority vote principle, is that rational ignorance within the electorate, ideology within the legislature, and vote-trading and logrolling of bills combine to enable minority factions to exert considerable influence over the output of legislation. For those concerned with protecting individual rights from the appetite of the uncontrolled majority, or even from logrolling minority factions, judicial restraint has nothing to offer but the predictable erosion of the written Constitution and the entrenchment of the rent-seeking society.

The weaknesses, briefly outlined above, associated with judicial activism, pragmactivism, and restraint as alternative views of the appropriate role of judicial process in a constitutional democracy, reinforce the importance of maintaining the integrity of the constitutional text. The Constitution contains provisions designed to ensure that some decisions will be made by elected representatives. It also contains provisions designed to limit those same elected representatives, to establish a system of laws to which all individuals, including legislators, are subject. If the United States truly is a constitutional democracy, then clearly its constitutional parchment must hold precedence over statutes and administrative regulations. In the policing of the parchment, the Supreme Court is accorded the dominant authority. Its role is the strict construction of the Constitution from which its oversight responsibilities emanate.

Strict constructionism implies that the Supreme Court is not bound by precedents that derive from judgments based earlier on activism, pragmactivism, or restraint. It requires instead that the judges be ruled by the wording of the Constitution, together with the notes and textual interpretations that surround it. Only where the Constitution is silent or ambiguous should law-making other than legal interpretation emanate from the bench. Even then, if the issues are suitably important, constitutional amendment is the preferred route of constitutional consolidation. Such an emphasis on the preeminence of the Constitution as the basis of the U.S. legal system and on the acquiescence of personal, social, and political agendas to the wording of that parchment would require a radical rethinking of many law school programs and the abandonment of an educational system that is highly geared to the achievement of programs of "reform" that run counter to the Constitution itself.

In the absence of sound, textually based constitutional interpretation, the law itself becomes subject to competing value preferences. For this reason, the actual words of the parchment are to be viewed as decisive, and not the presumed original interest of those who drafted the Constitution. Epstein (1987, p. xiii) has emphasized that one must be very cautious in dealing with the question of specific intent: it is fruitless to interpret the general provisions of the Constitution solely with reference to the particular legislative clauses that prompted their passage; and there are major difficulties in ascertaining constitutional intent when all that is available in the record is the inconsistent, ambiguous, and unreflective intentions of the large body of independent persons who participated in ratifying its clauses. Because the Constitution was drafted in the natural-rights, limited-government tradition, it has been suggested that modern commentators in that tradition "will be among those best able to explicate the principles that made the document so great and enduring a human achievement" (Epstein 1985).

4. The Constitutional Political Economy Perspective

In this section, two alternative approaches to constitutional political economy, one from a jurisprudential and the other from an economic perspective, are outlined and evaluated from the particular perspective of the takings issue. Both approaches attempt to steer the constitutional interpretations debate away from policy-oriented methodologies in favor of process analysis in an attempt to maintain the notion of a regime of law against the potential for its disintegration as a result of factional piecemeal attacks.

The first such approach—in my view the less convincing of the two—is the proposed reconciliation of views advanced by Manne (1991). The author rightly denigrates those who debate the success or failure of Supreme Court judgments about government regulations or taking of private property in terms of political attitudes rather than interpretational craftsmanship and constitutional propriety. He is correct in his judgment that the debate is about methodology, not political preferences. He is less than sure-footed in his own particular resolution over the debate on interpretation, particularly with regard to its public choice problems.

In Manne's view, original intent is unreliable because of the evident absence of consent among the participants at the Philadelphia convention. The logrolled compromises enunciated by those concerned may well reflect no more than the preferences of an agenda setter or the accident of some arbitrary resolution of a cycle in multidimensioned issue space. Given the uneven recording of the debate, no one can even be sure whether the record itself has not been doctored by agenda setters whose writings have surfaced and survived. Public choice, in these ways, supports Manne in his unwillingness to swallow the original intent doctrine.

Although the Constitution itself may be infused with similar compromises of public choice—indeed it clearly is—it has the advantage over original intent that a specific set of words was endorsed without contradiction by all representatives who did not absent themselves from the vote. For Manne, however, strict construction is an unreliable approach because the meaning of words is notoriously vague, ambiguous, and volatile. In such circumstances, the reach of their meaning quickly becomes a function of the reader's subjective attitude or preference, evidently a noninterpretivist position. In this judgment, Manne parts company with scholars who find little difficulty in attaching consistent meaning to words, even over the two centuries since many of them were written down and approved. However, his concern rests less with the ambiguity of words than with changes in the environment which substantially change the real allocation of legal power without at all affecting the meaning of the constitutional text.

By no means do these interpretivist criticisms convince Manne of the case for "living Constitution" arguments which indeed he rejects as "an abject intellectual failure." In his judgment, this approach has no compelling logical, scientific, semantic, or even moral foundation. It is an approach grounded in ideology both from the left and right of the political spectrum. Its deployment greatly politicizes the process of constitutional litigation. It is an approach that threatens the preservation of the republic by wrongly treating constitutional issues as policy issues to be addressed politically rather than as legal questions to be resolved judicially.

As a more promising alternative, Manne suggests that the Founding Fathers should be viewed as creating not a document but a structure of government composed of dynamically competing and interacting political parts. Constitutional interest should focus on the relative power position of all the various groups that comprise government in an attempt to preserve or to restore the balance initially imposed by the Constitution. In Manne's view, it is only the ratio of power that the Founding Fathers reasonably could have sought to stabilize, not the absolute value of power available to any particular branch. Under this view, the Supreme Court is responsible for preserving or restoring this original equilibrium ratio against exogenous shocks that would otherwise displace it and replace constitutional balance by a lottery. By centering attention on the structure of government created in 1787 and 1789 rather than on the words used in the document, the resolution of disagreements would be focused in a way that existing controversies self-evidently are not.

The importance of the power ratio for the Founding Fathers is evident in *The Federalist* as it is in the detailed determination within the Constitution concerning the separation of powers. Evidently, this ratio has shifted sharply in favor of the federal government and against the states and the people during the two centuries since the parchment was signed. In this respect, Manne's refocusing has a timely quality. Yet, the Constitution was concerned with limiting the power of government, as a whole as well as by ratio. To play down this constraint potentially is to unchain Leviathan, especially if the separate formal powers should collude rather than compete in order to expand the range of the polity. Public choice offers little scope for optimism concerning the predictable dominance of competition among the separate branches of government. Although Manne accords all groups, including the people, an indexed place within the power structure, the logic of collective action (Olson 1965) effectively precludes the practicality of this balance. The groups best able to privatize benefits and/or coerce membership contributions predictably will advance relative to those who cannot. As relative positions adjust, the absolute power of Leviathan predictably will rise. If the precise wording of the Constitution is played down or ignored, rent-seeking forces will profit and individual economic freedoms will become more vulnerable.

More promising is the constitutional political economy perspective advanced by Buchanan (1988) with its emphasis on the process of exchange (catallactics) rather than on the end-state goal of neoclassical economics. In this perspective, rules, law, and institutions that govern individual exchange are ranked in terms of their contribution to the contractarian paradigm, quite independently from end-state outcomes that exchange induces. The approach has implications for disputes over judicial activism and nonactivism; between judicial deference to legislative authority and judicial independence; between strict constructionism and pragmatism; between teleological and deontological conceptions of law.

If individuals, or organizations of individuals, are the units that enter into exchanges, the values and interests of those individuals are the only values that exist and, therefore, that count. There is no organic "public interest," no teleological conception of the law, of the constitution, or of the role of the judiciary. The "good society" is that which best furthers the interests of its individual members, as expressed by these members, and not the society that best advances some independently defined criterion for the "good." In politics, this shifts attention away from the in-period political process which is nonconsensual, even nonmajoritarian, to constitutional politics that may approach consensual agreement, at least in its ideal form. The question of legitimacy or justification shifts to the rules and, inevitably, to the role of the Supreme Court.

If the individualistic contractarian approach is endorsed, it has direct implications for judicial interpretation, notably with respect to the functional role for judicial review. In Buchanan's view (1989), the "state-as-umpire" function is properly assigned to a branch of the political order that is separated from those branches that operate within the rules. The judiciary, in this umpire role, must adopt a truth-judgment approach that would be unworkable in branches subject to the pressures of in-period politics. The judiciary must determine whether the rules have been violated, whether a rule exists, whether a rule applies to this case or to that—all by reference to truth judgments. It is absurd to involve arguments based on such irrelevances as "compromise among interests" or "proper representation of interests" in the judicial process.

In this perspective, the inclusive political order is classified in terms of three separate functions. The first, which embodies the role for judicial review, involves the enforcement of existing rules. The second, which embodies the role for in-period politics, involves taxing, spending, and other activities related to the financing and supply of public goods. The third function involves changes in the rules themselves, or the process of constitutional reform. The latter function is inappropriate both for the judiciary and for the legislative branch, at least in its majoritarian mode. For rules are to be changed only through well-defined procedures for constitutional amendment, procedures that are explicitly more inclusive than ordinary legislation or judicial review.

In Buchanan's interpretation, the judicial role, limited to interpreting rules that exist is akin to strict constructivism, but not precisely so. Certainly, the judiciary should not hesitate to denounce legislative decisions when these would modify the basic rules. In this sense, activism is required. However, in its constructivist role, the court must defend constitutional rules that exist in the status quo when the case at issue is adjudicated. These rules may have been modified significantly by the historic case record away from either original intent or the wording of the Constitution. Given stare decisis, however, the case record must stand and not the Constitution itself, even when the latter has been displaced by bad law.

In Buchanan's judgment (which I do not share), if the prior judicial interpretations have been in place sufficiently long as to form part of the rational expectations of individuals, then it is inappropriate for the judiciary to seek to change the rules. To move beyond deference to the status quo and to assume an activist role in deconstruction opens up judicial review to serious dangers of abuse, given ex post realities. On the other hand, judges should be entirely jealous in protecting existing rules from legislation and judicial intrusion that attempt to move the law ex ante in directions away from the Constitution. Any attempted change that upsets the legitimately held expectations of citizens should be interpreted as a change in the constitutional structure and, as such, should be prevented by the courts.

5. The Pressures of Public Choice and the Vulnerability Of Supreme Court Justices

The Supreme Court in recent times has neglected the high standing of economic rights in the text of the Constitution, in the U.S. political tradition, and in its moral theory (Macedo 1987, p. 47). Indeed, it has established a politically charged double standard that has offered, ostensibly at least, a high place to personal and civil rights, while ignoring—indeed overriding—economic rights that are at least as well grounded in the Constitution. This double standard flies in the face of the plain words of the Constitution and ignores or rejects important aspects of U.S. legal and political traditions. In large part, this outcome is a predictable response of the Supreme Court justices to rent-seeking pressures exerted by self-serving minority interest groups on all branches of the U.S. government. In their pursuits of the wealth of others, through the instrument of political pressure, rather than in efforts to create wealth for themselves and others, such interest groups have become a potent force destructive of economic liberties and harmful to capitalist wealth creation. They have been helped in their endeavors by important characteristics of the U.S. political and judicial marketplace (Gwartney and Wagner 1988).

The vote motive itself, the very basis of democracy, provides a weak and uncertain signal in any system of representative democracy (Tullock 1967). The individual voter, in any sizeable electorate, perceives only a minimal probability of supplying a decisive vote. With the value of his vote expected to be miniscule, there is no economic incentive for such a voter to become knowledgeable concerning the rival candidates and their policies, and no reason other than civic duty why he should incur the relatively high cost of voting in order to seek out a much smaller expected return. With abstention ratios as high as 40 percent in U.S. presidential elections and as high as 70 percent in state and local elections, the rational abstention theory cannot be ignored as a potent factor in the political marketplace. In combination with the rational ignorance theory, indeed, it constitutes the foundation of the interest group theory of political market equilibrium.

With much of the electorate rationally ignorant concerning politics, a significant opportunity is offered to well-organized interest groups to fill the market vacuum and to lobby and pressure the legislature to enact policies that are favorable to their respective memberships. Because many of the political benefits conferred on such groups have publicness characteristics—notably are available to individuals whether or not they have actively committed to the group endeavor—free-riding becomes a serious potential obstacle to effective collective action (Olson 1965).

In such circumstances, interest groups predictably will enjoy asymmetric access to political markets. Those groups that are relatively small, that can coerce their members into active support, that can provide significant private benefits, and/or that can effectively byproduct their political initiatives on significant private initiatives will fare disproportionately well in political markets and will constitute the effective factions feared by Madison and the other contributors to *The Federalist*. Legislators anxious to secure political action campaign support, and thus to enhance re-election probabilities, predictably will broker policies favorable to effective interest groups and will diffuse the costs of such programs across a rationally ignorant broader-based electorate and/or politically ineffective groups.

The same interest groups that rent-seek effectively in political markets predictably will seek out privileges within the judicial bureaucracy, most especially from the judgments of the Supreme Court. To this end, they perceive a vital interest in influencing nominations and confirmations of federal judges and, most conspicuously, of Supreme Court justices. Indirectly, they exert influence on this process by their impact upon presidential and Senate elections which determine the composition of the key players in the exercise.

More directly, they can exert influence upon the Senate and even the president, by offers of campaign funding and by orchestrated campaigns directed at the electorate and designed to manipulate rational ignorance to their own rent-seeking objectives. Ultimately, they may even attempt to intimidate the justices into rendering judgments favorable to their causes, by directing media pressure upon their deliberations, and/or by threatening civil disobedience if adverse decisions should prevail. Recent cases involving judgments on abortion rights and affirmative action have provoked powerful pressure-group lobbying and threats.

In principle, such pressures should not matter; the Supreme Court justices should be inured against them by the independence of their office, by the high distinction of their own legal careers, and by their oaths of office. In practice, however, pressures are effective—in some cases, significantly.

All judges are required to take an oath "to support the Constitution" and all federal judges another oath to decide cases "agreeably to the Constitution." So the lawful judge *is* constrained by the Constitution. Where the Constitution is unambiguous, the lawful judge in principle has no option but to uphold its meaning, even though he/she may be irked by his/her own judgments. The lawful judge is enjoined by an oath of office to deprive contemporary public opinion of any opportunity to shape its own destiny in areas that lie within the range prohibited by the Constitution, except through the cumbersome process of constitutional amendment.

If such a judge cannot accept the burdens of this constraint, he or she has two alternative solutions: to refuse or relinquish office, or to become unlawful and betray the oath of office. Few judges have chosen to reject or relinquish the valuable privileges that the Supreme Court offers. Many have taken the unlawful route and abandoned the parchment of the Constitution, whether in pursuit of their own political agendas or in deference to special-interest pressures.

The key personnel of the Supreme Court are the justices, though their staffs play an important role both in the choice among cases granted *certiorari* and in preparing the documents from which the justices reach their judgments. As Posner (1985, p 17) makes clear, "in a system in which judges are appointed by politicians, it would be unrealistic to expect all or most judges to be apolitical technicians." Indeed, the very independence of the Supreme Court justice makes such a position a prime plum and a particularly apt instrument of high-level political patronage.

It is not surprising, therefore, to find that the most influential judges in U.S. history—among whom Posner lists John Marshall, Roger Taney, Oliver Wendell Holmes, Louis Brandeis, Benjamin Cardozo, William Howard Taft, Charles Evans Hughes, Felix Frankfurter, Robert Jackson, Harlan Fiske Stone, Hugo Black, Earl Warren, William Brennan, William Rehnquist, Learned Hand, Roger Traynor, Jerome Frank, and Henry Friendly—have tended to be highly politically motivated. Few of those would have made their way to the supreme court of a European judicial system organized as a career bureaucracy or to the meritocracy of the English House of Lords or even the English court of appeal. Their minds, for the most part, are less rigorously trained in technical legal analysis and less tuned to detailed scholarly documentary research than to the techniques of political law creation, arguably with potentially damaging implications for constitutional democracy. Theirs, for the most part, are not the mindsets that scrupulously will comb the constitutional documents to uphold the wording of the parchment in determining the outcome of legal cases. A clear example of such resistance to the perceived chains of constitutional law was provided in 1958 by Learned Hand:

> For myself it would be most irksome to be ruled by a bevy of Platonic Guardians. . . . I should miss the stimulus of living in a society where I have, at least theoretically, some part in the direction of public affairs.

Posner (1990) further develops this path of reasoned resistance to the pedigree approach to judicial decisionmaking, especially in its most extreme form as idolatry toward the Constitution, signalling his own sympathy with the views of Learned Hand, and distinguishing himself from the views of his erstwhile Chicago colleague, Frank Easterbrook (1988, pp. 628–629) who has argued:

> The Constitution demands that all power be authorized. . . . Judges applying the Constitution . . . must take their guidance and authority from decisions made elsewhere. Otherwise they speak with the same authority they . . . and I possess when we fill law reviews with our speculations and desires: none. And the other branches owe no obedience to those who speak without authority. . . . Judges can legitimately demand to be obeyed only when their decisions stem from fair interpretations of commands laid down in the texts.

Posner (1990) challenges the normative validity of the "faithful agent" notion of the "good" Supreme Court justice. He notes that the natural answer (as well as the answer given by the natural lawyer) to the question as to why individuals have a duty to obey judicial decisions is that they should obey them because they are just. He evidences his own doubts whether there is any moral duty to obey law (Posner 1990, p. 137) and notes the many different criteria of "just" that in any event would vie for attention. Posner fails to recognize the very real prospect that the use of terms like "fairness" and "justice" serve a more deliberative, rhetorical purpose as techniques for justifying self-serving, even rent-seeking agendas (Crew and Rowley 1988).

Posner (1990) also challenges the positive validity of the "faithful agent" notion, noting that the main reason why judicial decisions are obeyed is that the consequences of disobedience are unpleasant. There are heavy penalties for flouting court orders, although these depend on the willingness of the executive branch to enforce judicial decrees and of the legislative branch to pay for these enforcement efforts. It would be naive to suppose that the willingness of the other branches to cooperate with the judicial branch depends on the courts confining themselves to fair interpretations of commands laid down in the texts. More likely, such willingness will be related to the level of public confidence in the courts which itself will be based on notions of justice or fairness that are independent of fidelity to texts. Predictably, public choice pressures will determine the political equilibrium which itself ultimately will dictate the degree of support provided by the executive and the legislative to the judiciary, though Posner does not make this point.

In Posner's view, the framers of the Constitution provided a compass and not a blueprint, recognizing that they themselves could not foresee the future and that, in any event, the unprecedentedly powerful judiciary that they were authorizing would exercise independent judgment. The most influential framers were lawyers and it is unlikely that they greatly feared an "imperial" judiciary, though such worries perhaps influenced the Seventh Amendment's guaranty of trial by jury in federal court cases. Furthermore, the framers were revolutionaries who had exceeded their own terms of reference in submitting the Constitution for ratification by the people. The "pedigree" itself thus begins in usurpation (Posner 1990, p. 141).

Posner (1990, p. 142) acknowledges that "the pedigree theory can lay claim to being the official theory of statutory and constitutional interpretation, by which I mean the theory that a plurality of judges subscribe to publicly." He suggests that may be due in part to the hold of formalist thinking on the legal mind, in part to the desire of judges to duck personal responsibility, and in part to the vagueness of the pedigree theory. In general, Posner is skeptical of the extent of true belief in this theory: "what could be more attractive to judges than a theory of judicial legitimacy that allowed them to do anything they wanted provided they employed a rhetoric determinedly self-abnegating?"

Posner is careful not to allow his skepticism concerning the relevance of judicial rules to run amok or to snuggle into bed with such critical legal studies scholars as Duncan Kennedy, Mark Kelman, or even (God forbid!) Roberto Unger. He fully recognizes that judges, unlike professors of ethics, are decisionmakers in a system of government, concerned not only with doing substantive justice in the case at hand but also with maintaining a legal fabric that includes considerations of precedent, of legislative authority, of the forming of issues by counsel, of the facts of record, and so on.

Still, Posner (1990) leaves it clear that judges, even Supreme Court justices, will not be bound by rules, at least not completely, and that they will impose their own preferences in the shaping of the law. In such circumstances, the mechanism whereby they are appointed and their terms of tenure on the bench become relevant to any theory concerning the nature of their judicial decisions. Posner (1985) has pertinent comments to make on these matters.

The American system, unchanged since the Revolution, he claims, is now almost at the opposite extreme from the meritocratic English system. Its federal judiciaries are not narrowly meritocratic and its judges are not (merely) technicians of the law. The interactions between legislation and the Constitution, between two houses of Congress and the Presidency, and between federal law and the law of 50 quasi-sovereign states have made many fields of American law immensely complex, offering opportunities for highly creative, judicial patchworking to avoid chaos. Moreover, when judges are required to make use of political concepts to resolve questions for which the technical legal materials of decision provide no answers, they are forced to choose among competing concepts because no one approach commands a consensus in a diverse and contentious society.

Judicial independence, which in England guarantees the insulation of judges from politics, in America fosters the exercise of political power by individual judges. This is achieved both by protecting judges from retribution by the executive and legislative branches of government, and by influencing the selection process in favor of politically well-connected lawyers, many of whom possess the skills and predilections for functioning as political judges. "Judicial independence has not taken our judges out of politics; in our political culture, it has put the judges securely in politics" (Posner 1985, p. 19). The provision in Article VI that "This Constitution . . . shall be the supreme law of the land" and the provision in Article III extending the judicial power of the United States "to all cases arising under this Constitution," together with the many affirmations of the judicial power to review the constitutionality of legislation in the debates preceding the adoption and ratification of the Constitution, "make clear beyond reasonable doubt that constitutional questions were indeed intended to be justiciable. Thus, the framers envisaged a judiciary of unprecedented power" (Posner 1985, p. 20).

The framers evidently did not intend that such judicial power be unlimited nor did they choose to remove all checks on that power from the other branches of government. The Constitution established a number of checks on the exercise of political power by judges. The first consists of the limitations on the nature of the federal judicial power itself. By restricting federal judges to the decision of cases, Article III limited the occasions for judicial intervention. Because judges must wait for cases to come before them, before they can make judgments, they are limited in the range of their judicial activism. Because cases arise in a somewhat random order, the judges will find it difficult to establish an agenda for political action. The judicial role, at least in its design, is a reactive and not an initiating one.

Even in this respect, the framers' expectations have not been entirely satisfied since they failed to anticipate the emergence of aggressive litigation on the part of special-interest groups employing the class action suit to enrich in timely fashion the portfolio of Supreme Court business with issues that might become part of a powerful political agenda. The framers also failed to anticipate the enormous caseloads of the Supreme Court that enables it to recover a political agenda, if it is so minded, by picking among the cases for review.

Other checks remain in place and remain somewhat effective at the present time. Congress can refuse to raise the salaries of judges in inflationary times, thus sidestepping the salary commitment of the Constitution. It can also curtail their prerequisites and restrict the appropriation of monies for essential support services. It can attempt to curtail their jurisdictions, though this would be subject to judicial review. It can initiate constitutional amendments. In conjunction with a like-minded President, it can attempt to reconstitute the court as retirements and deaths begin to offer such opportunities. Finally, the prestige and status of the Supreme Court justices can be undermined by hostility from the Congress (and indeed a popular President) especially if the court's judgments are unpopular within important special interest constituencies. The advantages of respect and the quiet life play a powerful role in inducing Supreme Court judicial restraint and/or judicial activism that fits squarely into the contemporary, politically correct legislative agenda.

The process through which justices are appointed to the Supreme Court is highly politicized, in some instances (Bork) almost comparable in media attention to presidential election campaigns. Since justices enjoy life tenure on the bench, once appointed, and pass judgment on a wide range of politically sensitive issues without any requirement to seek electoral support, the importance of once-for-all upfront evaluation is recognized by all involved.

The President has largely a free hand with Supreme Court justices if he is electorally popular and when the Senate is controlled by his own party. Otherwise, he may be severely constrained, forced to nominate candidates who appear unlikely to threaten the policy agendas of the majority party's political constituencies. The President's nominees must also submit themselves to evaluation by the American Bar Association's left-leaning Standing Committee on the Judiciary which places a high premium on judicial activism in favor of civil rights and judicial restraint concerning economic rights, and which is unduly biased in favor of trial lawyers. In the case of contentious appointments, mediocrities (Kennedy and Souter and Thomas) may succeed to the bench as some kind of lowest common denominator outcome. Otherwise, politically charged appointments are highly predictable. Ideological appointments are very common at the Supreme Court level (Posner 1985, p. 30).

High-quality Supreme Court justices must combine a range of scarce talents. They must be politically skillful in circumventing the highly charged minefield of the consent process. They must be well versed in constitutional law and widely experienced across the many fields of law within which they may be called on to pass judgment. They must be endowed with razor-sharp intellects that will unerringly lead them to the constitutional essence in each of a vast panorama of cases chosen for review. They must be skilled in writing judgments, whether majority, concurring, or in dissent, that provide clear guidance for those who must rely on them in subsequent litigation. The legal profession attracts individuals with such talents, given its pre-eminence as a highly paid, prestigious profession. The salaries of Supreme Court justices, however, are unattractive to high-flying lawyers who command incomes several times higher than the Chief Justice.

The annual salaries of Supreme Court justices (in the low $100,000s at the time of this writing) are substantially lower in real terms than they were in 1900 and about one-third lower than they were in 1940 (Posner 1985, p. 32) despite massive increases in per capita income in the United States over these periods. The constitutional commitment to maintain income while a justice holds office was couched in nominal and not in real terms, and its intent has been subverted by the inflation tax. The Supreme Court has become a victim of wealth-redistributionist pressures which have penetrated almost all dimensions of the U.S. federal bureaucracy. Such has not been the experience of lawyers in private practice where pretax annual earnings well in excess of $1 million are not at all uncommon. In a country that educates its young to worship at the Holy Grail of the dollar and to subjugate all other instincts in its pursuit, salary differentials in excess of 10:1 carry an unequivocal signal. Top lawyers are not in the market for Supreme Court office, notwithstanding the high prestige of such appointments.

6. The Takings Clause In Strict Constructionist Perspective

The eminent domain clause states: "nor shall private property be taken for public use, without just compensation." The clause comprises two prohibitions: (1) all takings must be for public use, and (2) even takings that are for public use must be accompanied by compensation. There is no real ambiguity in either prohibition and, as will be shown, the intent of the framers of this clause is entirely clear. Yet the clause has been subverted with respect to both clauses by a sequence of Supreme Court judgments rendered by self-serving, overly deferential justices in a sustained demonstration of contempt for the Constitution that by oath they have sworn to uphold.

By this process of constitutional disregard, the U.S. Supreme Court repeatedly has violated the precepts of classical liberal political economy in pursuit of an agenda that places little or no value on protecting economic property rights. Such rights were deemed to be inalienable to those individuals who had created them by John Locke (1690) whose writings powerfully had influenced the framers of the U.S. Constitution. Only by violating such rights could the Supreme Court justices unchain the legislature from the constraints that confined it to a night watchman function over a market economy. In a sequence of judgments that suppressed the takings clause, such justices enabled the legislature to suborn the U.S. economy from capitalism to socialism as that legislature pursued its own ambitions to become the presidium of a rent-seeking, transfer society.

As Richard Epstein (1985, p. 7) rightly has observed, the U.S. Constitution is best understood as a constitutional response to the problems posed by Hobbesian man in a Lockean society. In his book *Leviathan* (1651), Hobbes offered a principled defence of absolute sovereign power from a perspective which offered no illusions about the perfectibility of mankind, but instead emphasized the destructive behavior of selfish individuals in an environment that provided no external authority to restrain their appetites, passions, and ambitions.

In such a state of nature, which precedes any notion of society but which does not preclude the existence of custom and/or of tradition, there are no rights economic or other, and no system of rules to constrain individuals from acts of aggression against each other. Predictably, in such an environment, individuals will be diverted from productive effort into acts of predation and/or defense, with the consequence that their lives are likely to be "solitary, poore, nasty, brutish and short." The state of nature, in this perspective, is a state of war "of every man, against every man." The price justifiably to be paid for order is the surrender of liberty and property by each individual to an absolute sovereign. No intermediate position, such as minimal or even limited government, is feasibly sustainable between the absolute extremes of total subjection to a single authority or of anarchy.

Hobbes thus provided a crude utilitarian justification for the establishment of an absolutist state that he called *Leviathan* and his book is to be viewed as a reasoned defense of absolutist government, whether in monarchic or other form, in the aftermath of the demise of the religious justification of Divine Right monarchy following the military defeat and execution of King Charles I of England. The book was not written to defend the House of Stuart, nor was it designed to flatter the Lord Protector, Oliver Cromwell. Hobbes pleased neither party, since his purpose was to carry out what he called "the first and fundamental Law of Nature, which is to seek peace and follow it." His account of the state was meant to be scientific and not self-serving, deduced from the eternal nature of man, depending on immutable laws of nature and of universal applicability.

Hobbes' *Leviathan*, in affirming absolutism in government, denied any supremacy of the "law of nature," as formulated in common law, over the commands of the sovereign. In this regard, his doctrine found favor with Cromwell who had complained to the Levellers that the doctrine of the law of nature might be carried too far, but not with the great common lawyers like Coke who had sided with the parliament during the Civil War. Hobbes indeed enunciated the necessary supremacy of statute over common law which, Hayek (1973) notwithstanding, now is a commonplace of government. If the sovereign should violate a law of nature, as well he might, he should not be disobeyed, nor should there be any appeal to that law against the sovereign. In this sense, sovereignty is indivisible and unlimited, though it can be influenced by persuasive argument or overthrown by superior might.

The framers of the U.S. Constitution eschewed the Hobbesian conception but were influenced by two important insights central to his endorsement of the Leviathan state. The first, seized upon by the authors of *The Federalist*, was Hobbes' analysis of the dangers of unconstrained self-interest in any non-Leviathan environment. The second was his implicit appeal to some comprehensive, though hypothetical, covenant whereby all individuals surrendered liberty and property in exchange for security (Epstein 1985, p. 8). Taken together, these insights comprise an implicit utilitarian rationalization for the formation of the state, albeit one which, in strict Hobbesian form, does not allow a voting solution necessary for the Wicksellian approach of modern-day contractarians (Buchanan 1975), or even for the late 18th century federalists.

In the absence of any vote constraint, the Leviathan sovereign, predictably claiming a monopoly in the legitimate use of physical force within a given territory, will expropriate most of the gains from political union, allowing individual subjects no more surplus than is necessary to prevent successful revolution or coup d'etat. Selfish interest and not noblesse oblige will determine the behavior of the sovereign in the

Leviathan state. The terms of the social contract in a Hobbesian environment ensure the sovereign of relatively unconstrained taxation powers.

John Locke (1690) made full use of Hobbes' insights while forging an entirely different vision of the role of the state; his view has become the basis for classical liberal constitutional political economy. In the Lockeian state of nature, individuals live in peace and harmony with each other, governed by the powers of reason (Locke 1690, p. 19). Yet this peace and harmony, without government, exists precariously under the continuous threat of a Hobbesian state of war. Indeed, it is this recognized danger of aggression and the uncertain value of the right of self-defense that drive responsible individuals from the state of nature into a civil society.

Locke thus denied the view of Hobbes that all men are driven by base instincts while acknowledging that there existed a sufficient number of corrupt and vicious individuals as to make civil society imperative for the protection of the remainder. The degeneracy of the few justified the centralized control of power to resolve private disputes in an impartial forum, free of personal bias and animosity (Locke 1690, p. 125). Unlike Hobbes, however, Locke sought out a set of institutional arrangements that would enable individuals to escape social disorder without surrendering the full complement of their individual rights to a sovereign, without empowering the sovereign with rent-extracting authority.

Locke emphasized that individual rights, including rights to obtain and to hold property, are not derived from the sovereign but are the common gift of mankind. Individuals obtain rights in this common gift by the first-possession method of acquisition. They are allowed to keep that which they first reduce to their own possession by mixing their own labor with the property in question, "at least where there is enough, and as good left in common for others." On this basis, Locke justified private property in the form of natural rights that might be passed on from individual to individual. Subsequently, classical liberals dispensed with the idea of divine justification for private property and adopted the common-law view of the original position which used the first-possession rule alone to subject unowned things to ownership without requiring that rule to create individual ownership by ousting common ownership (Epstein 1979, p. 1221; 1985, p. 11).

Locke proceeded to argue that the organization of the state does not require the surrender of all natural rights to the sovereign. Instead, Locke proposed a system of governance that would leave the net benefits of civil society with the people at large. The key elements in this governance structure are his theory of representative government and his prohibition against the taking of private property by the supreme power of the state.

The private rights of the individual are preserved as much as possible within the civil society, modified only to secure the internal and external peace for which political power is necessary. The state is allocated only what it needs to rule—its costs—and nothing more:

> The supreme power cannot take away from any man any part of his property without his own consent. For the preservation of property being the end of government, and that for which men enter into society, it necessarily supposes and requires that the people should have property, without which they must be supposed to lose that by entering into society which was the end for which they entered into it, too gross an absurdity for any man to own. [Locke 1690, p. 138]

In Epstein's view (1985, p. 15), Locke's move from the state of nature to civil society incorporates two elements of the eminent domain equation. What individuals must surrender is their right to use force; what they receive in exchange is a superior form of public protection. There is no actual contract as such, but rather a network of forced exchanges designed to leave everyone better off than before. The public-use language of the takings clause is consistent with Locke's general conception that the surplus created by the establishment of political union should not inure solely to those individuals vested with sovereign power.

The Lockeian system dominated the Anglo-Saxon common law of property and contract at the time when the U.S. Constitution was promulgated. Locke's theory of the state was endorsed by Blackstone in his *Commentaries*, and the protection of property against its enemies was a prominent feature of contemporary political thought. Protection of private property was a central objective of the federalists as it was of the original constitutional scheme (Epstein 1985, p. 16). Yet, the eminent domain clause itself was not a part of the original parchment but was added when the Bill of Rights became a part of the amended Constitution.

The basic constitutional approach was one of limiting government by indirection, as outlined in section 2 above. Federal powers were not plenary, but enumerated and confined largely to matters of Lockeian public good: the army, the navy, the post office, and commerce. The separation of powers provided a system of checks and balances designed to constrain the exercise of powers granted to the federal government. The president may veto legislation, subject to override by Congress. The judiciary is independent, but subject to presidential nomination and Senate confirmation. Congress is independent, but subject to presidential veto power and judicial review. Congress is empowered to declare war, but the president is commander-in-chief, subject to the power of the armed forces' budget in the Congress. The Bill of Rights, not least in its eminent domain clause, moved beyond indirect controls by identifying the ends of government and the rights that the system was designed to protect. Some version of the eminent domain clause was included also in all state constitutions.

7. The Police Power, Takings Cases, and Supreme Court Judgments

Since the end of the Second World War, judicial activism—with some notable exceptions—has served to advance interests associated with the political agenda of the New Deal coalition, including those of minority group members and proponents of certain rights of privacy, most prominently the right to procreative choice. It has operated only rarely to protect economic rights despite the wording of the Constitution and the widespread evidence that the framers of the Constitution shared a special sympathy for private ordering and designed the Constitution at least in part as a means of guarding against democratic or collective control of property.

The prohibition against the taking of private property, as Epstein (1985, p. 35) has noted, has ancient and powerful roots in all legal systems. The early common law, for example, treated the carrying away of chattels and the dispossession of land as paradigmatic takings of private property. In this sense, the framers of the Constitution are to be viewed not as making new law in writing the eminent domain clause into the U.S. Constitution, but simply as codifying well-established common law principles as the fundamental law of the land. Thus, in its failure properly to enforce the eminent domain clause against governmental attacks, the Supreme Court not only has despoiled an important Lockeian element of the written Constitution but has also subverted an ancient common-law rule. In so doing, it has empowered those very factions that control the pluralist legislature, enabling them to seize the property of others without full compensation, despite the checks and balances carefully crafted by the federalists into the U.S. Constitution.

What is the evil at which the eminent domain clause is targeted? Although the history of the clause is sparse, the answer involves at least some sort of redistribution of resources (Stone, Seidman, Sunstein, and Tushnet 1986, p. 1445). The clause reflects a judgment that if government is seeking to produce some public benefit, it is appropriate that the payment should come from the public at large—taxpayers—rather than from identifiable individuals. The compensation requirement indeed operates as an insurance to that effect. Indeed, such compensation reduces the likelihood that a transfer has occurred merely to benefit A at the expense of B. The willingness of the public to pay for the taking suggests that some general public good is at work.

The fundamental public-choice issue at stake in the treatment of the eminent domain clause, broadly construed, is the predictable role of the state. If the taking of private property by goverment had been prohibited entirely—which, of course, it was not—the role of government would have been confined, more or less, to that of the minimal, night-watchman state, fortified by the powers of police and defense. By allowing for the taking of private property for public use, but with compensation, the stage was set by the framers of the Constitution for the emergence of the productive state, presumably to correct for market failures and to provide public goods.

What clearly was not countenanced by the framers—and was blocked by the takings clause—was any notion of the transfer state within which government acted as an agent of wealth redistribution. Evidently, the takings clause must be obliterated if the factions of special interest were to control the legislative marketplace to plunder the wealth of others and to establish the basis for the rent-seeking society. This almost inevitably became the battlefield of the second half of the socialist 20th century. Predictably, the Supreme Court would defer, employing extensive judicial restraint in the face of the rent-seeking legislative onslaught to which the constitutional parchment was exposed. It is against this back-cloth that the takings issue will be reviewed.

In reviewing the behavior of the Supreme Court with respect to the takings issue, certain institutional features are important. First, it is relevant to note that the Supreme Court adjudicates upon each case *en banc*, sitting as a whole of its nine members and not in parts. This ensures that the leadership structure is much sharper in the Supreme Court than it is among the appeals courts, where sittings are much more dispersed and where interaction among the judges is low and declining.

The chief justice is the appointed leader of the Supreme Court, and his power to assign the majority opinion in the cases in which he is in the majority provides him/her with a powerful lever for dealing with the other justices, always provided that he or she is not in dissent most of the time. To the extent that an agenda is discernible within the Supreme Court's adjudications, and to the extent that cycling is apparent within that agenda, the chief justice may become an effective dictator of the Court, by choosing the order of adjudications, by assigning majority opinions, and by logrolling among the associate justices.

For the most part, however, the reputations of the Supreme Court justices rest on their published opinions and not upon their teamwork. Indeed, few such justices can expect anyone to be interested in aspects of their judicial output other than their published opinions and their public votes. Inevitably, this is a force working against teamsmanship and the spirit of institutional responsibility (Posner 1985, p. 229). It is a strong impulse making for an excessive number of written opinions and, aided and abetted by the increased writing role of the law clerks, for excessive length, general verbosity, and self-indulgence of opinions.

An associated feature of this self-indulgence is the abuse of colleagues, usually unnecessary and often nasty, increasingly scattered among the written opinions of Supreme Court justices. Such abuse figures ever more prominently not only in dissenting and concurring opinions but in majority opinions as well, given the current fashion for the author of the majority opinion to attack the dissenting (and even, on occasion, the concurring) opinions of his/her colleagues. Indeed, the printed abuse of colleagues is far more common in the Supreme Court than in any court of appeals other than the District of Columbia Circuit (Posner 1985, p. 233). This in part is a reflection of the drift away from constitutional principles within the Court, leaving Supreme Court opinions as little more than expressions of personal preference on debateable questions of public policy.

The eminent domain clause is only one of several provisions in the U.S. Constitution that expressly restrict the power of the government to interfere with the private economic interests of individuals. The Fifth and Fourteenth Amendments, for example, provide that "No person shall be deprived of property without due process of law." Article 1, section 10, provides that "No state shall pass any law impairing the Obligation of Contracts." Although these provisions protect private economic interests against certain narrowly defined forms of government interference, they also reflect the fundamental importance of private property.

This doctrine of economic substantive due process came into full flower in *Lochner v. New York*, 1905. In this case, the Supreme Court (Mr. Justice Peckham delivering the opinion) held unconstitutional a New York statute providing that no employee shall "work in a biscuit, bread or cake bakery or confectionary establishment more than sixty hours in any one week, or more than ten hours in any one day." The statute clearly interfered with the right of contract between employers and employees concerning the number of hours of work.

The Court recognized the existence of certain powers, vaguely termed "police powers," in the sovereignty of each state, relating to the safety, health, morals, and general welfare of the public, and acknowledged that private property was subject to the exercise of such powers. However, in this case, the Court determined that the limit of the police power had been reached and passed. Statutes of the kind under review in this case were "mere meddlesome interferences with the rights of the individual," and the act constituted an illegal interference with the rights of individuals, both employers and employees, to make contracts regarding labor on such terms as they may think best.

In many ways the *Lochner* case represents the high point of the Supreme Court's defense of economic liberties against the encroachment of pluralistic politics, though it has become "one of the most condemned cases in United States history and has been used to symbolize judicial dereliction and abuse" (Siegen 1980, p. 23). In essence, the judgment reflected judicial activism against a statute that was arguably the product of a political process in which labor unions possessed an organizational advantage over consumers, who ultimately would pay for the regulation through higher prices for bread, and over nonunionized labor willing to accept jobs in unregulated transactions with employers. The Court acted entirely appropriately both in strict constructivist and in the Buchanan perspective, in rectifying this defect in the operation of the political process which culminated in unconstitutional legislation.

From the decision in *Lochner* in 1905 to the mid-1930s, the Court invalidated approximately 200 economic regulations, usually under the due process clause of the Fourteenth Amendment. These decisions centered primarily on labor legislation, the regulation of prices, and restrictions on entry into business. The Court employed substantive due process in an activist manner without departing from an essentially strict constructionist position, maintaining the classical liberal approach that underpinned the Constitution. For example, the Court sustained many regulations during this period, on the ground that they did not offend the Constitution. Moreover, the Court was often divided with Justices Holmes, Brandeis, Stone, Cardozo, and even Chief Justice Hughes not infrequently in dissent.

In the early 1930s the Supreme Court encountered overt political pressure from President Roosevelt's New Deal administration, whose policies its *Lochner* style judgments clearly jeopardized. This pressure became intense following the decision of the Court in *A. L. Schechter Poultry Corp. v. United States* (1935) which invalidated the National Industrial Recovery Act, in many ways the conceptual centerpiece of the New Deal. There can be little doubt of the Court's good judgment in this decision which struck down codes of "fair competition" affecting a live poultry code applicable in metropolitan New York. Because *Schechter* dealt with an activity near the retailing end of the economic activity spectrum, supporters of the New Deal believed that their program might survive in areas closer to the industrial base of the economy. Not so. The Bituminous Coal Conservation Act of 1935 was enacted after *Schechter*. It was invalidated in *Carter v. Carter Coal Co*. (1936). The National Labor Relations Act became effective after *Schechter* and supporters of the New Deal believed that the Court might hold it unconstitutional.

To protect his economic programs against Supreme Court devastation, and following his massive victory in the elections of 1936, President Roosevelt proposed changes in the structure of the Supreme Court. Seizing on the fact that six justices were over 70 years old in 1937, Roosevelt proposed that one additional justice, up to a total of 15, be appointed for each justice over 70 who did not resign or retire. He claimed speciously to Congress that older justices were unable to fulfill their responsibilities, thus increasing the workload of the younger justices. His real motive was to pack the Supreme Court.

The proposal met with strong resistance and was challenged as an attempt to subvert the Constitution. During the debate, Justice Van Devanter retired. The Supreme Court, in a complete *volte face* from *Schechter* and *Carter*, and in clear contradiction to *Lochner*, upheld a state minimum-wage statute in *West Coast Hotel Co. v. Parrish* (1937). Justice Roberts, who had joined the five-person majority in invalidating a state minimum-wage law for women in *Morehead v. New York et al.* (1936), switched sides and now voted with a new majority in favor of an almost identical statute. Regardless of whether his switch could be justified as internally consistent, it was widely characterized as "the switch in time that saved nine" (Stone, Seidman, Sunstein, and Tushnet 1986, p. 168).

In any event, the majority leader of the Senate, Joseph Robinson, who appeared to have accumulated enough votes to secure passage of a Court-packing bill, despite its emphatic rejection by the Senate Judiciary Committee, died of a heart attack before the vote was taken, and the plan was rejected in mid-July 1937. By that time, however, the damage had been wrought. Rarely after 1937 was the Supreme Court to exercise judicial activism in defense of the Constitution and against legislative encroachments on economics rights. The shadow of Roosevelt cast itself over the Court, not least with respect to the takings issue, until President Reagan's appointments to the Court began to shift the majority toward judicial activism in favor of economic rights during the late 1980s.

Central to the treatment by the Supreme Court of cases that purportedly involve the eminent domain clause are conflicting views concerning the nature of property rights in the United States. At the one extreme is the Lockeian notion that individuals hold natural rights in property with which they have been vested and that such rights are inalienable save only when eminent domain considerations justify a takings, for which compensation must be paid. This is the strict construction of the takings clause in the U.S. Constitution. This interpretation offers a principled defense of private property from seizure by the government and provides an indispensable constitutional pillar for a capitalist democracy.

At the other extreme is the notion popularized by Michelman (1981) that property rights are not at all inalienable in a majoritarian democracy but are transferable at the will of the political majority. In this vision, individuals are endowed only with political rights of participation in political action and are not entitled to obstruct the will of the political process by claiming rights to property that run counter to the majority vote. This view, which prevailed in the Supreme Court until the mid-1980s, has jeopardized capitalism in the United States and has provided a powerful foundation for the expansion of rent-seeking socialism.

It is to the credit of Presidents Reagan and Bush that they have out maneuvered the legislature and have succeeded, albeit at a significant sacrifice in the quality of legal scholarship, in appointing to the Supreme Court a chief justice and several associate justices who may prove capable, however unevenly, in holding to some line in the sand against the slide to socialism that has resulted from an inappropriate, if expedient, exercise of judicial restraint with respect to the takings issue. Whether such principled judicial activism at some future point in time will induce yet another Roosevelt-type attack upon the judiciary must depend on the outcome of the unavoidable eventual political battle between capitalism and the rent-seeking society, engaged by Margaret Thatcher in Britain during the 1980s but sidestepped by Ronald Reagan and (as yet) by George Bush in the United States. The issue at stake is whether property rights can be protected in a constitutional democracy, whether indeed capitalism can survive.

8. A Review of Selected Takings Judgments: Constitutional Political Economy or Public Choice?

The eminent domain clause provides "nor shall private property be taken for public use, without just compensation." The logically prior "public use" requirement will be reviewed first against an important unanimous opinion of the Supreme Court in *Hawaii Housing Authority v. Midkiff* (1984) with Justice O'Connor writing the opinion.

This case involved an effort to transfer ownership of property in Hawaii, a state in which land traditionally had been concentrated in the hands of a relatively few individuals. The Land Reform Act of 1967 had created a mechanism for condemning residential tracts and for transferring ownership of the condemned fees simple to existing lessees. By condemning the land in question, the Hawaii legislature intended to make the land sales involuntary, thereby making the federal tax consequences less severe while still facilitating the redistribution of fees simple.

Under the act's condemnation scheme, tenants living on single-family residential lots were entitled to ask the Hawaii Housing Authority to condemn the property. If HHA found that acquisition of such property served the public purposes of the act, it could acquire at prices, set either by condemnation trial or by negotiation between lessors and lessees, the former fee owners' full right, title, and interest in the land. After compensation has been set HHA may sell the land titles to tenants who have applied for fee simple ownership. The issue before the Supreme Court was whether the statute should be deemed unconstitutional on the ground that "public use" was not involved.

The starting point for the Court's review of the constitutionality of the act was the decision of the Supreme Court in *Berman v. Parker* (1954), a decision that was a model of judicial restraint and deference to legislative pressure. In *Berman*, the Court held constitutional the District of Columbia Redevelopment Act of 1945, which provided for the comprehensive use of the eminent domain power to redevelop slum areas and for the possible sale or lease of the condemned lands to private interests. In discussing whether the takings authorized by that act were for "public use," the court stated:

> Subject to specific constitutional limitations, when the legislature has spoken, the public interest has been declared in terms well-nigh conclusive. In such cases the legislature, not the judiciary, is the main guardian of the public needs to be served by social legislation.

Notwithstanding this statement, the Court in *Midkiff* recognized that a role remained for it to play in reviewing a legislature's judgment of what constitutes a public use, even when the eminent domain power is equated with the police power. But the Court in *Berman* made clear that it is "an extremely narrow one." On this basis, the Court had no trouble concluding that the Hawaii act was constitutional:

> We have no trouble concluding that the Hawaii Act is constitutional. The people of Hawaii have attempted [to] reduce the perceived social and economic evils of a land oligopoly. . . . Regulating oligopoly and the evils associated with it is a classic exercise of a State's police powers.

The Court emphasized that the mere fact that property taken outright by eminent domain was transferred in the first instance to private beneficiaries does not condemn that taking as having only a private purpose. The court long ago had rejected any literal requirement that condemned property be put into use for the general public. No purely private taking was involved in the case under review.

This judgment, reported unanimously, confirms the Court's deference to the will of the legislature. An unconvincing a priori case, bereft of serious economic logic, was mounted to determine that the taking indeed was beneficial. An equally unconvincing definition of public use in a case which pre-eminently was private was employed to satisfy the public-use requirement. The public-use requirement originally operated as a serious independent constraint on government action.

After *Midkiff* it is difficult to see how the constraint could be effective when the legislature is involved. This dramatic decline in the constraints imposed by the public-use requirement parallels the expansion in the police power that has played such an important role in constitutional doctrine under the due process clause after the *Lochner* decision. Both events evidence the immense power of special interests to effect naked wealth transfers in the so-called constitutional democracy of the United States. No Reagan effect on the Court is discernible in this judgment. It is now doubtful whether any condemnation of land can be attacked successfully for want of a public purpose.

The notion of exclusive possession, which is implicit in the basic conception of private property, accounts for perhaps the most important takings case in the Supreme Court literature, namely *Pennsylvania Coal Company v. Mahon* (1922). In this case, the owner of land containing coal deposits deeded the surface interest, but expressly reserved the rights to remove all the coal underneath the surface. The deed stipulated that the buyers and their assigns waived all rights to damage in the event that the surface should collapse. Subsequently, Pennsylvania passed the Kohler Act which prohibited any mining that caused damage to the surface owner. This statute was held correctly by the Supreme Court to constitute a taking. Prior to the enactment, the coal company was in possession of a mineral estate. After the enactment, that interest was lost. The Court's judgment was unequivocal and entirely supportive of the

Lockeian classical liberal position: "If [the city's] representatives have been so short sighted as to acquire only surface rights without the right of support, we see no more authority for supplying the latter without compensation than there was for taking the right of way in the first place and refusing to pay for it because the public wanted it very much." Although a case conceivably might have been made for a police power justification for the taking, the Court was unable to determine any external harm on which such a case could be made to rest. As Epstein has noted (1985, p. 64), the case was easy, although the opinion has generated an enormous amount of scholarship.

Such has not been the experience, however, with equally easy post-1937 cases on which the Supreme Court has passed judgments, through which, by dint of tortuous reasoning, it has succeeded in deferring to the legislature. Perhaps the most notorious of such judgments is that in *Penn Central Transportation Company v. City of New York* (1978). The issue before the Court was whether the City of New York, acting pursuant to its landmark preservation statute, was entitled to prevent the owners of Grand Central Terminal from constructing a new office tower over the existing structure. The owners claimed only the right to such airspace that effectively could be occupied. The Supreme Court, however, decided that as long as the use of the existing structures was not impaired, the city could wholly prohibit the occupation and use of airspace without payment of compensation.

The Court, dividing six to three in its majority, essentially in line with the apparent political dispositions of its members, and speaking through Justice Brennan, held that the state may exclude persons from the occupation of part of what they own and still not come under a prima facie obligation to pay compensation. It claimed that it was a fallacy to assume that the loss of any particular right of easement constituted a taking of property. It ignored the fact that ownership is divisible and that the rights over the existing building were property just as much as the air rights already occupied by the existing structure. The judgment demonstrated an appalling ignorance of the nature of property rights and of the meaning of the eminent domain clause, but a shrewd understanding of the dominant political agenda of the legislature and its special interests at that time.

The dissenting opinion of Justice Rehnquist exposed the intellectual weakness of the majority opinion. Nowhere does the Court offer a coherent account of the incidence of ownership, including exclusive possession. Certainly, in private cases it is not necessary to show actual damages in order to obtain an injunction against entry (Epstein 1985, p. 65). The entry itself is the violation of the right, for which the injunction is available for redress, even if no damages can or should be awarded. The question of whether the appellant's rights were negligibly impaired, therefore, is beside the point, just as it would have been in a private dispute. It does not reach out to the takings issue at all, but only to the issue of reliance damages. Justice Marshall, in his concurring opinion, had a better sense than Brennan of the normative conception that must underlie the constitutional interpretation of private property. But he could offer no such principle that would allow him to respect the external authority of the constitutional text, and with good reason. Private property gives the right to exclude others without the need for any kind of justification.

Not content with its judgment on the takings issue, the Court in its majority opinion proceeded to emasculate property rights further by advancing a theory of compensation for any actual taking that is little less than a justification for theft. This opinion, which has been widely cited, confirms the very real fear that no man's property is safe while the legislature remains in session. In the view of the *Penn Central* court majority, the state's obligation is discharged whenever its actions permit the owner of private property to enjoy a "reasonable return" upon his/her original investment. Thus, the property owner legitimately can be deprived of compensation for all or part of the appreciation in market value between the time of the original acquisition or improvement and the date of condemnation. To protect private property and to fulfill the unambiguous requirement of the takings clause, the Court should have insisted on market value as a universal standard, in the case of both outright takings and partial takings.

In *San Diego Gas and Electric Co. v. City of San Diego* (1981), the Supreme Court was able to revisit the takings issue in the new political climate that had ushered in the Reagan presidency consolidated by the Republican control over the U.S. Senate. The opportunity was not missed by Justice Brennan, in his dissenting opinion, to shift position rightward in political space and to countermand some of his earlier errors of judgment in *Penn Central*.

In this case, the gas company had assembled a large tract of land within the city limits on which it planned to construct a nuclear power plant. Although the acquired land was not zoned originally for industrial development, the requisite zoning changes were procured after purchase. Before development could take place, however, the city downzoned some of the land from industrial to agriculture, included a new "open spaces" requirement in its comprehensive plan, and prepared a map on which the land was designated for purchase by the city after passage of the appropriate bond issue. The company contended that these combined actions constituted a taking of private property for which just compensation was owed.

The California Supreme Court had held that all challenges to government regulation under the police power must be brought administratively by way of mandamus. By shifting the emphasis from that of *takings* of property under the eminent domain clause and *deprivations* of property under the police power, the court enabled the city to escape interim damages between imposition of the regulation and its subsequent invalidation as an uncompensated taking. On appeal, the U.S. Supreme Court failed to resolve any of the eminent domain issues because five justices held that there had been no final judgment from which an appeal was proper. Five justices (Rehnquist plus the dissent) did address the inverse condemnation question.

In a sharp reversal of his *Penn Central* opinion, Justice Brennan's dissent wiped out the arguments of the California Supreme Court. First, he noted that "just" compensation is required, no matter how the taking is effected, be it by formal condemnation proceedings, occupancy, physical invasion, or regulation. He added that the requirement extended to partial as well as to complete takings, to temporary and indefinite as well as to permanent takings. If this is so, then the *Penn Central* decision is rendered inexplicable. He further noted that judicial, legislative, or executive policy, with its evident penchant for land planning, could not oust the constitutional command: "Once a court establishes that there was a regulatory 'taking,' the Constitution demands that the government entity pay just compensation for the period commencing on the date the regulation first effected the 'taking,' and ending on the date the government entity chooses to rescind or otherwise amend the regulation."

Brennan's opinion sought to reconcile *San Diego Gas and Electric* with *Penn Central* on the ground that *Penn Central* only addressed the takings issue proper and *San Diego Gas and Electric* the just compensation question. As Epstein (1985, p. 192) has noted, however, the attempted reconciliation, at best, is cosmetic. The compensation question in *San Diego Gas and Electric* arose precisely because the erroneous strictures on the takings question in *Penn Central* were not followed. The Brennan of *Penn Central* emphasized that there is no principled formula for determining takings cases. Here was judicial deference and antiproperty rights activism at its combined peak. The Brennan of *San Diego Gas and Electric* considered the takings and compensation questions in logical sequence and moved to a much more principled position. The change in the climate of opinion is the only evident explanation of this intellectual metamorphosis.

With the replacement of Burger by Rehnquist as chief justice and with the appointments of O'Connor and Scalia (and then in 1988 Kennedy) as justices, President Reagan shifted the balance of the Supreme Court in a direction more favorable to the support of economic rights against the rent-seeking equilibrium that still dominated the legislative branch of the U.S. government. In 1987 and 1988, the consequences of this shift of balance became discernible as the Supreme Court adjudicated a sequence of cases in which the takings clause was an important bone of contention. Uncertainly at first, but with growing determination, the Court shifted direction and adopted a much less deferential stance in protecting property rights from legislative seizure.

The first test of the reconstituted Court came in March 1987 in its judgment in the case of *Keystone Bituminous Coal Association v. DeBenedictis*, in which coal companies challenged a Pennsylvania Subsidence Act requiring that 50 percent of the coal beneath certain structures be kept in place to provide surface support. In a 5 to 4 decision, the Court held that: (1) there was public purpose for the act; (2) there was no showing of the diminution of value in land resulting from the act; (3) the act did not work on unconstitutional taking on its face; (4) there was no showing of unconstitutional taking of the separate support estate recognized by Pennsylvania law; and (5) public interest in the legislation justified the impact of the act on coal companies' contractual agreements with surface owners.

This judgment clearly violated the strict construction of the Constitution, since no one denied that a taking had occurred without any payment of compensation to those concerned. Instead, debate concentrated on post-*Lochner* judgments of the Court designed to amend the Constitution rather than to uphold it. Specifically, it was argued that taking is more readily established when interference with property can be characterized as physical invasion by government then when (as in this case) interference arises from some public program adjusting benefits and burdens of economic life to promote common good. Furthermore, it was argued (again, against the wording) that the Pennsylvania Subsidence Act did not work an unconstitutional taking on its face in view of the fact that the 27 million tons of coal required to be left in 13 mines represented only 2 percent of the coal in the mines. The Court refused to treat the coal required to be left in the ground as a separate parcel of property to which all value had been lost.

In May 1987, *Hodel v. Irving* presented a favorable environment for the Supreme Court to deliver a unanimous judgment that a taking had occurred without just compensation in a case no more (nor less) compelling on the facts than that affecting the Keystone Bituminous Coal Association. The principal difference was that the decision in *Hodel v. Irving* affected *a minority group*, the designated heirs and devisees of three deceased members of Oglala Sioux Tribe. The heirs sued seeking declaration that a provision of the Indian Land Consolidation Act was unconstitutional inasmuch as it authorized a seizure of property without just compensation. That which the Court would not offer to a group of capitalists evidently was not to be denied to native Americans.

The judgment of the Court (O'Connor) explicitly acknowledged the ad hoc manner of judgment in the takings field and the general inability of the Court to develop any "set formula" for determining when "justice and fairness" require that economic injuries caused by public action be compensated by the government. In contrast of *Keystone*, where 27 million tons of coal were deemed to be of trivial value, in this case values of $100, $2,700, and $1,816 were deemed to be "not trivial sums." The fact that consolidation of Indian lands would benefit all members of the tribe, including the plaintiffs, rightly was not allowed to weigh. It is impossible to reconcile this return to strict constructionism by the Court so quickly on the heels of *Keystone* except in terms of the politics of race, which, of course, has no place in a court of law.

In June 1987, in *First English Evangelical Lutheran Church of Glendale v. County of Los Angeles, California*, a divided Court handed down a more aggressive strict constructionist judgment designed to open up litigation in the whole field of temporary takings by government. The appellant church sought to recover in inverse condemnation and in tort against an interim ordinance prohibiting the reconstruction of a retreat center for handicapped children following a 1978 flood that had destroyed its buildings. The California Supreme Court had ruled that there could be no recovery in damages for the time before it is finally determined that a regulation constitutes a "taking" of property. The Supreme Court (Rehnquist) disagreed concluding that the Fifth and Fourteenth Amendments would require compensation for that period.

In this judgment, Rehnquist ignored all ad hocery and returned to the precise and clear wording of the Constitution, concluding that the Fifth Amendment required the government to pay the landowner for the value of the use of the land during the interim period under consideration. The majority opinion recognized that the judgment undoubtedly would reduce the freedom and flexibility of land-use planners and municipal corporations when enacting land-use regulations. Such was the nature of the U.S. Constitution.

In dissenting from this judgment, Justice Stevens (with some support from Blackman and O'Connor) noted the long litany of judgments in which temporary takings arguments had failed to convince. This reflects the status quo perspective of Buchanan outlined above. Stevens was particularly concerned that the majority would not distinguish between a physical and a regulatory taking, concurring with the judgment of Justice Holmes that "[g]overnment hardly could go on if to some extent values incident to property could not be diminished without paying for every such change in the general law." Notwithstanding these concerns, such is the wording of the Constitution.

In June 1987, in *Nollan v. California Coastal Commission*, the Supreme Court divided further, once again essentially on partisan lines, to strengthen the reach of the takings clause as extended to the states by the Fourteenth Amendment. The California Coastal Commission had granted a permit to the appellants to replace a small bungalow on their beach front lot with a larger house on the condition that they allow the public an easement to pass across their beach, which was located between two public beaches. The appellants had been denied a writ of administrative mandamus, and a direction that the permit condition be struck, by the California State Court of Appeal. The majority of the Supreme Court—Scalia, Rehnquist, White, Powell, and O'Connor—found in favor of the appellants.

In Scalia's opinion, the right to exclude was viewed as "one of the most essential sticks in the bundle of nights that are commonly characterized as property." If California wanted to use its power of eminent domain and advance a comprehensive program of socializing its beaches, it could do so. However, if it desired an easement across the appellants' property, it must pay for it. Compliance with the Fifth Amendment's property clause was designed to be more than an exercise in cleverness and imagination. In Brennan's dissent, the Buchanan perspective is advanced and the majority is criticized for imposing "a standard of precision for the exercise of a State's police power that has been discredited for the better part of this century." The majority is condemned for employing reasoning "hardly suited to the complex reality of natural resource protection in the twentieth century." The line of battle between strict construction and the living Constitution scarcely could be more clearly drawn.

The final case here subjected to review—*Pennell v. City of San Jose*—

was determined by the Supreme Court in February 1988. A clear majority of the Court shied away from making a strict constructionist statement in a hard case involving potential poor tenants. Justices Scalia and O'Connor stood by the words of the Constitution, thus refusing to allow a hard case to embroil them in the making of bad law. Justice Kennedy, newly appointed, played no role in the case.

The case involved an appeal by a landlord and a landlord's association attacking the constitutionality of a city rent-control ordinance which allowed a hearing officer to consider "hardship to a tenant" when determining whether to approve a rent increase proposed by a landlord. Although no hardship ruling had been made, the Supreme Court acknowledged the standing of the appellants in view of the many hardship tenants served by them. However, the majority concluded that the takings argument was premature and that "the constitutionality of laws should not be decided except in an actual factual setting that makes such a decision necessary." In affirming the judgment of the Supreme Court of California against the appellants, the Court determined that it was premature to consider their claims under the takings clause and rejected their facial challenge to the ordinance under the due process and equal protection clauses of the Fourteenth Amendment.

Scalia and O'Connor accepted the latter part of the majority judgment but denied that the appellants' takings claim was premature. The Fifth Amendment clause was designed to bar government from forcing some people alone to bear public burdens which, in all fairness and justice, should be borne by the public as a whole. This was the effect of the hardship provision. The appellants did not contest the validity of rent regulation in general and indeed accepted the six "other factors" that must be considered by the hearing officer (cost of debt servicing, rental history of the unit, physical condition of the unit, changes in housing services, other financial information, and market value rents for similar units). They were correct in objecting to the additional hardship criterion as a taking, for the neediness of renters was not remotely attributable to the particular landlords that the ordinance singled out.

9. Conclusions

The Court sharply changed direction during the late 1980s away from the living Constitution ad hocery that characterized its judgments over the proceeding half-century. Where political correctness coincides with strict construction, the wording of the Constitution predictably now holds sway.

Where it does not, judgments remain in doubt. It still pays to be a native Indian or a poor tenant rather than a coal mine owner or a landlord, even in the highest court in the land. That this is so demonstrates the ongoing power of public choice and the weakness of the Constitution when challenged by the guns of special interests. Yet, in some judgments, the Court has gone well beyond the strictures of Buchanan and has ignored stare decisis in maintaining the words of the Constitution. In these uneven judgments we may discern the last best chance for the United States to reattain minimal government under constitutional law against the forces that favor *Leviathan*.

References

Ackerman, B. 1984. "Discovering the Constitution." *Yale Law Journal* 93: 1013–1072.

Barnett, R.E. 1987. "Judicial Pragmactivism: A Definition." In *Economic Liberties and the Judiciary*, J.A. Dorn and H.G. Manne, eds., 18–45. Fairfax: George Mason University Press.

Blackstone, W. 1766. *Commentaries on the Laws of England*. Reprint 1979. Chicago: University of Chicago Press.

Buchanan, J.M. 1975. *The Limits of Liberty: Between Anarchy and Leviathan*. Chicago: University of Chicago Press.

————. 1988. "Contractarian Political Economy and Constitutional Interpretation." *American Economic Review* 78(2):135–139.

————. 1989. *Explorations into Constitutional Economics*. College Station: Texas A & M University Press.

Crew, M.A., and Rowley, C.K. 1988. "Toward a Public Choice Theory of Monopoly Regulation." *Public Choice* 57:49–67.

Dorn, J.M., and Manne, H.G., eds. 1987. *Economic Liberties and the Judiciary*. Fairfax: George Mason University Press.

Dworkin, R. 1985. *A Matter of Principle*. Cambridge, MA: Harvard University Press.

Easterbrook, F. 1988. "Method, Result and Authority: A Reply." *Harvard Law Review* 98:622–629.

Epstein, R.A. 1985. *Takings: Private Property and the Power of Eminent Domain*. Cambridge, MA: Harvard University Press.

The Federalist, No. 10. 1937. New York: The Modern Library: 53–61.

The Federalist, No. 51. 1937. New York: The Modern Library: 335–340.

The Federalist, No. 78. 1937. New York: The Modern Library: 502–511.

Grey, T. 1980. "The Disintegration of Property." In *NOMOS*, Monograph No. 22, J.R. Pennock and J.W. Chapman, eds.

Gwartney, J.D., and Wagner, R.E., eds. 1988. *Public Choice and Constitutional Economics*. Greenwich: JAI Press.

Hand, L. 1958. *The Bill of Rights: The Oliver Wendell Holmes Lectures 1958*. Cambridge: Harvard University Press.

Hayek, F.A. 1973. *Law Legislation and Liberty*, Vol. 1: *Rules and Order*. London: Routledge & Kegan Paul.

Hobbes, T. 1651. *Leviathan*. Reprint 1965. London: Everyman's Library.

Locke, J. 1690. *Two Treatises of Government*. Reprint 1947. New York: Hafner Press.

Macedo, S. 1987. *The New Right v. The Constitution*. Washington, DC: the Cato Institute.

Manne, H. 1991. "A Proposal for Reconciling Different Views About Constitutional Interpretation." Fairfax: George Mason Law School-Working Paper: 1–32.

Michelman, F.I. 1967. "Property, Utility and Fairness: Comments on the Ethical Foundations of Just Compensation Law," *Harvard Law Review* 80:1165–1258.

Olson, M. 1965. *The Logic of Collective Action*. Cambridge, MA: Harvard University Press.

Pitkin, H.F. 1967. *The Concept of Representation*. Berkeley: University of California Press.

Posner, R.A. 1985. *The Federal Courts: Crisis and Reform*. Cambridge, MA: Harvard University Press.

————. 1990. *The Problems of Jurisprudence*. Cambridge, MA: Harvard University Press.

Rowley, C.K. 1987. "A Public Choice Perspective on Judicial Pragmactivism. In *Economic Liberties and the Judiciary*, J.A. Dorn and H.G. Manne, eds., 219–224. Fairfax: George Mason University Press.

————. 1989. "The Common Law in Public Choice Perspective: A Theoretical and Institutional Critique." *Hamline Law Review* 12 (Spring): 355–383.

Siegan, B.H. 1980. *Economic Liberties and the Constitution*. Chicago: University of Chicago Press.

Stone, G.R., Seidman, L.N., Sunstein, C.R., and Tushnet, M.V., eds. 1986. *Constitutional Law*. Boston: Little Brown.

Tribe, L.H. 1985. *Constitutional Choices*. Cambridge, MA: Harvard University Press.

Tullock, G. 1967. *Toward a Mathematics of Politics*. Ann Arbor: University of Michigan Press.

CASES

Berman v. Parker, 348 U.S. 26 (1954).

Carter v. Carter Coal Co., 298 U.S. 238 (1936).

First English Evangelical Church v. County of Los Angeles, 107 S. Ct. 2378 (1987).

Hawaii Housing Authority v. Midkiff, 104 S. Ct. (1984).

Hodel v. Irving, 107 S. Ct. 2067 (1987).
Keystone Bituminous Coal Association v. Debenedictus, 107 S. Ct. 1232 (1987).
Lochner v. New York, 198 U.S. (1905).
Marbury v. Madison, 5 U.S. (1 Cranch) 137 (1803).
Morehead v. New York ex rel. Tipaldo, 298 U.S. 587 (1936).
Nollan v. California Coastal Commission, 107 S. Ct. 3141 (1987).
Penn Central Transportation Co. v. City of New York, 438 U.S. 104 (1978).
Pennell v. City of San Jose, 108 S. Ct. 849 (1988).
Pennsylvania Coal Company v. Mahon, 260 U.S. 393 (1922).
San Diego Gas and Electric Co. v. City of San Diego, 450 U.S. 621 (1981).

5 THE DILEMMAS OF PROPERTY AND SOVEREIGNTY IN THE POSTMODERN ERA: NEW SOLUTIONS FOR THE REGULATORY TAKINGS PROBLEM

Gary Minda

1. Introduction

In the last decade an explosion of Supreme Court case law has struggled with the question of what makes a regulatory restriction on private property a taking for which just compensation is required by the Constitution.[1] Judges, policymakers, and legal scholars have offered various modern approaches to answer this question; but, notwithstanding their efforts, or perhaps because of their meddlings, the problem of regulatory takings has only become more confused and complex than ever. As one commentator of the Court's recent takings cases has aptly concluded: "[I]t is difficult to imagine a body of case law in greater doctrinal and conceptual disarray" (Peterson 1989, p. 1304).

Yet, despite the current state of confusion spawned by the legal rationales of regulatory takings doctrine, a surprising pattern of predictability can be found when one examines the outcomes of particular cases. When the leading Supreme Court cases are examined solely in terms of their outcomes, one can discover, as others have revealed, an unarticulated policy that is weighted in favor of a deeply conservative ideology, an ideology committed to the possibility of immunizing the status quo of many common-law prerogatives of property ownership against modern regulatory change (Michelman 1988a, p. 1625; Radin 1988, p. 1682). It is therefore not surprising that commentators are also discovering that "it is much easier to predict when the Court will find a taking than one would anticipate, given the state of the Court's current takings doctrine" (Peterson 1990, p. 58).

Judges, however, have been reluctant to articulate or even recognize the baseline political, moral, and social assumptions that critically structure their legal analysis of takings problems.[2] Instead, the trend of the recent case law in this area appears to be advancing toward the goal of formalizing a takings law under a doctrinal system that is consistent, determinant, and, above all, committed to upholding the "Rule of Law" against arbitrary government (Sterk 1988, pp. 1747–1751). More than anything else, it may be the felt necessity to protect a particular concept of "property" from the demands of the modern regulatory state that "explains" the recent development of the regulatory takings doctrine in the Supreme Court.

Today, most takings scholars, like most judges and lawyers, uncritically assume that it *is* possible to discover determinant and politically neutral baselines for determining when regulatory restrictions on private property impinge the substantive limitations of the takings clause of the Fifth Amendment. Classical liberals who have internalized a Hobbesian model of politics argue that the takings clause establishes a determinant rule of law that is essential for restraining the *Leviathan* of governmental regulation (Epstein 1985). For them, the takings clause establishes one big Rule of Law at the center of the constitutional universe—*any* legislative restriction on the property owner's right to possess, use, and dispose of property is a prima facie taking for which the Constitution requires just compensation (Schwartz 1990, p. 98). Economic analysts who have adopted a Benthamite view of human behavior argue that the takings clause must be structured by efficient rules of law that preserve the investment-backed expectations of private individuals who have committed their economic resources to capital projects (Blume and Rubinfeld 1984). Legal reformists who have adopted a characteristically eclectic approach to the takings problem argue that the takings clause must be structured by an instrumental policy that attempts to "reconcile" the tension between democracy and private property (Rose-Ackerman 1988). Despite their important methodological disagreements, all of these scholars share the common belief that a conceptual framework of analysis can be discovered for protecting private property against official state action under rules of law that respect the values of efficiency, equity, and political legitimacy.

In this chapter I will seek to uncover what I believe to be a different *critical* approach to the problem of regulatory takings, one that may help to explain both the current doctrinal confusion of the case law and the predictable pattern of the outcome of the cases. The approach I will describe argues that the general methodogical approach of takings scholars who advocate a "right answer thesis" may be leading down the wrong conceptual path. Indeed, my approach advances a different methodology—namely, that the question of what constitutes a taking can *never* be answered in the way that most commentators and judges believe that takings questions can be answered—that is, answered once and for all under an ideal set of rules that avoid the fear of arbitrariness posed by a government of men, and not law.

For lack of a better term, I will use Jean-Francois Lyotard's idea of *postmodernism*[3] to characterize what I believe to be the emergence of a new era in takings scholarship, an era in which a growing number of scholars have rejected the attempt to solve any number of legal problems under an ideal set of legal or economic parameters. I will attempt to explain why I believe *postmoderns*,[4] and their characteristically *postmodern temperament*,[5] might be useful for inspiring a new framework of analysis that may offer not just another way of analyzing a difficult and complex legal problem, but one that may offer a transformed conception of what it means to solve the legal and constitutional issues posed by regulatory takings. In order to understand why some takings scholars have adopted a postmodern temperament in their takings scholarship, we must first examine what seems to be the hopelessly confused, yet predictable, state of current takings doctrine.

2. The Dialectic Structure of Regulatory Takings Doctrine

The law of regulatory takings has *always* been in a hopeless state of doctrinal disarray because judges have been unable to agree on a legal test or doctrine for reconciling the tension between the rights of private property, which the takings clause of the Fifth Amendment seeks to protect, and the interests of the community, which government is constitutionally committed to advance under its police power. As Richard A. Epstein (1985) has forcefully argued, nearly all regulatory restrictions on the use and disposition of private property could be seen as a prima facie taking for which just compensation is required by the Constitution. However, if all regulation affecting property entitlements is a prima facie taking, then we are faced with a serious constitutional dilemma since, as even Epstein has acknowledged, some recognition of the police power is necessary if we are to make any sense of the Constitution (Espstein 1988a, p. 59). The legal dilemma raised by the regulatory takings cases can thus be understood in terms of a basic contradiction posed by constitutional imperatives that restrict *and* advance the power of government to regulate private property.

The dialectical structure of takings law can be traced to the 1922 landmark Supreme Court decision of *Pennsylvania Coal Company v. Mahon*. In *Mahon*, the Court was asked to invalidate Pennsylvania's Kohler Act which forbade the mining of coal if it would damage surface habitats. Pennsylvania Coal conveyed its interest in a surface estate to the plaintiffs, but expressly reserved its right to remove all the coal underneath the parcel. The plaintiffs, relying upon the Kohler Act, sued to enjoin any mining that would undermine the support of the ground surface and their house. The legal question presented was whether the act constituted an unconstitutional taking of the coal company's property (the mineral rights) without just compensation.

Justice Holmes, writing for the majority, stated that "[t]he general rule at least is, that while property may be regulated to a certain extent, if regulation goes too far it will be recognized as a taking" (*Pennsylvania Coal Company v. Mahon*, p. 325). Justice Holmes concluded that Pennsylvania's law "went too far" because the regulation resulted in a substantial diminution of value of the property owner's right to use his/her property for profit. "To make it commercially impracticable to mine certain coal has very nearly the same effect for constitutional purposes as appropriating or destroying it" (*Mahon*, p. 325).

In dissent, Justice Brandeis argued that the state's coal-mining regulation was premised on the exercise of valid police powers necessary to protect the public interest. To Justice Brandeis, restriction on private property "imposed to protect the public health, safety or morals from dangers threatened is not a taking" (*Mahon*, p. 326). According to Brandeis, the regulatory restriction imposed by the Kohler Act involved a "noxious use" which interfered with the "paramount rights of the public "[6] (*Mahon*, p. 327).

For Holmes, the Archimedean point separating legitimate governmental regulation from an unconstitutional taking was to be determined by the degree of diminution in property value caused by governmental regulation. Only substantial diminutions in value would constitute a taking. For Brandeis, however, it was the concept of public interest that was the key for determining whether or not regulation amounted to a compensable taking. Regulation serving important public interests such as health, safety, or morals would not be a taking. Holmes and Brandeis thus saw the takings clause as grounded in two totally different legal principles. While Holmes focused on the economic effects of the regulation of property, Brandeis looked to the nature of police power and the concept of public interest.[7]

The Holmes versus Brandeis debate in *Mahon* can be understood in Hegelian terms—a dialectic swirling around a contradiction posed by the necessity of maintaining an economic system committed to the institution of private property, on the one hand, and a system of government committed to the values of democracy and popular sovereignty on the other. Holmes, in emphasizing the importance of protecting property value from the substantial effects of regulation, was advancing a property-like perspective for analyzing regulatory takings questions. Brandeis, on the other hand, in emphasizing the importance of allowing government to act for the common good, was asserting a community-like perspective for analyzing the same takings questions. Takings doctrine has since exemplified an unceasing dialectical movement oscillating between new but surprisingly similar variations of these two fundamental ways of understanding the role of law in protecting property in the modern regulatory era.

Today, state and federal governments have established new forms of regulations that make it difficult for the courts to discern intelligent boundaries between what is private property and what belongs to the community. The traditional common-law distinctions between state power and private property (the public-private distinction in liberal legal thought) have disintegrated as cities and states have come to perform proprietary functions, to use property ownership to achieve governmental objectives, and to establish new forms of regulations through licenses, franchises, and the like (Michelman 1988a, p. 1627). Actions by governmental officials can no longer be separated from private sector interests. "Every public act is, in part, a response to the desires of private individuals, while every private desire is, in part, a response to publicly created incentives, rules and institutions" (Frug 1984, p. 681).

Judges have nonetheless insisted on maintaining a public-private distinction in their takings analysis under doctrinal devices that reflect either a Holmesian or Brandeisian perspective to regulatory takings cases. Currently, a majority of the Supreme Court appears to employ a Holmesian property-like perspective in deciding most, but not all, of the recent regulatory cases considered since 1987. The property perspective of current takings law has served the rhetorical purpose of reinforcing the view that government action is different from private action, that state power is inherently coercive, and that private power of property must be protected because it is freedom-enhancing. Brandeis' view, establishing a community-like perspective favoring state action advancing the public interest, once dominant during the Warren Court era, now appears to have become a minority view of the Rehnquist Court. But, as I shall show, the community-like perspective still plays an important role in influencing the way judges define property interests under the Holmesian approach. Hence, while general trends can be discerned, important exceptions to this pattern do arise.

A prime example of this can be seen by comparing the Supreme Court's 1987 decision in *Keystone Bituminous Coal Association v. DeBenedictis*, with *Mahon*. In *Keystone*, the Court concluded that the Pennsylvania Subsidence Act of 1966 did not give rise to a taking of private property even though the act required coal mine operators to leave about 2 percent of all the coal to which they had legal title in the ground.[8] This regulation, like the Kohler Act invalidated as a taking in *Mahon*, was designed to prevent or minimize the environmental damage to surface estates caused by *subsidence*, that is, "lowering of the strata overlying a coal mine, including the land surface, caused by the extraction of the underground coal" (*Keystone*, p. 1236).

In *Mahon*, the Court, following Holmes' property-like perspective in evaluating takings claims, held that the Kohler Act's restriction on coal mining's having a subsidence effect constituted a taking because it made it "economically impractical" for the coal company to use its ownership interest in the mineral estate. In *Keystone*, the Court, while appearing to adopt a Holmesian view of takings, nevertheless reached the opposite result. As in *Mahon*, the *Keystone* Court concluded that the Subsidence Act of 1966 would constitute a compensable taking if it resulted in a substantial diminution of value in the landowners' property. Did the regulation in *Keystone* result in a diminution of property value? The *Keystone* majority, without overruling *Mahon*, concluded that the Susidence Act of 1966 did not. Why?

The *Keystone* Court was able to reach a contrary result because it defined the property interest of the landowner differently. The majority reasoned that the 1966 act, unlike the Kohler Act invalidated in *Mahon*, did not make it "commercially impracticable" to mine coal because the value of the support estate, affected by the regulation, was insubstantial when measured in relation to the value of the coal in the total parcel. In the majority's view, a restriction that merely required the coal miners to leave two percent of their coal in the ground was insufficient to constitute a "taking" of private property. By defining the property interest broadly as the entire mineral estate owned by the coal-mining company, the Court was able to utilize the property-like perspective of Holmes in *Mahon* to reach an outcome substantively different from the one actually reached by Holmes in *Mahon*.

The dissent in *Keystone*, on the other hand, argued that because the act abrogated the value of the support estate owned by the coal companies, the regulation resulted in a one hundred percent diminution in value. In other words, by narrowly defining the property interest to include only the "support estate" owned by the mining company, the dissent was able to conclude that the regulation effected a total diminution of value giving rise to an unconstitutional "taking" of property. The majority and dissent both followed the test advocated by Holmes in *Mahon* but reached different conclusions which were perfectly defensible based on their different definitions of the property interests involved.

What enabled the majority in *Keystone* to define the affected property interest differently was the different judicial perspectives the justices adopted in their takings analysis. Justice Stevens, who wrote the opinion for the majority in *Keystone*, appearing to follow the Holmesian view of takings in *Mahon*, implicitly adopted the public interest or community-like perspective of Justice Brandeis in shaping the contours of the property interest involved. Justice Stevens was able to do this by treating Justice Holmes' analysis of the economic effect in *Mahon* as nothing more than "advisory opinion."

According to Justice Stevens, the "holdings and assumptions" of *Mahon* provided "obvious and necessary reasons for distinguishing" *Mahon* on the basis of two critical factors which Stevens saw as integral parts to the Court's takings analysis. In his view, land-use regulation may constitute a taking if it "does not substantially advance legitimate state interests . . . or denies an owner economically viable use of his land" (*Keystone*, p. 1242, quoting *Agins v. Tiburon*). Stevens concluded that *Mahon* could be distinguished from *Keystone* because the "character of the governmental action involved . . . leans heavily against a taking," and because there was insufficient proof to show that the Subsidence Act makes it impossible for petitioners to profitably engage in their business . . ." (*Keystone*, p. 1242).

Justice Rehnquist, joined by Justices Powell, O'Connor, and Scalia, dissented on the ground that Justice Holmes' decision established a binding precedent that should have been followed in evaluating the economic effects of the Subsidence Act. Justice Rehnquist concluded that the fact that the act served a public purpose was insufficient to release the government from the compensation requirement given his conclusion that private property had been taken by the state. The dissenters' definition of property interest, unlike that of the majority, remained faithful to the property-like perspective of Justice Holmes in *Mahon*. As Justice Rehnquist explained in his dissent: "Though the government's direct benefit may vary depending upon the nature of its action, the question is evaluated from the perspective of the property holder's loss rather than the government's gain" (*Keystone*, p. 1258).

One might approach the takings problem in *Keystone* from a different angle by looking, as Justice Brandeis did in *Mahon*, to the concept of police power as a basis for delimiting valid governmental regulation from illegitimate regulatory takings.[9] In *Keystone*, Pennsylvania's Subsidence Act was seen by the majority to be necessary to prevent socially harmful or nuisance-like uses of property.[10] Hence, at least one reason for upholding the act was based on the view that the regulation was an environmental measure needed to permit the state to prevent the harmful or nuisance-like consequences of subsidence. The *Keystone* dissent, on the other hand, defined the regulation narrowly as an economic measure seeking to maintain the community's tax base from eroding land values. Because the dissent saw the challenged regulation as undermining the property owner's investment backed expectations in property, the dissent focused on a different policy. In their view, the nuisance exception does not apply if the regulation works to "extinguish *all* beneficial uses" of the property because such regulation would impair investment-backed expectations or the ability to utilize the property for profitable purposes (*Keystone*, p. 1257).

The majority and dissent were able to reach different legal conclusions about the significance of the state's police power by adopting either a property or community-like perspective in their analysis of public interest. Justices principally concerned about protecting private property against significant governmental regulations adopt a Holmesian property-like perspective, which enabled them to focus on property versus community interests. The public purpose to be served by state regulation is either ignored altogether or is narrowly defined. Justices concerned about upholding public purposes adopt a community-like perspective, which permits them to find that state regulation is necessary to remedy a nuisance or a public harm.

Decisions like *Mahon* and *Keystone* illustrate how easy it is for judges to manipulate takings doctrine to accord with their perception of the relative merits of property and community. Judges have been able to reach satisfactory outcomes by adopting either a property-like or community-like perspective, whichever takings doctrine is predominant, and then manipulating the chosen perspective to reach their objective by defining the interest that the perspective protects either narrowly or broadly. What separates majority and dissenting opinions, influences judicial choices, and determines legal outcomes are the underlying judicial perspectives and attitudes about the importance of upholding either property or community interests. While these judicial perspectives set the terms of the takings discourse through which legal arguments and judicial decisions are made, they fail to transcend the contradictions of takings doctrine because they merely represent partial and incomplete views about the nature of property and governmental regulation. While the legal rationales appear confused and incomplete, the underlying the arguments follow a consistent argumentative pattern or structure. When seen in the light of the legal dialectic established by Holmes and Brandeis in *Mahon*, modern decisions such as *Keystone* evoke an ironic sense of deja vu.

3. Doctrinal Shifts and New Dialectic Patterns

Until recently, the Supreme Court seemed resigned to accept the notion that no single legal test or principle could ever be devised for resolving all regulatory takings cases. Instead of seeking to establish hard and fast rules to decide takings issues, the Court adopted a flexible judicial attitude based on the idea of case-by-case balancing. In the 1978 decision in *Penn Central Transportation Co. v. City of New York*, for example, New York City's landmark-preservation law was challenged as an unconstitutional taking by Penn Central because it was used to prevent Penn Central from developing its property as Penn Central desired. Penn Central argued that the law constituted a taking of its airspace development rights in that the city had relied on the law in denying it the right to build on top of its terminal. The Supreme Court upheld the Landmark Preservation Act under an "essentially ad hoc" analysis that attempted to mediate the conflict between the common-law property rights of the owner and the community interest in preserving historical landmarks.

Justice Brennan, who wrote the majority opinion for the Court, analyzed the takings claim in *Penn Central* by considering the benefits and burdens of the regulation on the "parcel as a whole," rather than focusing solely on the airspace rights of the property owner. According to Justice Brennan, "'taking' jurisprudence does not divide a single parcel into discrete segments and attempt to determine whether rights in a particular segment have been entirely abrogated" (*Penn Central*, p. 2662). Justice Brennan concluded that whether the landmark law's restriction constituted a taking had to be determined by looking to a three-factor test.

That test required the Court to consider the character of the governmental action, the extent to which the government action interfered with reasonable, investment-backed expectations, and the severity of the economic impact of the regulation on the property. The Court balanced the right of the property owner against the needs of the state and concluded that the act represented a reasonable accommodation of conflicting rights and interests that merely prohibited Penn Central from developing the airspace above the Penn Central Terminal until an acceptable development plan was accepted. Penn Central was, of course, permitted as the owner to use the remainder of its parcel in a "gainful fashion."[11]

More recently, however, Supreme Court doctrine has exhibited a trend toward a more formalistic takings jurisprudence, one that appears to be moving away from case-by-case balancing toward rules based on *per se* categories[12] (Michelman 1989, p. 1625, Radin 1988, pp. 1681–1682). This new type of doctrinal formalism in the law of takings has been fostered by the judicial development of a new method for analyzing regulatory taking claims, one aimed at upholding common-law prerogatives of property ownership against regulatory change. The modern idea of regulatory takings can be attributed to the Supreme Court's recent reliance on what Margaret Jane Radin has called the method of *conceptual severance* (Radin 1988, p. 1676) or what Frank I. Michelman has dubbed *entitlement chopping* (Michelman 1989, p. 1601).

"Conceptual severance" or "entitlement chopping" is premised on the idea, rejected by Justice Brennan in *Penn Central*, that a parcel of property can be conceptually divided into a bundle of rights and uses, and that the significant regulation of any particular right or use might constitute a prima facie taking.[13] By narrowing its definition of property to discrete entitlements, the Court has applied a heightened level of judicial scrutiny in the course of finding categories of property entitlements to be immune from regulatory change, thereby reaffirming Justice Holmes' approach to takings in *Mahon*. The possibility that governmental regulation of particular "sticks" in the property rights bundle constitute a taking has opened the door to an ever-increasing number of Fifth

Amendment challenges to state and federal regulatory schemes. Three important Supreme Court decisions handed down during the 1987 term illustrate this trend.

In *Hodel v. Irving*, for example, the Court held that provisions of the Federal Indian Consolidation Act of 1983 abrogating the right of Indian property owners to devise property interests upon their death constituted a per se taking of a property interest that could not be justified by the public interest in holding tribal lands in trust by the federal government. Regulation of the right to pass on property was found to be a per se taking because the right was found to be "the most essential stick in the bundle of rights that are commonly characterized as property" (*Hodel*, p. 2083).

In *First English Evangelical Lutheran Church v. County of Los Angles*, the Supreme Court acknowledged that a church could raise a takings claim to challenge a flood control ordinance that prohibited the construction or reconstruction of buildings in an area that had been washed away by a flood until a flood control study had been completed.[14] The Court in *First English* premised its takings analysis on a strategy that "severed" the temporary restriction on the church's right to build as an estate for years, and then treated the restriction as a taking of a "separate whole thing" (Radin 1990, p. 1676).

In *Nollan v. California Coastal Commission*, the Supreme Court, in an opinion authored by Justice Scalia, again relied on the method of conceptual severance in finding that a public access easement constituted a taking of property even though the easement was merely a partial restriction on the parcel as a whole. *Nollan* involved a challenge to California's Coastal Act of 1976 which permitted a state commission to condition the issuance of a building permit upon the grant of a public right of access or lateral easement along the shoreline. The Court held that the state regulatory action imposed a permanent and unconditional occupation of property which constituted a taking.

What is significant about *Nollan* is that the Court was willing to find a compensable taking even though the state regulation was in reality a less restrictive alternative (the state could have refused to issue a permit without specifying conditions; see Radin 1988, p. 1677) that sought to accommodate substantial state interests while allowing the property owner to enjoy the prerogatives of private ownership. According to Justice Scalia, the Court was willing to find that the California regulation constituted a taking even though it was agreed that the state interest in protecting and maintaining the right of public to have access to the shore was sufficient to uphold a permanent state seizure of the land with compensation.[15] Instead, what the Court objected to was the fact that the state granted a building permit on the condition that the Nollans cede to the state a public easement allowing lateral access between two public beaches located on either side of the Nollans' property.

The method of conceptual severance was utilized by the Court in *Nollan* to find that a conditional and partial public easement was a taking. The lateral easement, demanded as a condition for a building permit, was found to be a compensable taking by the state because the Court treated the condition for the permit—the easement—as a restriction of a whole thing, separate from the parcel as a whole (Radin 1988, p. 1677). By rejecting Justice Brennan's understanding of property as the owner's parcel as a whole, Justice Scalia was able to reason quite persuasively that a public easement across a landowner's premises was not a "mere restriction on use" but rather a taking of a whole thing.

In *Nollan* the Court failed to engage in mean-ends scrutiny of the regulation that had been utilized in cases like *Penn Central* to evaluate the degree of property deprivation and the nature of governmental purpose. According to Michelman, the Court applied a new per se rule in *Nollan*: "[W]hen state regulatory action imposes permanent physical occupation conditionally rather than unconditionally, the aggrieved owner can challenge state regulatory action 'as' a 'taking,' and thereby obtain a certain form of intensified judicial scrutiny of the condition's instrumental merit or urgency" (Michelman 1988a, p. 1608). In short, the Supreme Court appears to have developed a new per se takings category in cases like *Hodel*, *First English*, and *Nollan* in order to protect the common-law property prerogatives of right of exclusion, transferability, and profitability from threatened, albeit limited, regulatory change.[16]

4. Predictable Legal Outcomes and Doctrinal Collapes

One thing that appears certain in current takings law is that conceptual severance or entitlement chopping has escalated the possibility that many land-use regulations will be invalidated as unconstitutional takings. In the 1988 decision of *Pennell v. City of San Jose*, for example, the Supreme Court was asked to invalidate a local rent control ordinance which provided that "hardship to a tenant" be considered when determining whether to approve rent increases proposed by landlords. The claimant argued that the hardship provision constituted a taking of the landlord's property without just compensation, a forced subsidy for poor tenants. The Court refused to decide the takings issue because the majority found the case to be "premature" in that the hardship provision had never been applied against the claimant.[17] Justice Scalia, however, joined by Justice O'Connor, wrote a separate opinion indicating that his reading of existing Supreme Court precedent supported the conclusion that the hardship provision constituted an unconstitutional taking of private property. Justice Scalia's views are significant in that they serve to illustrate where the strategy of conceptual severance is "*taking*" the Court's takings jurisprudence.

In *Pennell* Justice Scalia relied upon the method of conceptual severance in finding that the hardship provision of the San Jose rent control ordinance was a taking of property for public use without just compensation. Justice Scalia reasoned that the "thing" taken was the freedom of individual landlords to charge their poor tenants the prevailing market rate. He found that hardship restriction constituted a taking of private property because he found that landlord's property could be severed into discrete economic rights.

According to Justice Scalia, the hardship restriction was offensive because it required landlords to support a public welfare program through reduced rents for economically disadvantaged tenants. In placing the burden on landlords, the handship provision was found to violate what Scalia saw as a "guiding principle" of the Fifth Amendment—that "public burdens . . . should be borne by the public as a whole" (*Pennell*, p. 863). In Justice Scalia's view, the hardship provision of the statute was objectionable because it unfairly made "one citizen pay, in some fashion other than taxes, to remedy a social problem that is none of his creation" (*Pennell*, p. 864).

To bolster his disproportionate impact argument, Scalia advanced a political process objection which, when linked to his takings argument, condemned the San Jose ordinance as an undemocratic, unfair, and hence unconstitutional welfare measure. In Scalia's view, the rent control ordinance failed to comport with "normal democratic processes" because it permitted wealth transfers to be achieved "off budget," that is, the ordinance transferred wealth from one class to another as a disguised and relatively invisible form of taxation (*Pennell*, p. 863). Scalia's political-process objection was that the state was utilizing "the occasion of rent regulation (accomplished by the rest of the Ordinance) to establish a welfare program privately funded by those landlords who happen to have 'hardship' tenants" (*Pennell*, p. 863).

As even Justice Scalia's staunches allies recognize, however, Scalia's argument in *Pennell* rests on a debatable normative component (Epstein 1988b, p. 754). Scalia seems to believe that "normal democratic process" do not involve "off budget financing." Yet, Epstein notes, "[t]here is nothing more commonplace than having democratic processes generate systems of 'off budget financing . . . designed to create the mismatch between the benefit and burdens of public programs . . . To say that off budget legislation is not part of normal political processes is to place a very powerful normative constraint on what legislatures can do and how they can behave" (Epstein 1988b, p. 754). Scalia's political process objection simply fails to establish an argument that makes sense in the modern regulatory state.

It should also be apparent that the logic of Scalia's arguments in *Pennell* has wider ramifications. Indeed, conservatives such as Epstein find within Scalia's *Pennell* opinion a more general "capacity to transform the structure of modern takings law" (Epstein 1988b, p. 755). As Epstein explains: "Scalia's approach cannot be confined to the objectionable 'hardship' features of the San Jose law. His political process objection to the San Jose ordinance applies to all forms of rent control—indeed to all forms of regulation generally" (Epstein 1988b, p. 755; Schwartz 1990, p. 133). Scalia's political process objection can have such consequences because when it is linked with the method of conceptual surveyance the courts will begin find unconstitutional takings *everywhere*.

Once the courts begin to analyze the effect of regulation in terms of its effect on discrete and well-defined privileges of property ownership, the easier it will be for them to find that the consequences of regulation impose unfair political burdens and unconstitutional takings.[18] If the burdens of regulatory consequences must match the benefits bestowed on particular regulatees, as Scalia's disproportionate impact test suggests, then very little governmental regulation will be safe from constitutional challenge. Scalia's disproportionate impact takings test would thus work to favor the interest of individual property owners by erecting a constitutional roadblock for existing state and federal regulation.

There are compelling reasons for challenging Scalia's suggestion that rent control legislation unfairly burdens landlords and thereby constitutes a form of compensable state taking of private property. For one thing, Scalia assumed that only landlords would be burdened by rent regulation involved in *Pennell*. The impact of the San Jose ordinance, however, calls for a more complicated analysis since the legislation also affected the class of would-be tenants who would like to rent the premises at a higher rent. Indeed, it is precisely the impact of rent control on a more affluent class of would-be tenants that provides a prescriptive and normative rationale for upholding rent control regulations as necessary public policy measures.

Without rent control, higher-income tenants displace lower-income groups, bidding up the rental price of existing rental properties and leaving the poorest-income class "shelter poor" and frequently homeless. Indeed, studies have shown that the sharp decline in affordable housing for low-income families has been exasperated by the process of gentrification—movement of more affluent classes into older, poorer neighborhoods and the rehabilitation of those neighborhoods into high-priced residential areas (Note, 1988, p. 1835, n. 2). In gentrifying housing markets, a comprehensive system of rent control legislation can serve to check the escalation of housing prices fueled by speculation and thus preserve the amount of housing stock available for low-income groups (Note, 1988). Normative arguments about the justice of rent control restrictions should thus require a much more rigorous analysis of welfare consequences than the one advanced by Scalia in *Pennell*. Such arguments should demand a legal inquiry that looks beyond the bundle of property sticks that the landowner possesses in determining whether state interests justify property regulation.

Of course, Scalia's argument in *Pennell* could be read as advancing a purely political objection to rent control legislation "—landlords have the right to set the price at which they choose to rent their property—period" (Radin 1986, p. 355). The analysis of the costs and burdens of rent control would under such a view be irrelevant. If this is the rationale for Scalia's position in *Pennell*, and I believe it is, then it should be apparent that beneath Scalia's legal arguments lies an ideological perspective that reproduces merely one of several contested positions in the debates about welfare redistribution programs now taking place in the political arena.[19] Takings law may merely reflective of particular ideological viewpoints about governmental regulation.

5. The Ideology of Current Takings Law

Takings law appears to be following a predictable pattern only because the Court has recently favored a particular set of unstated assumptions about the nature of property and the role of government in relation to property. Andrea L. Peterson, for example, has recently argued that the takings decisions of the Supreme Court follow an "unarticulated pattern" that is premised upon a conception of property as *liberty* interest—"freedom to behave in a certain economically valuable manner with respect to . . . land" (Peterson 1990, p. 71). According to Peterson, governmental regulation of property will constitute a compensable taking "if the government is not seeking to prevent wrongdoing, but is simply forcing the developer to give up her property to promote the common good" (Peterson 1990, p. 79). Peterson thus argues that the "pattern to the Court's takings decisions . . . is not attributable to the announced doctrine, but rather to the fact that the Justices evidently are deciding [takings] cases according to their sense of when it is fair for the government to take something of economic value from a private party without paying for it" (Peterson 1990, pp. 161–162).

Margret Radin has in turn argued that the Court's "sense of fairness" is tilted by a general trend toward conceptual severance which has been employed primarily to protect the property prerogatives of *exclusion*. In focusing on issues of exclusion, the current court has sought to protect the *negative* liberty of the landowners to exclude intruders. Radin argues that "[t]he Court's solicitude for exclusion may correspond to the picture, at the core of liberal ideology, of the individual's right to use property to express her individual liberty, which means using property to fend off intruders into her space" (Radin 1988, p. 1678). The Court has thus come to understand property as a bundle of discrete entitlements that are treated as "sovereign islands" that must be protected against state occupations[20] (Radin 1988, pp. 1678–1679). The cases recognize the right of state to prevent the landowner from doing certain things that might harm others, but the state is otherwise forbidden from affirmatively establishing conditions or restrictions on property ownership without just compensation, even if they are otherwise justified by important state interests, and regardless of whether the requirement of just compensation might prevent the state from achieving its stated purposes.

Critics also argue that the takings clause has thus been read by the Court in a conservative and limited way—mainly as a negative restriction protecting the status quo of property entitlements (Michelman 1988a, p. 1625; Radin 1988, p. 1682). When one considers the outcomes of the recent takings cases, one finds support for such a view. In *Nollan* the Court concluded that the state could not regulate in ways that interfered with the right of the Nollans' interest to exclude strangers from walking on "their beach." In *First English* the Court suggested that the state regulation could not abrogate the interest of a church to build on "its property." In *Hodel v. Irving* the Court concluded that federal regulation of Indian land was unconstitutional because it precluded the common-law interest of the owner to pass on "his or her property" upon death. Finally, in *Pennell*, Justice Scalia suggested that rent control legislation was impermissible if it imposed a disproportionate financial burden on landlords, thereby interfering with "their property interest." In each case, the Court appears to have focused on the importance of protecting property interest, as a negative economic liberty, from governmental regulation (Radin 1988, pp. 1678–1680).[21]

It may well be that the Court's commitment to an alternative understanding of economic liberty, one that understands freedom as a negative right and sees property as a "sovereign island," best explains why the commentators find the law of takings to be following a certain confused, yet predictable, pattern of development. The explanation for this development may be the result of a conflict between two world-views of property—the 19th century world of the common law and the 20th century world of the modern regulatory state. If this is true then the current Supreme Court appears to be defending a 19th century common-law understanding of property and a 19th century form of legal rationality—formalism—from threatened extinction in the modern regulatory state.

This is not to say that the Court's law of takings will prove successful in upholding particular legal ideologies against change. While the method of conceptual severance seeks to erase the boundaries between property and community under per se categories, countervailing arguments pressure the Court, as they did in *Keystone*, to uphold the values of self-government and the community interests embodied within challenged governmental regulation. Justice Scalia's conception of property, while gaining judicial ground, is vulnerable to normative arguments presenting the ethical case for redefining the "sovereign island" property picture to take into account the interests and values of democratic government and popular sovereignty (Radin 1988, pp. 1679–1680).[22] Some recognition of the right of the state to regulate without having to pay property owners just compensation is necessary if government is operate effectively in the modern regulatory era.

Takings doctrine will likely remain frozen in a confused doctrinal state because legal analysis has failed to instruct judges how they should fix the boundaries between property and community or address the difficult analytical problem of evaluating the respective interests involved under the ideal of a determinant constitutional rule of law. Instead, the result of current law is what Michelman has called a "troubled and limited judicial protection of property, carried on in the name of the Constitution" (Michelman 1988a, p. 1628). The Court's recent takings decisions are "limited" because "the claims of popular sovereignty and classical property cannot, in truth, be stably reconciled at a very high level of abstraction or generality." The cases are "troubled, because the rule-of-law idea still pushes towards the high formality of a few, simple, abstract rules; and the price of such high formality, in a dynamic and impacted world, is obtuseness" (Michelman 1988a, p. 1628).

6. The Approach of Traditional Takings Scholarship

The problem posed by the seven takings cases that are the focus of this book is that their key holdings and their doctrine fail to decide anything; knowing that regulation is not a taking if it advances the public interest or avoids a noxious use fails to tell us anything about regulation prohibiting developers to filling wetlands for commercial use. Is prohibiting the development of wetlands beneficial to the public interest or is it merely an encroachment on the wetlands owners' property interest? To answer such questions intelligently, judges must look beyond the legal concepts of takings law in order to determine the boundaries between property and community. Regulation prohibiting the filling-in of wetlands may be seen to be justified under a concept of taking that embraces a community-based understanding of property and/or one that emphasizes the importance of regulation to preserve and protect property interest of future generations. The question to be asked is whether it is fair to ask the current generation of property owners to bear the cost for the benefit of the community, present and future.

Ultimately, all takings questions require pragmatic ethical answers about what resources should be kept in state hands and what type of community should be fostered by the particular conception of property to be upheld against state regulation. The takings clause commits the courts to protect private property against uncompensated takings, but the clause allows judges to decide which concept of property may be appropriate in particular cases. Because the concept of property is a "contested concept" (Radin 1988, p. 1688), takings questions, like questions of justice, are inextricably bound up with moral, philosophical, and political debates that have remained persistently immune to scholarly and judicial "solutions."

Most modern legal scholars have, however, persisted in advancing new theories and methods for "solving" the regulatory takings problem. The goal of traditional scholarship has been aimed at developing conceptual solutions that would permit judges to decide takings issues under rules of law that respect the competing values of efficiency, equity, and political legitimacy. Traditional legal scholars have thus sought to aid the effort of the Supreme Court to bolster a particular concept of property and save it from regulatory disintegration.[23] Their solutions to the takings problem have sought to do what judges since *Mahon* have failed to do—namely "solve" the takings problem by devising an ideal rule of law to mediate the tensions of property and popular sovereignty. Before considering the alternative approach of postmoderns, who reject the idea that takings problems can be "solved", it is necessary to review the dominant scholarly approach now followed by traditional takings scholars.

For example, one solution advanced by Epstein relies on the tradition of the common law to determine which government actions constitute "takings" of property for which just compensation must be paid. For Epstein, "Blackstone's account of private property explains what the term means in the eminent domain clause" of the Fifth Amendment (Epstein 1985, p. 23). In his view, Blackstone's *trilogy* of rights (contract, property, and tort) is the dividing line for distinguishing legitimate public regulation and private right (Paul 1986, p. 752). The common law categories of tort, property, and contract (and apparently the 19th century manifestation of these categories) become for him the principal framework for analyzing takings problems. The common law is seen to establish the limits on state regulatory powers over individuals.

Epstein believes that the common law that permits a landowner to exclude trespassers from his/her property establishes the justification for forbidding the state from interfering with rights of exclusion without just compensation (Epstein 1985, p. 65; Paul 1986, pp. 751–752). While Epstein recognizes that some exercise of police power is necessary to make sense of the Constitution, he believes that governmental regulation over private property must be narrowly drawn. Epstein believes that the role of governmental action must be restricted to defending common-law prerogatives and to enacting general regulations for the common good as long as they do not result in a "disproportionate impact" on a particular class of taxpayers. Hence, general revenue measures would not constitute a taking under Epstein's view because they have a proportionate impact on all classes. On the other hand, the vast majority of existing social-welfare legislation, including nearly all state and federal labor legislation (including child labor laws), rent control, unemployment compensation, black lung disease compensation regulation, and even certain forms of progressive income taxation, would, in Epstein's view, be deemed a prima face taking because of the disproportionate impact of such legislation (Epstein 1985, pp. 177, 257–259, 297–299; Epstein 1988a).

Unlike Holmes, who recognized merit in Brandeis' view that all takings questions were matters of "degree" that required judges to determine if "regulation goes too far," Epstein "wants us to believe that Holmes' approach [and by implication the approach of Brandeis] must be wrong because the Constitution prohibits all uncompensated takings, not merely those that go too far" (Paul 1986, p. 752). Hence, for Epstein, the word "property" in the Fifth and Fourteenth Amendments provides the "obvious solution" to all regulatory takings problems. What is obvious, however, as Epstein's many critics point out, is that Epstein's solution to the takings problem is premised upon a "naive conceptualism" that assumes that language has an "objective timeless meaning." Epstein refuses to admit that the word "property" has meanings that change over time (Radin 1988, pp. 1669–1670). Thus, one flaw in Epstein's theory is that the very language he seeks to rely on, the language of the common law of tort, property, and contract, is a dynamic language pushed and pulled by legal and political forces that are neither natural in design nor invariably frozen in time.[24]

Indeed, Epstein's theory is premised upon controversial and contested assumptions about the nature of property within a political and moral regime fostered by a common-law system infected by a Hobbesian fear of government. Reasonable persons would fiercely debate the wisdom of Epstein's baseline legal and political assumptions, especially his tough-minded willingness to countenance poverty and homelessness (Epstein 1985, pp. 315–323; Radin 1990, p. 1713). Those assumptions are now part of the political debate taking place in our political culture as we assess the excesses of deregulation following the Reagan era. Judges who might be tempted to employ Epstein's takings theory should therefore be politically self-reflective of other views and theories.[25]

An alternative approach to the legal problems of regulatory takings has been offered by law and economic scholars who advocate the value of efficiency as the basic concept for distinguishing legitimate regulation from unconstitutional takings. These scholars argue that the state should be required to provide just compensation whenever it is necessary to promote efficient (i.e., wealth-maximizing) regulation (Beerman and Singer 1989, p. 911). Economic analysts thus seek to devise rules of law for distinguishing between efficient and inefficient regulation. For example, in considering the impact of regulation on private investment, efficient takings doctrine requires judges to consider three relevant factors: "(1) the possibility of over or underinvestment by private individuals (the 'private-investment issue'); (2) the problem of government-created uncertainty (the 'insurance' issue); and (3) the impact of takings doctrine on the decisions of public officials (the 'public-investment' issue)" (Rose-Ackerman 1988, p. 1702).

Efficient takings doctrine utilizes these three factors to identify and isolate efficient regulation. Like natural-law theorists, legal economists argue that they have discovered the scientific laws that instruct them regarding what should be done about legal problems. The "private investment issue," for example, instructs these analysts to consider the effects of regulation on private investment on capital projects. Regulation that was anticipated by investors is not a taking since the regulation is unlikely to affect the price of capital projects (Blume and Rubinfeld 1984, pp. 584–587). The insurance issue tells the analysts to identify the risks of governmental regulation that are wholly unforeseeable and thus not easily protected by insurance. Only governmental actions that are unforeseeable and arguably uninsurable are takings, according to the efficient takings theory (Blume and Rubinfeld 1984, pp. 584–590). Finally, the "public-investment issue" instructs the economic analyst to ascertain the economic impact of takings law on the behavior of public officials. Here, the goal is to force public official to take into account the opportunity cost of their regulatory decisions. "Policies that 'take' private property would then have concrete budgetary impacts that would be immediately reflected in tax bills or borrowing capacity" (Rose-Ackerman 1988, p. 1706).

Efficient takings doctrine, however, fails to provide determinant solutions to takings problems. The problem is that the economic solutions offered by these analysts seeks to describe takings problems under a particular understanding of property, one that views property as merely a medium for maximizing private wealth. Economic theory is nothing more than a description of economic "practices" that seeks to develop an improved method for understanding the instrumental role of private property, but in a very special and, some would say, narrow way. The goal of such analysis is to develop an instrumental understanding of the takings clause that would serve to maximize the accumulation of private wealth. However, because the key economic concepts such as property, efficiency, and risk are indeterminant, efficient takings doctrine is capable of generating multiple conflicting solutions to legal problems depending on the definitions the analysts give to the critical terms of the analysis.

The current state of efficiency analysis of takings problems is currently too simplistic to offer meaningful guidance for the legal bench and bar. Any determination that regulation is more efficient can be intelligently made only if the costs and benefits to all affected groups are considered. For example, in the case of rent control legislation, the interests of would-be tenants, as well as other groups, should be considered in addition to the interest of landlords in determining the efficiency of such legislation (Note, 1988, pp. 1853–1854). The required analysis should also be a dynamic one that takes into account special and temporal factors, and it should also acknowledge the assumption of diminishing marginal utility of money as well as determine whether to use offer or asking prices in evaluating costs and benefits. The task of making intelligent decisions based on a more robust, dynamic efficiency analysis would raise insurmountable difficulties for most judges and lawyers.[26]

Efficient takings doctrine also says little, if anything, about the important legal concerns of fairness and justice. Efficient takings doctrine may lead to regulation that is wealth maximizing, but the doctrine may also serve to justify politically illegitimate levels of regulation. Regulation serving the interests of economic efficiency may serve to establish a rhetorical base justifying existing income inequalities and social injustices, and lead to what Radin has called "bad conceptual coherence" (Radin 1990, p. 1720).[27] As nearly everyone seems to agree, "[e]fficiency is not the whole story in analyzing takings doctrine" (Rose-Ackerman 1988, p. 1707).

A third, more sophisticated, scholarly approach to takings seeks to "develop a comprehensive answer to the takings question" by developing a principled framework of analysis that expressly takes into account the interests of efficiency, equity, and political legitimacy (Rose-Ackerman 1988, 1989). Legal reformists such as Susan Rose-Ackerman have advanced the case for a comprehensive law of takings "formalized" under clear and certain rules that would expressly take into account all the factors and approaches of other takings scholars as well as respond to the conflicting goals of efficiency, equity, and political legitimacy. Scholars who follow Rose-Ackerman thus seek to "sketch" a realistic policy analysis that would enable them to mediate the contradictions of takings doctrine. Rose-Ackerman, however, has so far failed to devise a firm theoretical base in theory to support her eccentric policy approach nor has she been able to devise a set of formalized rules that enable judges to mediate the conflicting goals of takings law.

The problem is that the sophisticated "policy" analysis of liberal legal reformers is hard to reduce to black-letter rules of law that judges can apply with ease. If anything, the work of these scholars falls prey to their own criticism of current takings law. Liberal legal reformists who advocate a high-tech policy approach to takings question are thus criticized by the political right on the ground that their policy analysis lacks scientific rigor and economic realism. The political left can argue that liberal legal reformists' commitment to the positivistic ideal of a neutral concept of law prevents them from appreciating the way law itself reproduces a particular ideological picture of social relations (Peller 1985). While liberal legal reformers advance more sophisticated formulations of takings doctrine, they have been unable to escape the criticism of both the left and right who advance methodogical and political reasons for believing that liberal reformers will fail in developing takings rules that avoid the type of policy decisionmaking required of political institutions. As Michelman argues, in commenting on Rose-Ackerman's proposals, it is unlikely that her proposals will be "judicially adopted whole, in one swoop, or by judges strictly professing to gain their authority to overrule the judgments of sitting legislators from a body of natural or positive higher law" (Michelman 1988b, p. 1713).

Hence, in deciding what constitutes a taking or alternatively in deciding whether a form of regulation is a valid exercise of the state's police powers, traditional legal scholars continuonsly search elsewhere for new concepts and ideas in their attempt to mediate the tension between property and community. This reference "out" to tradition, economics, or liberal forms of policy instrumentalism, however, never escapes the dilemmas of property and sovereignty posed by regulation of private property. Instead, the analysis of traditional scholarship merely serves to reproduce the dilemmas of property and community without ever solving the tension. Instead of solving the contradictions of takings law, traditional scholars merely offer new devices for either restating the partial and incomplete perspectives of Holmes and Brandeis, or ascend to a higher synthesis wherein each perspective is seen as a "factor" to be considered in some instrumental legal calculus still to be worked out. The contradictions of takings doctrine are unlikely to be resolved any time soon by the advance of traditional scholarship. Traditional scholars, however, continue their search for new conceptual foundations for takings law because they, like judges, long for certainty, and fear the arbitrariness of a system of law unrestrained by reason *or* the rule of law.

7. The Turn to Postmodernism

Rejecting the possibility of a solution to the takings problem based on conceptual formulations of some ideal Rule of Law, a new breed of takings scholars has appeared on the academic scene arguing the case for new forms of judicial solutions to the takings problem—solutions derived from an understanding of takings law that accepts the inevitability of making choices between irresolvably opposed principles and ideals. What is different about postmoderns is their unabashed acceptance of the impossibility of solving the takings problem under an ideal set of conceptual solutions.[28] One way to get a feel for postmodernism is to consider how these scholars understand the relationship between law and the human personality.

Duncan Kennedy, for example, captures the essence of postmodern temperament in his description of the normative contradictions that structure American legal doctrine (Kennedy 1976, 1978). According to Kennedy, these normative ideals "reflect a deeper level of contradiction. At this deeper level, we are divided, among ourselves and also within ourselves, between irreconcilable visions of humanity and society, and between radically different aspirations for our common future" (Kennedy 1976, p. 1685). In his view, law reproduces and reflects the irreconcilable and ambivalent views that human beings have about competing desires and longings for independence and security. He asserts that legal doctrine is generated by these competing and fundamentally contradictory impulses of human motivation because judges, like all human beings, are subject to these deeply felt urges (Kennedy 1986).

Roberto M. Unger, sharing Kennedy's critical perspective, has sought to describe how the idea of contradiction permeates and structures the way human beings think about law and politics. According to Unger, human beings are pulled by opposing and conflicting values and desires: "One is the need to preserve independence from the outside world. The other demand is the equally basic need of the self to live in a world transparent to its mind and responsive to its concern, a world with which it can therefore be at one" (Unger 1975, p. 205).

Unger and Kennedy thus argue that the history of American legal theory can be understood as a symbolic reproduction of the internal struggle of the personality. The law, like the individual, has struggled to combine the negative felt experience of alienation and isolation with the positive yearning for connection and community. Their insights can be helpful for understanding how particular legal doctrines such as takings doctrine seem to be trapped in a dialectic that oscillates between the two perspectives of property and community. Holmes' property-like approach to takings law may reflect the deeply rooted need of the individual to separate from others to experience true identity; whereas Brandeis' community-like perspective may respond to the opposing psychic desires that we all have for maintaining connection with others.

The postmodern temperament of these scholars is also helpful for understanding why legal doctrinal fields such as regulatory takings reproduce the same structural arguments over and over. Postmoderns argue that traditional approaches to doctrinal analysis in the law are locked within a repetitive dialectic because the law itself is a product of the contradictory impulse that structures all human endeavors—legal, political, and emotional. Postmoderns argue that there are no new tales to tell in the law even though law seems constantly to develop new theories and legal approaches. Postmoderns argue that what appears to be new about legal developments are the new twist, the new words, and the new emphasis given to a standard argumentative story. Postmoderns would argue that Supreme Court decisions like *Mahon* and *Keystone* evoke strong feelings of deja vu for good reasons.

Advancing a form of pragmatic philosophy, postmoderns thus exhibit what Thomas Grey calls "freedom from theory-guilt" (Grey 1990, p. 1569); a scholarly temperament liberated from the necessity of devising a foundational theory of law rooted in some absolute total perspective.[29] Legal postmoderns argue that there is no universal perspective "out there" that we can turn to for discovering an interpretative theory of takings untainted by its own particular "interpretive framework" (Peller 1985, p. 881). Postmodernism is thus not a theory but rather a recognizable temperament or ethic for understanding law and the world.

Postmoderns who write about the takings question, for example, can be recognized by their scholarly effort to demonstrate that the key takings questions—What is a taking? What is a public use? What is the property interest involved?—require judgment calls and trade-offs that cannot be reduced to fixed, determinant legal rules that avoid the dangers of official *arbitrariness*. As Jeremy Paul has put it, the strategy of these scholars is not to attempt to legitimize any particular set of solutions to the takings problem but rather "simply to prove over and over again that the 'problem' can never be 'solved'" (Paul 1986, p.785).

Michelman's analysis of the recent Supreme Court takings cases, for example, seeks to explain how the Supreme Court's strategy of conceptual severance has forced the Court to "recognize in every act of government a redefinition and adjustment of a property boundary" (Michelman 1988a, pp. 1627–1628). This realization has created, in Michelman's mind, an infinite-regress problem. As he explains: "The war between popular self-government and strongly constitutionalized property now comes to seem not containable but total" (Michelman 1988a, p. 1628). Hence, Michelman's goal is to show how the Court's current strategy toward regulatory takings will only exacerbate the legal problems the courts are now struggling to solve.

Yet, Michelman stops short of arguing that current doctrine lacks a coherent rationale. To the contrary, Michelman argues that the Court's current takings strategy makes "sense ideologically as [doctrinal] tokens of the limitation of government by law" (Michelman 1988a, p. 1628). He argues that the judicial focus on the common-law prerogatives of property ownership make sense because the Court's concept of property has "both the feel of legality and the feel of resonance with common understanding of what property at the core is all about" (Michelman 1988a, p. 1628). Michelman's strategy is to reveal how the current takings doctrine reflects an important, albeit limited, socially constructed understanding of property.

Postmoderns thus advance an indeterminacy thesis about takings doctrine, but one that argues that it is possible to discover predictable patterns of legal doctrine. While they assert that the law of takings is indeterminant, postmoderns do not claim that takings law lacks meaning or lacks a sense of coherence. Instead, postmoderns argue that meaning and coherence can be discovered in takings law in terms of the socially constructed understandings that judges have adopted in fashioning takings doctrine. Postmoderns argue that what judges do is translate their favored ideology into the doctrinal theories they devise for constructing takings law. Postmoderns thus provide an angle for understanding why commentators today have discovered that takings law is following a predictable pattern of development.

Postmoderns, while critical in their perspective, offer guidance for restructuring takings law so that new legal solutions might be discovered. Michelman, for example, has argued that the law of takings would be better served if judges ceased their endless quest for devising formalized rules to deal with takings cases and instead implemented a pragmatic judicial practice of "situated judgment" or "practical reason" (Michelman 1988a, p. 1629). By these terms Michelman means judges should resolve takings questions by assessing the contradictions of takings doctrine in terms of their actual consequences on all sorts of people. Instead of choosing between the stereotypic property and community-like perspectives, Michelman wants judges to consider the consequence of their decisions within the messy historical and social context in which takings law operates.

Michelman's commitment to situated judgment and practical reason is not meant to be a endorsement of Justice Brennan's case-by-case balancing approach nor is it intended as an alternative to "legality." Instead, Michelman's argument is that judges should be forthright in acknowledging that the takings cases require a thoroughly pragmatic form of reasoning that accepts, and even valorizes, the contradictions of takings doctrine. Instead of seeking to mediate the traditional dichotomies of takings law, Michelman can be read as arguing that judges should devise a new way of talking about takings problems that accepts the inevitable conflicts between opposing perspectives. Such a view is characteristically postmodern in temperament because it accepts the role of self-creation and imagination in judicial decisionmaking and rejects the claims of traditionalists like Justice Scalia who equate legality with legal formality and antiquated 19th century conceptions of property rights.

Other postmoderns offer concrete proposals for reformulating takings doctrine. Radin, for example, argues that judges should distinguish between property objects that are utilized solely for purely economic gain and those objects that individuals experience as being "almost part of themselves" (Radin 1982, p. 959).[30] The law of takings should, in her opinion, show more willingness to protect what she calls the personhood perspective—that is, "that to achieve proper self-development—to be a *person*—an individual needs some control over resources in the external environment" (Radin 1982, p. 957). Whether a compensable taking has occurred would thus depend on whether the government has restricted an individual's freedom to control a personal item such as one's home, which is for most people an integral part of their personhood. In Radin's view, such a re-description of property would provide a stronger rationale for the willingness of judges to uphold some regulations such as land-use restrictions (Radin 1982, p. 1008; Paul 1986, pp. 781–782). Radin does not, however, argue that her personhood perspective offers a better lens for synthesizing takings doctrine. Instead, she admits that "[t]he personhood perspective cannot generate a comprehensive theory of property rights vis-a-vis the government; it can only add another moral inquiry that helps clarify some cases" (Radin 1981, p. 1002).

A personhood perspective to the law of takings would nonetheless serve to provide the courts with a stronger rationale for providing protection to aspects of property that are essential to human self-development and realization. The interest in one's home and minimum welfare entitlements would be a prime examples. A personhood perspective provides a normative answer to Justice Scalia's argument in *Pennell* that landlords cannot be taxed to support the welfare of their poor tenants. As Radin argues, "the private home is a justifiable form of personal property, while a landlord's interest is often fungible." The landlords' interest is fungible and not personal because the landlords' claim is normally based on a sum of money.[31] While landlords whose property is personal should be treated differently, the class of landlords who merely claim a commercial interest in obtaining higher rents do not have the same claim of moral entitlement than that of a tenant whose personhood interests, and human existence, may depend on having shelter. Radin thus presents the case for giving greater normative weight to the personhood interests of people and less weight to the pecuniary interest in money.[32]

Legal scholars who have exhibited a postmodern temperament in their scholarship do not claim to have a completely worked-out theory about what judges should be doing in the takings cases. Instead, postmoderns advocate the case for a new way of understanding how such problems might be approached. Hence, postmoderns seek to redescribe regulations in ways that make it possible to imagine how takings law might be restructured to take into account other interpretations based on different social and political perspectives about property and power in the land-use context.

Gregory S. Alexander, for example, has shown how the regulatory takings cases tell a story of "power and fear," one that "describes local regulators as empowered, possessing enormous leverage over private landowners, who are depicted as unempowered" (Alexander 1988, p. 1752). Alexander finds that the current takings law is influenced by a common narrative about the dangers of regulatory power that works to justify the protection of private property: "[C]ourts must develop constitutional norms aimed at controlling the behavior of government landuse regulators because only regulators, not landowners, are empowered" (Alexander 1988, p. 1752). Alexander also reveals how counter-narratives can be found, such as Justice Brennan's dissent in *Nollan*; who found that it was the private landowners who disrupted the settled public expectations and who were the true "interlopers" (*Nollan*, p. 3153). Alexander's lesson stemming from these competing judicial narratives is that the question of who is empowered and who is coerced in the land-use planning context is always an open question that cannot be determined by legal rationality alone.

In recognizing that judges accommodate different perspectives and attitudes about power and regulation, postmoderns have argued that judges should attempt to redefine property so that the tensions between constitutional property and regulation could be reduced without having to make zerosum choices between "property" and "community" (Frug 1984). Postmoderns, though they are critical in their scholarly perspective, are not nihilistic. They argue that it is possible to make sense of regulatory takings only if judges come to recognize that the "law" fails to embody a commitment to a particular conceptual or methodological approach to takings problems and that the key legal questions of the takings cases invite judicial experimentation and imaginative solution.

For the postmodernist, the dilemmas of property and sovereignty cannot be solved through legal formulations based on the ideal of a rule of law alone. Moreover, instead of seeking to affirm either a property-like or community-like perspective in takings analysis, postmoderns seek a "middle way" that advocates the importance of giving consideration to both perspectives, as well other perspectives not embodied by such views. For postmoderns, what is important is the creation of a legal dialogue for engaging in a new form of takings dialogue, one that accepts the indeterminacy of values and one that embraces the value of "otherness". The aim of such a dialogue is not consensus-building in the global theory sense, but rather the discovery of a pragmatic way of judging that accepts the wisdom of developing temporary contextual, but nonetheless workable, solutions to regulatory takings problems.

8. Conclusion

Postmoderns believe that the ideal of the rule of law is important, but they want the law to respect the ideals of diversity and the humanity of an inquisitive desire for the unknown. This is not to suggest that postmodernism is not open to question by those who fear relativism and legal nihilism. The rejection of rational foundation in law is frightening to many observers, especially in light of the dominant mind-set demanding scientific-like answers for nearly every legal problem imaginable. Postmoderns cannot assuage such fears; instead what postmoderns do is remind us again that there is no universal, rational foundation "out there" that we can turn to for resolving those fears.

Fear of the unknown is understandable. But a commitment to the ideal of the rule of law cannot avoid the contradictions of American legal doctrine. The problem with ideal of the rule of law is that the ideal is itself a product of the dialectic reflected in the argumentative patterns found in American legal doctrines, such as takings law. Legal arguments about the ideal of the rule of law, like those about regulatory takings, reflect a deep contradiction between opposing world views and moral and ethical perspectives. Judges, policymakers, and legal scholars, like all human beings, seek freedom and security, and desire autonomy and attachment. It should not be surprising that these contradictory human impulses infect their conception of the ideal of the Rule of Law or, at a more mundane level, the development of takings doctrine. What postmoderns offer is a new way to approach the underlying source of these dilemmas. Postmoderns also offer new solutions based on a transformed concept of what it means to solve legal problems generally. What post-moderns cannot do is offer a blueprint for mapping the future course of law's development. They leave that task to traditional metaphysicians.

Notes

1. The Fifth Amendment to the U.S. Constitution prohibits the federal government from "taking" private property "for public use, without just compensation." The Supreme Court has held that the substantive limitations of the Fifth Amendment apply to state governments through the due process clause of the Fourteenth Amendment which prohibits the states from "depriving" citizens of property "without due process of law" (*Chicago B. & Q.R. Co. v. Chicago*, 1897).

2. The baselines of the observer's perspective define the normative starting points of legal analysis. These starting points explain why certain, rather than other, answers are favored (Beerman and Singer 1989, p. 913). Jeremy Paul (1986), for example, has demonstrated how the choice of common law baselines has influenced the development of the regulatory takings doctrine.

3. According to Lyotard, *postmodernism* describes a recognizable temperament of contemporary thinkers—one that accepts fluidity, uncertainty, and disagreement as the only "natural order" of things (Lyotard 1984, Kolh 1986, p. 257). By *postmodernism*, Lyotard sought to describe what he saw as a breakdown of modernity and a movement toward a new world view rejecting cognitive mastery under fixed rules in favor of a perspective that understands technical, scientific, and artistic knowledge as "meta-narratives" that lack a determinant or grounded foundation.

Modernity describes the perspective of the generation of traditional thinkers in art, architecture, sculpture, literature, and culture who shared the belief that it is possible to systematize human knowledge and conditions of life under coherent and verifiable theoretical propositions about the nature of truth and reality (Unger 1976, pp. 37–43, 134–137, 265–266).

4. Sometime in the early 1980s there appeared within *left* legal scholarship a body of writing associated with *The Conference on Critical Legal Studies* (Minda 1989a and b). Some of the people who associated with CLS identified themselves as working within a form of legal criticism associated with "deconstruction," or simply "postmodernism." The writing and discourse of these postmodern legal critics is recognizable in their commitment to ideas of contradiction, contingency, and interpretative reversals in their approach to legal interpretation. CLS postmoderns claim that legal interpretations are like interpretations of poems or stories from literature—they are subject to alternative interpretations or story "tellings." This chapter seeks to reveal how the work of these CLS postmoderns has influenced the development of scholarly discources on the regulatory takings problem.

5. By *postmodern temperament*, I mean the commitment of some legal scholars to the discovery of contradiction, contingency, and indeterminacy in the legal analyses of the takings problem; the use of metaphor, narrative, and story telling for discovering surprising new insights within the authoritative texts of the takings cases; the embrace of a pragmatic understanding of takings questions; and a search to justify "situated judgments" premised upon an open questioning of competing values of particular communities (Michelman 1988a and b; Singer 1990, p. 1822).

6. Justice Holmes, recognizing the validity of Brandeis' view, agreed that the takings clause must be interpreted so as to preserve the constitutional responsibility of state government to regulate for the common good. As Justice Holmes stated: "Government hardly could go on if, to some extent, values incident to property could not be diminished without paying for every such change in the general law. As long recognized, some values are enjoyed under an implied limitation, and must yield to the police power" (*Mahon*, p. 413).

7. Apparently, both Holmes and Brandeis believed that judges could intelligently mediate the tension between property and community by focusing either on the rights of property or the nature of legitimate police power. Neither approach or perspective, however, has successfully mediated the conflicts presented by the takings cases. The view of each justice sought to transcend the contradiction of property and community, but both views failed because each was committed to a partial and incomplete "perspective" of the role that law might play in protecting property in an increasingly regulatory state. There were also internal problems endemic to both views.

The problem with Holmes' solutions was that a *diminution-of-value* test was so openly textured and indeterminant that it could justify nearly any conclusion. Assuming that judges could agree that "property" has been adversely affected, the *diminution-of-value* depends on how judges define the property interest involved, broadly or narrowly (Singer 1991, p. 910). Brandeis' public interest test suffers from a similar weakness. The Achilles heel of the public interest test lies in the definition of public interest. Even assuming that judges could agree on what constitutes the public interest, judges would still have to determine if the challenged regulation is necessary to achieve that interest.

8. The regulation prevented the coal companies from removing coal from the strata of ground constituting the support estate of their property.

9. For example, Bernard Schwartz has recently argued that the majority opinion in *Keystone* "indicates that the Supreme Court itself now agrees more with the Brandeis than the Holmes *Pennsylvania Coal* view" (Schwartz 1990, p. 118). Schwartz argues that the majority's decision in *Keystone* vindicates Brandeis' dissent in *Mahon* because the Court chose to rest its decision on importance of upholding the state's police power to regulate a threatening nuisance-like activity. Whether *Keystone* represents a triumph over Brandeis' view of takings is doubtful. As Michelman has noted in a slightly different context, it is highly unlikely that judges can "distinguish cogently and non-'politically' between regulations that legitimately prevent harms and those that (if unaccompanied by compensation) illegitimately expropriate benefits" (Michelman 1988a, p. 1603, n. 18). Schwartz's idea of a public interest takings analysis uncritically assumes that judges can agree on which regulations are in the public interest. The problem is that what is in the interest of one group is frequently economically disadvantageous to another. A noxious use to one person is economic development to another.

10. According to Michelman, the *Keystone* Court "reaffirmed a longstanding notion that regulations of uses classed as socially harmful or nuisance-like ordinarily cannot be considered takings despite any specially onerous consequences they may carry for regulated owners" (Michelman 1988a, p. 1602).

11. Justice Brennan's "essentially ad hoc" approach has not been found to be particularly helpful to those committed to finding consistent right answers to takings problems (Peterson, 1989). Susan Rose-Ackerman, for example, has argued that judicial decisions based on the "ad hochery" of multifactor balancing are bad because they introduce an irrational and uncertain element into investors' choices about how best to utilize their property. In her view, "[t]akings law should be predictable . . . so that private individuals confidently can commit resources to capital projects" (Rose-Ackerman 1988, p. 1700). If

legal predictability is the key value to be maximized, then ad hoc balancing should not be the preferred legal method for determining the legitimacy of takings claims. The value of predictability, however, may lead judges to reach results that fail to take into account the particular circumstances of specific cases and thus reach unfair results. Predictable rules may lead to the opposite danger of balancing standards. In other words, arguments in favor of formalized rules merely state one side of a dialectic posed by the tension between predictable rules and flexible standards (Kennedy 1976, p. 1712).

12. Whether the Supreme Court is moving away from the balancing method of the *Penn Central* decision is the subject of some scholarly debate. Margaret Jane Radin has argued that the current Supreme Court is searching for "conceptual bright lines and per se rules" in its takings jurisprudence (Radin 1988, p. 1682). Michelman, agreeing with Radin, has argued that the Court is now moving away from a "multi-factor balancing method" toward a new legal "reformalization" based on a categorical "either-or" frame of analysis structured by relatively formalized rules of law (Michelman 1988, p. 1622). Rose-Ackerman, however, believes that the Court has continued to maintain its embrace of ad hoc balancing standards. In her view, what the law of taking needs is "a good dose of formalization" based on clear and predictable standards (Rose-Ackerman 1988, p. 1700). While Rose-Ackerman is right to point out that the Court has not totally abandoned balancing in its takings decisions, the trend of the case law, especially the important decisions decided in the 1986–1987 term, evince a judicial temperament in favor of per se categories.

13. A zoning regulation that prohibits the owner to build on the property or to use the property for a particular use would certainly be experienced by the property owner as a governmental taking since the regulation would have the same consequences as a state seizure (Singer, 1991, p. 903). And this is exactly what the Supreme Court has concluded in number of recent regulatory takings decisions. Hence, regulation requiring landlords to grant cable carriers access to run cables across the roofs of their buildings has been held to be a taking because the regulation subjects property to permanent physical occupation by strangers (*Loretto v. Telepropter Manhattan CATV Corp.*, 1982). It has also been recognized that regulation is a taking if it "denies an owner economically viable use" of the affected property even if it does not involve a physical occupation (*Agins v. City of Tiburon* 1980).

14. The Court failed to decide the takings issue and instead remanded *First Evangelical* to determine whether the ordinance actually denied the property owner substantial use of its property requiring just compensation as a taking of private property.

15. The lateral easement the state required the Nollans to dedicate to the public as a condition to obtaining a building permit may have actually applied to land already owned by the state. Expert testimony indicated that the lateral access path may have been below the high-tide line and hence was subject to public use under California's public trust doctrine (*Nollan*, p. 3161, nn. 11–12; Radin 1988, p. 1677, n. 55).

16. The method of conceptual severance was also pressed in the 1981 decision of *San Diego Gas & Electric Co. v. San Diego*, but the Court declined to decide whether the method was relevant for deciding the takings issue for purely procedural reasons.

17. This aspect of the Court's decision can be several criticized since the challenge in *Pennell* was a facial challenge which, unlike "as applied" challenges, does not require that the challenged legislation was actually misapplied to the litigant (Epstein 1988b, p. 752, n. 30).

18. The dilemma posed by conceptual severance is that the strategy creates a "slippery slope" that collapses the distinction between compensable takings and legitimate state regulation. As Radin explains: "Every curtailment of any of the liberal indicia of property,

every regulation of any portion of an owner's 'bundle of sticks,' is a taking of the whole of that particular portion considered separately. Price regulations 'take' that particular servitude curtailing free alienability, building restrictions 'take' a particular negative easement curtailing control over development, and so on" (Radin 1988, p. 1678).

19. Different normative perspectives would could lead the Court to different legal conclusions. Contrary to the views of Justice Scalia in *Pennell* and conservative academics such as Epstein, there is respectable and persuasive opinion to support the view that rent control regulations, properly structured, can reduce the social cost attributed to poverty and homelessness (Note, 1988); and persuasive normative arguments regarding the justice of entitlements can be made to justify such regulation (Radin, 1986). The problem with Scalia's opinion in *Pennell* is that it ignored the coercive power of private property. His analysis failed to recognize that "[c]oercive power is part of the definition of property rights and the exercise of property rights is an integral part of governmental power" (Frug 1984, p. 686). The disproportionate advantages of private economic power may justify the imposition of disproportionate burdens because the exercise of private property entitlements is itself an integral part of public power (Cohen 1927).

20. As Radin notes, this ideological picture of property was first revealed by Charles Reich (Radin 1988, p. 1678).

21. What tends to go unprotected or not considered is a positive, humanistic view of economic liberty, one that embraces a personhood perspective and acknowledges the value of self-development as an integral property interest to be protected by the Constitution. If we adopt a positive concept of liberty, then freedom must be understood in terms of the right of the individual to self-realize his or her human potential (Radin 1988, pp. 1687–1688). A positive concept of economic liberty would encourage the courts to recognize more fully that forms of governmental regulation seeking to address problems of substantive inequality are freedom-enhancing even though they may also place restrictions on the prerogatives of private property.

22. Radin, for example, argues that "[t]he Court has applied this ideological picture only to traditional property interests, and has not taken into account the difference in the ethical case for a 'sovereign island' depending upon whether the property holder is a person or a corporation" (Radin 1988, pp. 1679–1680).

23. The current law of regulatory takings can be seen in a similar light. As Michelman has put it, "[p]ermanent physical occupation, total abrogation of the right to pass on property, denial of economic viability—all of these may be regarded as judicial devices for putting some kind of stop to the denaturalization and disintegration of property" (Michelman, 1988a, p. 1628).

24. The meaning to be attached to particular common-law principle can be fixed only if judges agree to refer to a particular historical period, and then only if they look to a particular jurisdiction and perhaps a particular judge. Moreover, even if agreement can be found on the meaning to be attributed to some common-law principle, there is no objective reason for favoring the definitions of property bequeathed by unelected judges over other definitions reflected within democratically promulgated regulation (Singer 1991, p. 911).

25. Epstein's theory has failed to garner a consensus of opinion among judges, mainly because his baseline political assumptions are rightly understood to be extreme and unacceptable, although an occasional glimmer of his theory does shine through in opinions like that of Justice Scalia in *Pennell*.

26. As an alternative to the theory of efficient takings, economic-oriented analysts might advance arguments drawn from public choice theory of economics to question the ability of the legislative process to enact efficient legislation. Public choice theorists argue

that the market for legislation is subject to the rent-seeking pressure of special interest groups, who seek to capture the benefits for their own special advantages (Minda 1990, pp. 945–948). These analysts argue that there is no reason for assuming that the market for legislation could ever duplicate the ideal efficient market in a capitalist economy. When applied to the regulatory takings problem, public choice theory would seem to offer a reason for discounting the political legitimacy of most regulation. Alexander, for example, has argued that one could read the recent takings decisions of the Supreme Court as illustrations of how public choice theory has served to reinforce "a new era of judicial activism in takings jurisprudence, carried out in support of the interests of individual landowners, from whom members of the Court gain advantages, albeit indirectly, such as landowners urging Congress to raise the Justices' salaries or perhaps to support their nominations to higher office" (Alexander 1987, p. 1772). Public choice theory, however, has been criticized for its unrealistic assumptions about political behavior; assumptions that critics claim overlook important aspects of the nature of preference selection in politics (Kelman 1988). Critics also assert that public choice theory has failed to establish empirically its central claims about political behavior (Farber and Frickey 1987). Public choice theory is also indeterminant. The theory could be invoked to reveal the ideology of current takings jurisprudence.

27. By "bad conceptual coherence," Radin means the standpoint from which one can argue that a system is conceptually coherent in terms of prevailing world views, but nevertheless "bad" in the sense that the system perpetuates an unjust state of affairs. Slavery in ancient Greece (when slaves felt convinced of the natural state of their bondage) is an example.

28. Postmoderns are difficult to pigeon-hole because postmodernism is not a single, clearly defined movement, but a multifaceted association of scholars who identify with other movements such as critical legal studies, feminism, law and literature, and others (Minda 1989a p. 620, n. 103).

29. Unlike the postmoderns characterized by Grey, however, legal postmoderns avoid being caught up in what Grey calls the "logical paradoxes of perspectivist self-reference" (there are no universal truths) or "perspectivist dogmatism" (my truth is the *real* truth) (Grey 1990, pp. 1576–1577). Instead, legal postmoderns accept the idea that it is possible to know the truth without accepting the idea of universal essences *and* that it is possible to reach principled decisions even though there are *no* right answers. Legal postmoderns argue that there is more than one way to skin a cat (Radin 1990).

30. Personhood interests depend on the relation a physical object has to a particular individual. Radin provides the example of a lost wedding ring to illustrate her point: "[I]f a wedding ring is stolen from a jeweler, insurance process can reimburse the jeweler, but if a wedding ring is stolen from a loving wearer, the price of a replacement will not restore the status quo—perhaps no amount of money can do so" (Radin 1982, p. 959).

31. As Radin explains the distinction: "When a holding is fungible, the value for the holder is the exchange or market value, not the object *per se*; one dollar bill is as good as another, or the equivalent in stocks or bonds, or any other item with market value. When a holding is personal, the specific object matters, and the fact that it matters is justifiable" (Radin 1986, p. 362).

32. According to Radin, the personhood perspective requires us to evaluate claims to property in terms of the relationship some object has to the person. Radin's theory of personhood is derived from Hegel's insight that human personality is embodied in the relationship the person has to things. Hegel's insight would suggest that we should not make normative judgments about individuals apart from their material position in the

world. Such a view would suggest that the definition of what counts as property cannot be determined in the abstract, without considering the context of a particular person. Libertarians like Epstein, however, who insist that "every person should count for one and only one," argue that abstraction is essential if we are to make meaningful comparisons between individuals (Epstein 1988b, p. 771). Epstein's view fails to acknowledge that coercive power is affirmed by the exercise of private property rights, and that unequal distributions of property establish unequal power advantages. Postmoderns, by advancing the case for redescribing what counts as property, offer new normative solutions for regulatory takings cases.

References

Alexander, G.S. 1988. "Takings, Narratives, and Power." *Columbia Law Review* 88(8):1752–1773.

Beerman, J.M., and Singer, J.W. 1989. "Baseline Questions in Legal Reasoning: The Example of Property in Jobs." *Georgia Law Review* 23(4):911–995.

Cohen, M.R. 1927. "Property and Sovereignty." *Cornell Law Quarterly* 13(2): 8–30.

Blume, L., and Rubinfeld, D.L. 1984. "Compensation for Takings: An Economic Analysis." *California Law Review* 72(72):569–624.

Epstein, R.A. 1985. *Takings: Private Property and the Power of Eminent Domain*. Cambridge, MA: Harv and University Press.

————. 1988a. "Unconstitutional Conditions, State Power, and the Limits of Consent." *Harvard Law Review* 102(1):4–104.

————. 1988b. "Rent Control and the Theory of Efficient Regulation." *Brooklyn Law Review* 54(3):741–774.

Farber, D., and Frickey, W. 1987. "The Jurisprudence of Public Choice Theory." *Texas Law Review* 65(5):873–927.

Frug, G.E. 1984. "Property and Power: Hartog on the Legal History of New York City." *American Bar Foundation Research Journal* 3:673–691.

Grey, T.C. 1990. "Hear the Other Side: Wallace Stevens and Pragmatist Legal Theory." *Southern California Law Review* 63(6):1569–1595.

Kelman, M. 1988. "On Democracy-Bashing: A Skeptical Look at the Theoretical and 'Empirical' Practice of the Public Choice Movement." *Virginia Law Review* 74(3):199–273.

Kennedy, D. 1976. "Form and Substance in Private Adjudication." *Harvard Law Review* 89(4):1685–1778.

————. 1978. "The Structure of Blackstone's Commentaries." *Buffalo Law Review* 28(4):205–382.

————. 1986. "Freedom and Constraint in Adjudication: A Critical Phenomenology." *Journal of Legal Education* 36(4):518–562.

Kolb, D. 1986. *The Critique of Pure Modernity: Hegel, Heidegger, and After*. Chicago and London: University of Chicago Press.

Llewellyn, K. 1930. *The Bramble Bush*. Oceana Press.

Lyotard, J.F. 1984. *The Postmodern Condition: A Report on Knowledge*, G. Bennington and B. Massumi, trans. Minneapolis: University of Minnesota Press.

Michelman, F.I. 1988a. "Takings, 1987." *Columbia Law Review* 88(8):1600–1629.

———. 1988b. "A Reply to Susan Rose-Ackerman." *Columbia Law Review* 88(8): 1712–1713.

———. 1989. "Conceptions of Democracy in American Constitutional Argument: The Case of Pornography Regulation." *Tennessee Law Review* 56(3):291–319.

Minda, G. 1989a. "The Jurisprudential Movements of the 1980s." *Ohio State Law Journal* 50(3):599–662.

———. 1989b. "The Law and Economics and Critical Legal Studies Movements in American Law." In *Law and Economics*, ed. N. Mercuro, 87–122. Boston: Kluwer Academic Publishers.

———. 1990. "Interest Groups, Political Freedom, and Antitrust: A Modern Reassessment of the *Noerr-Pennington* Doctrine." *Hastings Law Journal* 41(4):905–1028.

Note, 1988. "Reassessing Rent Control: Its Economic Impact in a Gentrifying Housing Market." *Harvard Law Review* 101(4):1835–1855.

Paul, J. 1986. "Book Review: Searching for the Status Quo." *Cardozo Law Review* 7(2):743–785.

Peller, G. 1985. "The Politics of Reconstruction." *Harvard Law Review* 98(4): 863–881.

Peterson, A.L. 1989. "The Takings Clause: In Search of Underlying Principles, Part I—A Critique of Current Takings Clause Doctrine." *California Law Review* 77(6):1299–1363.

———. 1990. "The Takings Clause: In Search of Underlying Principles, Part II—Takings as Intentional Deprivations of Property Without Moral Justification." *California Law Review* 78(1):55–162.

Radin, M.J. 1982. "Property and Personhood." *Stanford Law Review* 34(3): 957–1015.

Radin, M.J. 1986. "Residential Rent Control." *Philosophy and Public Affairs*, 15:350–380.

———. 1988. "The Liberal Conception of Property: Cross Currents in the Jurisprudence of Takings." *Columbia Law Review* 88(8):1667–1696.

———. 1990. "The Pragmatist and the Feminist." *Southern California Law Review* 63(6):1699–1726.

Rose-Ackerman, S. 1988. "Against Ad Hocery: A comment on Michelman." *Columbia Law Review* 88(8):1697–1713.

———. 1989. "Law and Economics: Paridgm, Politics, or Philosophy." In *Law and Economics*, ed., N. Mercuro, 233–258. Boston: Kluwer Academic Publishers.

Schwartz, B. 1990. *The New Right and the Constitution: Turning Back the Legal Clock*. Boston: Northeastern University Press.

Singer, J.W. 1990. "Property and Coercion in Federal Indian Law: The Conflict Between Critical and Complacent Pragmatism." *Southern California Law Review* 63(6):1821–1841.

———. 1991. *Property Law: Cases and Materials* (forthcoming).

Sterk, S.E. 1988. "*Nollan*, Henry George, and Exactions." *Columbia Law Review* 99(8):1731–1751.

Unger, R.M. 1975. *Knowledge and Politics*. New York: The Free Press.

———. 1976. *Law in Modern Society: Toward a Criticism of Social Theory*. New York: The Free Press.

CASES

Agins v. City of Tiburon, 447 U.S. 225 (1980).

Chicago B. & Q.R. Co. v. Chicago, 166 U.S. 226 (1897).

First English Evangelical Lutheran Church v. County of Los Angeles, 107 S. Ct. 2378 (1987).

Hodel v. Irving, 107 S. Ct. 2076 (1987).

Keystone Bituminous Coal Association v. DeBenedictis, 107 S. Ct. 1232 (1987).

Loretto v. Teleprompter Manhattan CATV Corp., 458 U.S. 419 (1982).

Nollan v. California Coastal Commission, 107 S. Ct. 3141 (1987).

Penn Central Transport Co. v. New York City, 98 S. Ct. 2646 (1978).

Pennell v. City of San Jose, 108 S. Ct. 849 (1988).

6 THE PUBLIC USE OF PRIVATE PROPERTY: A DUAL-CONSTRAINT THEORY OF EFFICIENT GOVERNMENTAL TAKINGS

Thomas S. Ulen

1. Introduction

There are very few absolute, inviolable proscriptions in the law. Exceptions almost always exist. This is true for both criminal law and for the law governing private relations. For example, homicide is forbidden but is excusable in self-defense. Breaking and entering another person's property is forbidden but may be excused if the perpetrator is attempting to save someone's life. In the law of private relationships, a person is held liable for the foreseeable consequences of failing to keep a contractual promise but may be excused if the performance has become commercially impracticable. A person whose actions proximately cause harm to another will be held liable for the victim's harms but may be excused if the victim him/herself was careless or the injurer took as much precaution as a reasonable person would have. Much of the great work of the law consists of trying to elucidate the principles that consistently explain both the central proscriptions and the exceptions.

The law of property exhibits this tension between grand principles and their exceptions, and this tension has given rise to extensive attempts to reconcile the two. The conventional wisdom among nonlawyers, including many economists, is that rights to property are among the most sacred and inviolable of all legal rights. While it *is* true that the law of property establishes a broad area of inviolability for the private property owner, it is also true that the law in its great practical wisdom has also imposed important constraints on individual property rights. These constraints arise from the presence of competing rights and protected interests. To the extent that these other rights and interests are being re-examined and are periodically expanding and receding, the constraints on individual property rights will also expand and contract. The limits between individual property rights and other valuable legal rights and interests are continually shifting through both litigation and commentary. While it is unlikely that a bright line marking the inviolable limits of individual property rights will or can ever be defined, there are, nonetheless, better and worse arguments for defining the limits at one point rather than another.

This chapter focuses on one of the most important constraints on the use of private property: the power of the government to compel the private property owner to sell his/her property to the government. In fact, the eminent domain power, that is, the power to take private property, is the most extreme example of a broader set of constraints that the government imposes on private property owners. This broader set of powers, which might be collectively called "the public-use constraint," includes not only the compelled sale of property to the government but also collectively imposed limits on an individual property owner's enjoyment of his/her property. For instance, society may through zoning ordinances legitimately restrict the commercial use of property, the right of a landlord to bar political protesters from his/her property, the manner in which the property is kept, the ability of unrelated persons to occupy the same establishment, the terms and conditions by which an individual may sell or transfer his/her property to another person or organization, and much more. Clearly, these public-use constraints lie on a spectrum, at one end being trivial and amounting virtually to no constraint on individual property rights at all and at the other end being so extreme as to require the individual to surrender his/her rights to the property altogether.

The taking power has been a particularly vexatious constraint to justify and limit. Both the courts, who have had to try to design practical guidelines on the taking power, and legal commentators, who have tried to design theoretical justifications for this constraint, have devoted years and remarkable effort to the taking power. Despite all this extensive practical experience and theorizing, I believe that it is fair to say, and somewhat surprising to discover, that there is consensus on neither the theoretical justification for nor the practical application of the taking power. Instead, the taking power is being exercised by governmental bodies with increasingly less constraint.

It is bad enough that there is no common wisdom about so important a matter. But private property rights being as important as they are, this legal uncertainty has also had noteworthy consequences on the use of both governmental power and private property. To put the matter bluntly, the government has over-reached in its use of the public-use constraint to affect individual property, and—the other side of the same coin—individual property owners' rights to the enjoyment of their property have become too contingent (by reference to their reasonable expectation of what the government may do to constrain that enjoyment). Indeed, despite pieties from both courts and commentators about the sanctity of private property rights and the limits of legitimate government, it is difficult to discern in practice today any principled limit to the taking power specifically or to the other less intrusive aspects of the public-use constraint.

In this chapter I shall attempt to provide both a theoretical justification for the taking power as well as a workable definition of its limits. I shall proceed by first showing, using the tools of law and economics, why, if the only meaningful constraint on the taking power is the requirement that the government pay the private property owner just compensation, the taking power is likely to be exercised inefficiently. Next I shall try to show that there is, nonetheless, an efficiency case for there being a taking power but one that is constrained by more than the just-compensation constraint. An important part of this demonstration—one that is, I think, conspicuously lacking in other theories of the taking power—will be an attempt to define the limits of this most extreme form of the public-use constraint. My emphasis in talking about these limits will be on providing a workable, not merely theoretically sensible, definition of the limits. I propose a second constraint on the taking power, a constraint I call the "public-good" constraint. Taken together with the just-compensation constraint, this additional constraint—a dual-constraint on the taking power—more nearly guarantees that the use of the power of eminent domain will be efficient. I shall also evaluate some alternative constraints, including a system of privatization of eminent domain, and find that none of them is as persuasive or as workable as is the dual-constraint theory. I shall then try to show the strengths and weaknesses of this theory by applying it to a well-known case in modern takings law, *Poletown*

Neighborhood Council v. City of Detroit (1981). Finally, using the dual-constraint theory, I shall discuss several recent U.S. Supreme Court cases that form the focus around which the discussion in this book is organized.

My conclusion, in brief, is this. The government's power to take private property is currently limited only by the government's duty to pay fair market value to the individual whose property has been taken. That constraint, while necessary, is not sufficient to confine the taking power to circumstances in which it is more efficient to take than not to take. An additional constraint must be imposed, and the one for which I argue restricts the government's ability to compel the sale of private property to circumstances in which the acquisition of property for the provision of a public good might be frustrated by high transaction costs. Thus, my conclusion is that the taking power will be efficiently exercised only under dual constraints, the just-compensation constraint and the public-good constraint.

2. The Dual-Constraint Theory of Governmental Taking[1]

All private property owners hold their property subject to the contingency that they may at some time be required to sell it to the government. Unlike the negotiations with a private buyer, the private property owner cannot, in general, decline to sell to the government. Nor can he insist that he or she be paid his/her reservation price for his property, that is, the price that compensates him/her for the subjective, as well as the market or objective, valuation of his/her property. The most that the private property owner who contests a compelled sale to the government can hope for is to be paid the fair market value of the property.

This is an extraordinary power, one that flies in the face of what most people take to be the near sanctity of private property rights. One of the great liberties of the English was said to be that each yeoman was so secure in the enjoyment of his property that the law would protect him if he chose not to admit the king when he came calling. But the taking power appears to make this same individual powerless to resist the king if he comes not to call but to purchase the yeoman's cottage. Clearly such an extraordinary power requires an extraordinary justification and considerable constraint against abuse.

Fears of this nearly unconstrained power in English common law[2] led the framers of the U.S. Constitution to include as part of the Fifth Amendment a duty of the federal government to pay "just compensation" when it took private property for a public use. Nearly all the states have in their constitutions imposed similar constraints on the ability of their agencies of government to take private property.[3] Despite over 200 years of litigation and commentary on this extraordinary power, there is no widely accepted justification for its existence, nor for the reasonable limits on its exercise. The remarkable cases having to do with governmental taking decided by the U.S. Supreme Court in the late 1970s and the 1980s and the extensive scholarly literature on the subject in the past decade both provide eloquent testimony to this lack of consensus.[4] The justification and limits of the taking power are still ripe for analysis.

I propose to sketch here an economic analysis of the taking power. I shall proceed in three stages. First, we shall see that if the only real restriction that exists on the taking power is that the private owner be paid just compensation, the taking power is likely to impose net social costs. Second, I shall argue that a second constraint—the public-good constraint—must be added so as to limit the use of the taking power to those circumstances in which there are likely to be net social benefits of the taking. Third, we shall compare the efficiency of this dual-constraint theory of the taking power to some alternative policies designed to correct the inefficiencies of the single-constraint theory.

2.1. The Costs of Governmental Taking

Allowing the government to compel a private property owner to sell his/her property to the government may create an economic inefficiency that can rarely be attributed to voluntary transactions: the compelled sale may move the property from a higher-valued use to a lower-valued use. A property owner who willingly sells his/her property to another is presumed to do so only if in his/her estimation he or she is thereby made better off. It follows that if a property owner is *compelled* to sell his/her property, he or she may well not be better off. Because, generally speaking, we want property to be put to its highest use, this potential inefficiency of a compelled transaction raises a serious objection to allowing the taking power at all.

To see what the inefficiency might be, consider a simple example. Suppose that Samson owns a plot of land. His ancestors have occupied that land for time out of mind so that the property has a special sentimental value to him, although it is not likely that anyone else would share that sentimental attachment. Although he has never thought about what precise monetary value he would place on this attachment, assume that a private real estate developer has recently offered Samson $100,000 for his property and that Samson has declined the offer. Further assume that the government has the power to compel Samson to sell his property to the government so long as it pays him just compensation and that "just compensation" means "fair market value." An assessor tells the government that Samson's lot is worth $105,000 on the open market.

The government, let us suppose, wishes to use Samson's land to build an access road to a new multiple-lane public highway. Without that particular parcel the access will have to be moved to a less convenient place, and the entire route of the highway may have to be altered. The government's economists calculate that the benefit of having the access at the point of Samson's land and the additional costs to its building project of moving the access elsewhere and of, perhaps, redesigning the entire route of the highway are such that it makes sense for the government to spend up to $110,000 of public funds to purchase the lot from Samson. Therefore, the government—thus far indistinguishable from a private purchaser—approaches Samson and offers to purchase his property for $110,000. If Samson accepted the offer, we would have no hesitation in concluding that, as in nearly all voluntary exchanges, both the general public (through its agent, the government) and Samson were better off after the transaction than they would be in the absence of the exchange.

Thus far, there has been no taking, that is, no compelled sale. The transaction described is no different from any other mutually beneficial voluntary exchange. Whatever monetary value Samson places on the sentimental attachment he has to the parcel is apparently less than about $5,000 (the difference between the sale price and the assessor's determination of the fair market value of the property). And we know by assumption that the value that the general public, through the government, attaches to the property is at least $110,000. The property has apparently moved from a lower-valued to a higher-valued use.

The potential inefficiency arises if Samson refuses the government's $110,000 offer, and the government then forces him to sell at that price. First, what inference can one draw from Samson's failure to accept the $110,000 offer? The most plausible inference is that the value to Samson of continuing to own the property himself is greater than the highest value that the other party anticipates from being the owner of the property.[5]

But what might we conclude if the government can compel the transaction to go through at the $105,000 figure? At first blush, we might conclude that the transaction is inefficient in the sense that it has moved property from a higher-valued (Samson's) to a lower-valued (the government's) use. While this is surely the most likely conclusion, it is not the only possible one.[6] And if this is the most likely outcome of allowing the government to compel a private owner to sell to the government at fair market value, why do we allow it to occur?

I have said that the principal reason for not allowing compelled sales to go forward is that they are very likely to move property to less valuable uses. But there are additional inefficiencies that this single constraint on the power to compel a sale may induce. First, let us briefly consider those that arise in governmental behavior.

If the government can transfer resources from private owners to itself at fair market value, this creates a strong incentive for the government *always* to acquire whatever property it may need by this means. The alternative of simply dealing at arm's length with the private owner and concluding voluntary exchanges only when both parties agree on the price and other terms of the transaction will be the exception rather than the rule. I do not mean to suggest that government agencies are motivated solely or even largely by a desire to maximize the difference between the value to them and the general public of a particular project and the cost of the property inputs necessary to complete the project. Still, this opportunity is likely to be of considerable importance in governmental decisionmaking. But maximizing profit is usually taken to be a good thing. Why would it be bad for the government to behave in that fashion with regard to property purchases? The short answer is that government decisionmaking may be distorted by the taking power away from efficiency. Because private property will have become a relatively cheaper input into public projects, there will be two distortions: one toward using more land and fewer other inputs than is optimal, and a second in which government projects appear to be cheaper, and therefore more desirable, than they ought to, with the result that there are too many public projects—that is, too many compelled sales of private property.[7]

Just as certainly, the behavior of private property owners will be adversely affected if the only constraint on the government's taking power is the requirement to pay just compensation. For the sake of analyzing this issue, let us divide private property owners into those who do not and those who do attach a subjective value above the fair market value to their property and look at the effects of taking on these separate groups.

Consider first those who attach no subjective value to the ownership of their property. Let us assume that if the government were to take their property, they would be fully compensated if they were paid the fair market value of the property plus whatever reasonable relocation costs the taking would impose.[8] Allowing the government to compel them to sell their property subject to this full compensation will have no adverse efficiency effects. That is, this class of private property owners will probably not use their property differently because of the risk of taking. What they will lose as a result of the compulsory sale to the government is the opportunity to make whatever profit they could have realized from a sale of the property at a higher price. But the conventional wisdom is that this loss does not have any efficiency consequences; rather, it simply redistributes wealth from the individual whose property has been taken to the beneficiaries of the governmental taking.

Matters are different for those who attach a subjective value to their property. For that class of individuals, governmental taking under the single constraint of just compensation imposes an efficiency loss because the single constraint leads to an increase in the amount of taking and each taking *under*compensates the private property owner.[9] If they are aware of this risk of loss of subjective value, these individuals will try to insure themselves against this loss. Market insurance for such a loss is not available, so that the individuals subject to this risk of loss will simply have to suffer the loss or take self-insuring measures, many of which may be inefficient. An example of such an inefficient self-insurance mechanism would be investing resources in lobbying the relevant governmental decisionmakers not to take one's property. In addition to all the distortions that such activity would impose on both individual and governmental decisionmaking, there are the additional costs of organizing a lobbying effort. Another form of inefficient self-insurance is avoiding physical and emotional investments in one's property that would give it a subjective value that would be lost in the event of a taking. It is likely that even partial compensation for some of these subjective losses would improve the investment decisions of individuals and those of the government.[10]

To summarize thus far, I have asserted that if the only constraint on the government's ability to take private property is that it must pay just compensation to the private owner, then there is a strong likelihood that inefficiencies will result. The greatest of these is that because the just-compensation formula excludes any subjective values that the private owner may attach to the property, the compulsory sale at fair market value may well move the property from a higher-valued to a lower-valued use. But there are additional inefficiencies if the only constraint on the taking power is that of paying the rightful owner just compensation. Governmental bodies may misbehave, for example, by using the ability to acquire property at fair market value to pay off political debts. Moreover, because of the losses of subjective value that private owners may suffer as a result of the compelled sale to the government, some private citizens may find inefficient means of insuring against the loss of this value or may forego certain attachments or improvements to their property that might result in uncompensated losses.

2.2. An Economic Justification of the Taking Power and Its Limits: A Dual-Constraint Theory of Governmental Taking

Thus far, I have suggested that if the only constraint on the taking power is a requirement to pay just compensation, then the exercise of that power is likely to impose costs on society in the form of inefficiently skewed governmental and individual decisionmaking. I now want to address the possibility that there are social benefits that the taking power confers. We shall see that there are, in fact, such benefits and that they are likely to arise in an identifiable class of situations. That there are both social costs and benefits to the taking power raises a policy design issue: are there policies besides the single constraint of paying just compensation that will constrain the taking power to those situations in which there are positive net social benefits? I shall address that issue in the following section.

Another way of looking at the question posed in this section is to ask why, with regard to the purchase of property, the government should *ever* be allowed to behave in a manner that is different from that of private persons. Couldn't we eliminate the social costs of the taking power most obviously simply by eliminating the taking power? The social costs we identified above would vanish if the government could acquire property only through the consent of the seller. But would there be other social costs—perhaps better characterized as social benefits foregone—if there were *no* circumstances in which the government could compel private parties to sell their property? This is, it seems to me, the central question to answer in trying to find a justification for the taking power.

There *is* a class of social benefits that might not accrue if the government did not have the power to compel sales at fair market value. These are transactions for the provision of a large-scale, complex public good. By this characterization I mean to designate transactions that require the simultaneous purchase by the buyer of a large number of parcels for the purpose of providing a public good. The reason that this class of transactions merits special attention is that it is extremely difficulty to complete a transaction that requires the simultaneous consent of a large number of people. Each individual owner whose consent is required to complete the transaction would very much like to be the last person with whom the purchaser must settle. If everyone else has consented and agreed to terms with the purchaser, then the last seller is in a marvelous bargaining position. In the extreme this final seller will be able to charge the purchaser a much higher price than would any of the other sellers.[11] This final seller is usually referred to in the economic literature as a "holdout," and the general problem is referred to as the "holdout problem."

Another way to characterize the holdout problem in multilateral transactions is to say that the "transaction costs" of these numerous transactions are likely to be high. The fear is that these costs of putting a multilateral transaction together may be so high as to prevent the project from being completed. Without some means of compelling all the parties to conclude a deal, an otherwise mutually beneficial transaction may not be possible. As applied to the government, these considerations suggest that there is a close connection between a multilateral exchange with its high transaction costs and the power to take private property.

What do I mean by "high transaction costs"? There are three elements of transaction costs—search costs, bargaining costs, and enforcement costs. Search costs are the costs of finding someone with whom to exchange. In the case of fungible goods or those sold in a highly competitive market, the resources expended in finding a seller or a buyer are trivial. But in the case of a unique good—for example, the only manuscript copy of Shakespeare's *Twelfth Night*—the costs of finding a seller or buyer may be large. "Bargaining" costs include the costs of concluding the transaction. When the transaction is a simple one-off exchange, as with the purchase of a diet drink, there is virtually no bargaining: one pays the posted price or does not transact. For a transaction that is complex—for example, a construction contract that will take many months or years to complete and requires a high degree of coordination among the parties—these costs may be high. Also, multilateral transactions are likely to involve high bargaining costs, as we have seen, because of the holdout (or free-rider) problem. The final element of transaction costs is enforcement cost. These are the postexchange costs of seeing that the terms of the exchange are fulfilled by both parties. Presumably these are higher the more complex the exchange, the more unique the subject of the transaction, and the more parties that are involved.

In each of the very brief examples of the elements of transaction costs the emphasis was on the *objective* characteristics of transaction costs. There are two reasons for this. First is the fact that if it is to be useful to legal decisionmakers, the notion of transaction costs must be applicable in a relatively easy way. For instance, if, as I am asserting, governmental taking ought to be associated with circumstances in which transaction costs are high, then a case-by-case investigation of the aptness of the taking power should begin with an examination of the level of transaction costs existing between the government and the private property owners involved. Second is my desire to distinguish *objective* transaction costs from what might be called *subjective* transaction costs, where the latter is taken to indicate such seeming impediments to exchange as a distaste by one party for dealing with the other. These are not really, by reference to my previous definition, costs of transacting; they are not search, bargaining, or enforcement costs per se. Rather, subjective transaction costs are really elements of the parties' utility functions. Whether society is better or worse off if someone is allowed to block a transaction because they derive utility from not dealing with the person or class of persons on the other side of the transaction is a huge question well beyond the scope of this examination of the taking power. Nonetheless, throughout the analysis here, the distinction between objective and subjective transaction costs will be maintained. I shall also maintain that an economic justification for the taking power is premised on the existence of high objective transaction costs. Subjective elements of transactions will have little role to play in what follows.

Thus far I have asserted that the presence of high (objective) transaction costs is a necessary condition for an economic justification for the taking power. But this is not a sufficient condition. This is because there are circumstances in which there may be high transaction costs but the government has little justification for compelling private property owners to sell their property to the government. Suppose, for instance, that someone wants to put together a large tract of land currently owned by tens of independent owners for the purpose of operating an amusement park. Or that a developer wants to buy all the existing interests on a large downtown block for the purposes of destroying all the existing buildings and putting up an office building on the entire block. Assume further that the transaction costs involved in assembling either of these unified parcels are high. Would anyone seriously maintain that the government would be justified in either case in taking these parcels simply because the transaction costs facing the private parties were high? Clearly there is more to an economic justification of the taking power than high transaction costs.

The final element in an economic justification of the taking power and its limits is that the government must encounter these high transaction costs in the course of assembling a parcel of property for the provision of a public good.

A public good is one that has two closely related characteristics. First, the good exhibits nonrivalrous consumption. This means that many people may simultaneously consume the good. Examples are fireworks displays, over-the-air (but no cable) radio and television signals, and national defense. Second, public goods are those for which private profit-maximizing suppliers have a difficult time excluding nonpaying consumers. Again, fireworks displays and national defense are good examples. While those goods may be valued by consumers, it is unlikely that private profit maximizers will be able to induce enough consumers to pay for them: most consumers will prefer to "free ride," that is, to enjoy the goods without paying for them. Typically, those suppliers can earn greater profit elsewhere. Because an unregulated market fails to provide a socially optimal amount of public goods, there is a strong case for the government to intervene into private decisionmaking regarding public goods to correct this "market failure." The government may generate the optimal amount of public goods by either producing the goods itself or subsidizing their private provision.

This important responsibility to provide public goods provides the missing constraint on the government's taking power. Indeed, I contend that there is a vital but little-recognized connection between this responsibility and all the puzzles that have surrounded the government's power of eminent domain. We have already seen that the requirement to pay just compensation does not sufficiently constrain this power to take to those cases where the taking is more likely than not to be efficient. If we were further to constrain the taking power so that it were to be applied only in circumstances in which the government was very likely to encounter high (objective) transaction costs in the course of its efforts to provide a public good, we should be very nearly guaranteed that the exercise of the taking power would confer net social benefits. That is, if the "public use" for which the government could take private property and pay just compensation were defined to be the provision of large, complex public goods, the taking power would likely be exercised efficiently.

There are strengths and possible weaknesses of imposing this second constraint on the taking power. The greatest strength of this dual-constraint formulation is that it is both theoretically sound and practically applicable. The soundness of the theory stems in part from the previous observation that if the only constraint on the taking power is the requirement to pay just compensation, then the power is likely to be used inefficiently. From that point we saw that what was needed was an additional constraint on the exercise of the taking power. The constraint I have proposed combines the well-known troubles associated with high transaction costs and the government's legitimate responsibility to provide public goods. With regard to applicability, this second constraint provides a straightforward benchmark against which to evaluate whether a taking was efficiently exercised: was this a situation of high (objective) transaction costs incurred in the course of the provision of a public good?

Another strength of the dual-constraint formulation is that it reasonably clearly defines the limits to the taking power. As an example, consider "quick take" statutes. The Illinois "quick-take" statute[12] permits the plaintiff-government in a taking action "at any time after the complaint has been filed and before judgment is entered in the proceeding, [to] file a written motion requesting that, immediately or at some specified later date, the plaintiff either be vested with the fee simple title (or such lesser estate, interest or easement, as may be required) to the real property, or specified portion thereof, which is the subject of proceeding, and be authorized to take possession of and use of such property." The statute applies to condemnation proceedings brought by the State of Illinois, the Illinois Toll Highway Authority, the St. Louis Metropolitan Area Airport Authority, sanitary districts in the State of Illinois, any public utility subject to the jurisdiction of the Illinois Commerce Commission, and other governmental bodies. In essence, the statute creates a two-step process in the exercise of the power of eminent domain. In the first step the state takes title to the private property before final judgment has been rendered. In the second step the court determines the level of just compensation. The government takes now and pays later. Presumably if the State of Illinois took possession under this quick-take statute but was later determined *not* to have legitimately exercised the taking power in this instance, compensation would be due the private property owner.[13] This is a powerful addition to the government's arsenal of tools for use against the private property owner. I suspect strongly that this provision enhances the general bargaining position of the government in its negotiations with private property owners. This in itself would be cause for concern, given my contention above that because the only real restriction on the exercise of the taking power is the requirement to pay just compensation, the government is likely to use that power excessively.[14] However, if the second constraint that I have proposed were to be added (and perhaps combined with a thorough airing of the appropriate level of compensation in the event that the quick-take was exercised in violation of my second constraint), then an efficiency case could be made for the quick-take statute. The gist of that case would be that the statute allowed the government to make investment and other decisions in a more timely fashion than it otherwise would. I leave the development of that case for another day. My principal point in bringing up the quick-take statute is that it raises efficiency alarms if the only constraint on the government's taking power is the requirement to pay just compensation but that it is (perhaps) an efficiency-enhancing statute if the second, public-good constraint for which I have argued further constrains governmental taking.

The addition of the public-good constraint also helps to clarify the distinction between legitimate and illegitimate takings. Briefly put, the constraint allows us to argue that neither of the following is a legitimate taking: one in a situation of high transaction costs associated with the provision of a private good and one in a situation of (possibly) low transaction costs associated with the provision of a public good. An example of the former would be the purchase of a large number of private parcels for the purpose of opening a profit-maximizing amusement park. Under the theory that I am proposing, no matter how persuasive the demonstration of high transaction costs made by the private party, the fact that there is no public good involved makes the setting an inappropriate one for the exercise of the taking power. The private developer should use whatever tools he or she can (e.g., option purchases and purchases through a series of buyers that masks the identity of the true buyer so as to minimize the hold-out problem) to assemble his or her lot.

This example raises a question that is worth a moment's reflection. Why not allow private parties to exercise the taking power upon demonstration to the government that the benefits of their taking the property at fair market value rather than at each owner's reservation price exceed the costs of this action? (The costs would principally be the lost subjective value of the private property owners.) Should we allow assignment to private parties of the taking power upon a demonstration that the net social benefits of a private taking are positive? My answer is no, we should not. The short reason is that private negotiations are the best tool of which we know to make relative valuations (e.g., of whether the property at issue here is more valuable to its current owners or consolidated in the hands of another private owner). We should adopt other methods only where there is a compelling reason for so doing—for example, the provision of public goods. There is a fairness or distributive justice question at issue here, too. I shall address this matter more fully in my discussion of the *Poletown* case.

As an example of the second limiting point noted above, consider the government's seeking to acquire title to a single piece of private property for the provision of a public good. One can imagine two variants on this situation, either of which allows me to make a qualification to my proposal for a public-good constraint. First, the public good is a large one, say, an airport, but the large amount of property that is required for the government to provide the airport is in the hands of one person. Should the taking power be exercisable against that single owner? If the (objective) transaction costs are not large, the answer is no. There are only two parties involved, and that fact would seem to argue that transaction costs are low. But there may be an additional complication that necessitates a qualification on the constraint that I am proposing. Suppose that despite the fact that there are only two parties involved, the private property owner is, in essence, a monopolist. This might be the case if his property is the only one suitable for the airport that the government wants to build. One might treat this as a variant on my high transaction costs position—on the grounds that the private seller's monopsony position creates high transaction costs—or as a separate class of cases in which the taking power is legitimately exercised.

The second variant on the situation of (possibly) low transaction costs associated with the provision of a public good has to do with the government's incremental addition to an already existing public good. Suppose that a local government wants to add a playground adjacent to a public school or to expand an existing public park and that to do so involves the purchase of only a few parcels. The question that this situation poses is whether the small number of purchases involved presents a situation of such low transaction costs that the government should not be allowed to exercise the taking power, despite the acquisition's being done pursuant to the provision of a public good. Should, rather, the government be required in this setting of low transaction costs to deal at arm's length with the private property owner? The answer to this question is not obvious. As in the previous example, the private property owner may be a monopolist, what is sometimes referred to as a "situational" monopolist.[15] If, for example, the setting of the public school and the public park are such that there is only one direction and therefore one lot into which expansion may be made, then the monopoly position of the private property owner may make out a strong case for the governmental exercise of its taking power. On the other hand, if the playground or public park could conceivably expand in any or several directions, then there may be sufficient competition among the potential sellers that the transaction costs of the government's successfully completing the expansion of its public good are low, and, therefore, there is no need for the government to exercise its taking power.

While I believe that the addition of a public-good constraint defined as I have proposed helps to answer many of the puzzles that have surrounded the exercise of the taking power, I do not believe that this addition clearly answers *all* the questions. Let me here suggest some of those questions that deserve, I believe, closer attention under the dual-constraint theory. First, there is the matter of regulatory takings. This is so important a qualification of my theory that I will devote an entire section to it below. Second, I mentioned above that private parties, when faced with a situation of high transaction costs arising from the presence of many sellers whose unanimous consent must be had for the completion of a large private project, frequently employ option purchases and blind purchases through intermediaries as means of minimizing the frustrations of the holdout problem. Why shouldn't the government do the same? My intuition is that there is something to be said against the government's behaving in the secret fashion that this method of putting together large parcels would require. There is a strong sense in our system that the government's actions should routinely be open and above board, and that secrecy should be a rare exception. Whether government purchases of land for the provision of public goods is one of those rare exceptions—and whether, therefore, the taking power ought to be scrapped in favor of the government's emulating private developers' methods for assembling large parcels—is an interesting question. I strongly suspect that more reflection on the matter would conclude that government purchases ought not to be secret and that, therefore, what is appropriate for a private purchaser is not appropriate for the government. But I grant that the question is still open. Third, there will have to be further refinement of what are sufficiently high transaction costs to justify governmental taking of private property for the provision of public goods. Fourth, there will have to be further discussion of the degree to which being a public good justifies the exercise of governmental taking in its provision. "Pure" public goods are almost as rare as pure or perfect competition. Many goods and services are "mixed" goods in that they are intermediate between pure public and pure private goods. For instance, elementary education is a mixed good, and the supply of elementary education reflects this mixture. There are both public and private elementary schools. Could it be argued that a private school is providing, in part, a public good and should, therefore, be allowed to exercise the power of eminent domain? Or could it be argued that the public schools are public only by historical accident, not for reasons of economic theory, and that, therefore, they, like other essentially private parties, ought not to be allowed to exercise the taking power? Fifth, there is the question of the circumstances in which the efficient use of the taking power would be advanced by the government's assigning that power to private parties such as public utilities.[16] To the extent that public utilities are providing a public good and that their land acquisition for that purpose is attended by high transaction costs, the taking power ought clearly to be delegated to them. There is the related question of whether the taking power can ever be efficiently assigned to a private party that is not a public utility. The theory I am propounding would seem to suggest that the answer is yes, when the private party is engaged in providing a public good and there are high transaction costs associated with the acquisition of land for that provision. Sixth, and finally, how might the considerations of efficiency on which I have focused be tempered by a consideration of issues of distributive justice? While fairness and justice are tremendously important constraints on the taking power, they are beyond my explicit subject matter in this chapter. Nonetheless, we shall return to a brief discuss of fairness in our discussion of both the *Poletown* case and *Hawaii Housing Authority v. Midkiff* (1984).

2.3. A Summary of the Dual-Constraint Theory

We have reached two conclusions thus far. First, if the only constraint on the taking power is the requirement of paying just compensation, the exercise of the taking power is likely to impose considerable net social costs. But second, if the government confines its use of the taking power to situations involving high transaction costs associated with the provision of a public good, the exercise of the taking power is likely to confer substantial social benefits. I conclude that the taking power will be efficiently used when that power is exercised under two constraints: (1) the taking is for the purpose of prividing a public good and the transaction costs of acquiring the property for the provision of that public good are high, and (2) the government compensates the private property owner by paying him/her the fair market value of the property taken.

2.4. Alternative Correctives

In this section I want to investigate any alternative constraints on the taking power that would confine its exercise to circumstances in which there are net social benefits from a compulsory sale of private property. I shall consider three alternative correctives: (1) super-compensation for taking (a requirement that the government pay not just fair market value plus relocation costs but that amount plus, say, 25 percent); (2) creating a mechanism for allowing the individual property owner to present a case that he or she would lose subjective value in the event of taking, leading to full compensation of that lost subjective value; and, finally, (3) the privatization of eminent domain. My conclusion will be that each of the first two alternatives is flawed by comparison to the dual-constraint theory and that, despite its great attractions, there are still many questions about how to operate the privatization theory and about its political acceptability.

2.4.1. Super-compensation. One alternative to the suggestion for imposing a public-good constraint on the exercise of the taking power is to change the method of determining compensation for the private party whose property has been taken. If the contention is that the single constraint of paying fair market value is insufficient to deter inefficient taking, then perhaps the appropriate corrective is to define just compensation to be equal to something more than fair market value (plus reasonable relocation costs). For example, suppose that the government retained the power to compel a private party to sell his or her property to the government but that the owner were entitled to receive 125 percent of the fair market value of that property. How would that alternative compare to the single constraint of fair market value and to the dual constraint I have proposed?

Arguably, the requirement of super-compensation leads to greater efficiency than the simple requirement of paying fair market value. The greatest shortcoming of the single constraint is that it tends to under-compensate private property owners for any subjective value they attach to the continued ownership of their property and, therefore, causes both the government and those private parties to behave inefficiently. Paying 25 percent more than fair market value has the virtue of more efficiently compensating those property owners who have a subjective value associated with continued ownership. To that extent the government is more efficiently constrained in its use of the taking power, and private property owners, being more nearly completely compensated under the 125 percent formula, feel less necessity to take inefficient self-insurance actions to protect against a loss of subjective value when their property is taken.

However, super-compensation is not unambiguously better than the payment of fair market value. This is because a blanket requirement of paying 125 percent of fair market value plus reasonable relocation costs *over*compensates those whose reservation price is equal to their property's fair market value. This creates a moral hazard problem.[17] For some private property owners, having their property taken now becomes better than continued ownership or sale to another private party, and this fact may induce those owners to expend resources in attempting to acquire property that is likely to be taken. Suppose, for instance, that the super-compensation plan is in place and the government announces that it will build a new courthouse somewhere in the downtown area. This could set off a scramble for ownership claims in that area in an effort to be the recipient of super-compensation in the event that one has guessed right about the parcels that will be taken for the provision of the new courthouse. Moreover, depending on how fair market value is determined—is it simply the most recent price at which the property voluntarily changed hands?—super-compensation could lead to a frenzied inflation in real estate prices in the hopes of realizing an immediate 25 percent gain if the property is taken.

Another obvious shortcoming of this proposal is the determination of the appropriate premium over fair market value. I assumed a 25 percent premium, but there is no reason to believe that figure is the optimal one. It is conceivable that a more thorough analysis could suggest a figure that minimizes the moral hazard problem for those with no or little subject value while more nearly compensating those who do have a subjective value attached to ownership, but I am skeptical.

These problems with the blanket super-compensation corrective are considerable and make this alternative, despite its initial attractions, less satisfying than one might have thought.

2.4.2. Allowing a Demonstration of Loss of Subjective Value. The problem with the previous proposal was its universal character: *all* property when taken was entitled to super-compensation, however determined. Perhaps a better idea is to pay super-compensation only to those who can demonstrate in a formal setting a loss of subjective value from governmental taking and put a plausible dollar figure on the extent of that loss. One can imagine a special hearing designed to allow private owners to make this case in the event that their property is taken. The default level of compensation would continue to be fair market value. Presumably those whose valuation is close to fair market value would have only a modest incentive to incur whatever costs would be involved in making a showing that fair market value was undercompensatory. Only those whose subjective losses would be large if they were to be paid only fair market value have an incentive to mount such a showing. To this extent the proposal surmounts the most serious objection to the blanket super-compensation proposal: it creates an incentive-compatible mechanism for the revelation of subjective value greatly in excess of fair market value, and one may presume that this incentive is stronger, the greater the loss would be.

However, this proposal also has problems. While it reduces the incentive for inefficient gaming with respect to the taking power, it does not remove that incentive. Some property owners who do not have a large subjective valuation will attempt to persuade the tribunal that judges these matters that they would suffer greatly if only paid fair market value. The overriding reason for this is that an adversarial hearing, as this certainly would be, is an exceedingly crude method of determining subjective value. Everyone will have an incentive to manufacture such a value whether they truly have any or not. Determining which claims are genuine will not be easy. Those private owners with great histrionic talents may be highly likely to receive super-compensation whether their reservation price is the same as or much greater than fair market value.

An ex post demonstration of subjective valuation on property is extraordinarily difficult to validate. The costs that will be incurred by private parties in attempting to legitimate their claims of subjective valuation and by the government in attempting to disprove those claims could be large—so large, in fact, as to erase any social benefits that the scheme might seem to have. What would be far preferable would be a system of establishing and validating subjective valuation of property ex ante a taking. In the next section I shall discuss a method of doing just that.

2.4.3. The Privatization of Eminent Domain. In a recent intriguing article Professor Peter Colwell suggested that some of the inefficiencies associated with the taking power would vanish if the power were to be privatized.[18] Under this proposal each property owner assesses the value of his or her property for the purpose of paying property (and any other relevant) taxes. This self-assessed value determines both the amount of property tax for which the owner is liable and the price at which the property can be purchased by the government if it wants to purchase the property. The private property owner would presumably assess his or her property at a price that reflects not just its fair market value but also its subjective value, discounted by his/her estimate of the likelihood of governmental taking. In exchange for paying property taxes on this self-assessed value, the property owner would be guaranteed that this subjective valuation would be protected in the event that the property were taken.[19]

This proposal is an attractive alternative to the taking power, but it does raise some perplexing but not insurmountable problems. For instance, should the self-assessment value be held in secret between the owner and the government or should it be public information? If it is public information, should it be the case that anyone, not just the government, can take title to the property if he or she is willing to pay the declared self-assessment value? Notice that this would amount to a system of *private* taking, so that there would be little if any distinction between governmental and private taking. Allowing private taking would create a very strong incentive for private property owners to reveal the true subjective value of their property. Only if they were truthful would they be indifferent between a private or public taking and continuing to live in their property. Another question that the privatization proposal raises is how often property owners could make changes in their self-assessments. The changes cannot be made too frequently without inviting overly burdensome administrative costs. Moreover, if changes were allowed to be made too often, government property tax revenues would become highly variable. Also, private owners would be tempted to vary their self-assessments not because their underlying valuation had truly changed but because something like their estimate of the likelihood of private or public taking had changed. This is not necessarily inefficient but does deserve much closer attention than I can give it here. Finally, would there be any adverse effect of a declaration of self-assessment on the government's regulatory power?

Until these questions are adequately answered, I suspect that the self-assessment or privatization alternative is one that, despite its great attractions, lies far beyond the bounds of political possibility.

3. The Complication of Regulatory Takings[20]

In the introductory section of this chapter, I mentioned that the taking power is the most extreme policy lying along a spectrum of policies that I called collectively public-use constriants on private property ownership. I want in this section to discuss the relationship between my dual-constraint theory of the taking power and a closely related, but less intrusive, policy—land-use regulation.

The government's police power allows it to regulate the use of property in such a way as to promote the general health, welfare, safety, and morals. Zoning ordinances are an example, as are regulations forbidding building power plants on earthquake fault lines and those requiring commercial lots to set aside a percentage of their area for public parking.

Regulations do not transfer title of the property to the government, and generally they do not greatly reduce the value of the property that is being regulated. However, in some instances a regulation can so greatly reduce the value of private property as to amount to a taking.[21] Where a private property owner feels that his or her property's value has been so significantly reduced by a legitimate government regulation as to amount to a taking, he or she may bring an inverse condemnation action against the government. The purpose is to have the regulation declared a taking, in which case the government will have to compensate the owner for the fair market value of her property. If the court determines that the reduction in the value of the property is not substantial enough to amount to a taking, then the plaintiff receives no compensation for the reduction in the value of his or her property. The fact that there is no compensation owing for reductions in value owing to the imposition of a regulation but there is fair market value owing for a taking may introduce a significant complication into our analysis of the taking power. To the extent that a police power regulation and an eminent domain taking are substitute policies for achieving a given governmental goal, the government will use whichever policy is less expensive, all other things equal.

The incentives for the government to take or to regulate and for private property owners to make use of their property are likely to be affected by the courts' views on what constitutes a compensable taking. Consider a private property owner's decision to convert his residence into a commercial establishment. Assume that this conversion would be costly, would violate no existing government regulations, and is anticipated to make substantial profits for the owner. Further assume that a later change in the relevant governmental zoning ordinance might make the operation of a commercial establishment in this area illegal. The issue is whether such a regulation will be deemed a taking or not.

If the regulation is almost certain to be deemed a compensable taking, then the private investor bears no risk of loss from making the large investment in his/her property. The result is that he/she may make a larger-than-appropriate investment since any loss in value that results from a subsequent government regulation will be fully compensated. For the government a heightened risk of having to compensate more private property owners for lost values due to government regulation may have an inefficient chilling effect on the government's exercise of the police power. For instance, the government might inefficiently fail to regulate for fear of incurring large compensatory expenses.

However, if the governmental regulation is almost certain to be deemed a noncompensable regulation, then the inefficiency of the incentives are reversed. Private property owners now bear all the risk that the value of any investment they make will be lost due to a change in government regulation. As a result, private owners may become overly cautious about investment and inefficiently forego some improvements to their property. For the government the reduced risk of being held liable for compensating owners for the loss of their property due to regulation may well lead to overregulation. Certainly it will induce the government to try more assiduously to accomplish through regulatory means what might alternatively be accomplished through means of taking.

The upshot of these considerations is that policies of always compensating and of never compensating are inefficient. The optimal policy would involve a policy of sometimes compensating and sometimes not, with the dividing line between compensable and noncompensable regulatory takings being determined on a case-by-case basis according to whether the decline in the private property value was substantial.[22]

The question arises whether the introduction of the possibility of a regulatory taking affects the case above for the efficiency of the dual-constraint theory. The answer, I believe, is a qualified no. If the ability of the government to take private property were constrained by both the requirement to pay just compensation and that the taking be for the provision of a public good in a situation of high transaction costs associated with the acquisition of property, then I do not see how the government's choice of policy instrument as between a taking and a regulation affecting land use would be inefficiently biased. Quite to the contrary, my suspicion is that the choice of policy is inefficiently biased today when there is effectively only the single requirement to pay just compensation. The exact nature of that bias is a complicated issue requiring much further inquiry. However, as a first approximation I would speculate that because the only constraint on the taking power today is the requirement to pay just compensation and because that may lead to an inefficiently large amount of taking, the imposition of a second and more binding constraint will lead to less taking and, probably, an increase in the amount of land-use regulation.[23]

4. The Dual Constraint Theory Applied to the Poletown Case

One of the most widely discussed cases involving the taking power in recent years is *Poletown Neighborhood Council v. City of Detroit*, a case that came before the Michigan Supreme Court in 1981. I shall take some time to discuss this fascinating case because I believe that it illustrates the shortcomings of the just-compensation constraint theory of the taking power and the theoretical and practical strengths of the dual-constraint theory that I proposed above.

In 1980 the General Motors Corporation informed the City of Detroit that it intended to close its two Cadillac plants in the city and to move to a new manufacturing facility near Dallas. Fearing the loss of 6,000 jobs and the consequent problems of unemployment as well as the loss of related businesses and corporate income tax revenues, the City of Detroit entered into negotiations with General Motors designed to discover if there were any improvements that could be made to the current Cadillac facilities that would induce GM not to move to the Sunbelt. In addition to pointing out the inherent attractions of the Sunbelt location and the benefits that the governments in that new location were offering, GM noted the age of the Detroit facilities and the inadequacy of the freeways, streets, and sewers around the factories. The city, like many others, had established the Detroit Economic Development Corporation, a governmental organization authorized in Michigan's Economic Development Corporations Act. That act empowered the corporation to engage in planning, zoning, and other activities directed at improving the general health, safety, and welfare of the citizens of the State of Michigan by attracting and retaining industry, reversing urban blight, and fostering urban redevelopment. Among the powers that the Michigan legislature assigned to bodies like the Detroit Economic Development Corporation was the power to acquire property by condemnation. The legislature specifically meant this to cover the acquisition of industrial and commercial sites that might be taken by the Development Corporation for transfer to private parties.

The corporation induced General Motors to stay in Detroit by taking property near the Cadillac plants worth $200 million and transferring title to that property to GM for $8 million for the purpose of building a new assembly plant and of improving the freeways, streets, and sewers in the area.

The property that the city took consisted of a large number of individual homes that belonged principally to first- and second-generation Poles, who contended that they were a closely knit ethnic community. They argued that it would be impossible for them to relocate in such a way as to replicate the cohesive ethnic neighborhood that was being turned over to the General Motors Corporation. These individuals organized themselves into the Poletown Neighborhood Council and sought to block the takings.

A majority of the Michigan Supreme Court held that the takings were a legitimate application of the taking power: "The power of eminent domain is to be used in this instance primarily to accomplish the essential public purposes of alleviating unemployment and revitalizing the economic base of the community. The benefit to a private interest is merely incidental."

How would this taking have fared under the dual-constraint theory? It would not have been allowed. Recall that to pass muster under that theory the taking must occur in the course of the government's provision of a public good and that the acquisition of property for that provision encounters high transaction costs. Certainly the element of high transaction costs was present: there were apparently many individuals whose consent to sell would have to have been secured in order for General Motors to have assembled the tract on which to build the new assembly plant and the access roads and sewers. But it is impossible to discern any aspects of a public good in the use to which the government put the taken property. Continued employment for the Cadillac assembly workers, however desirable that may be, is not what an economist would call a public good, and, therefore, the taking should not have been permitted.

This conclusion may strike many as excessively harsh. Let me explain further why the fact that the taking was not for the purpose of providing a public good, even though transaction costs were high, makes out a compelling case for voiding the taking.

Stripped to its essentials, the Court in *Poletown* is saying that this taking is justified on the grounds of a balancing test: whatever the losses in subjective value to the private property owners in this cohesive ethnic neighborhood, they are offset by the benefits that accrue to the workers who continue in their jobs, the social benefits to other firms, the unemployment compensation that is not drawn out of the public fisc, and so on. This theory that the court should permit a taking if it passes this balancing test and void it otherwise is not something that the Michigan Supreme Court made up out of whole cloth. It is precisely what the single-constraint theory of the taking power recommends.

There are four strong reasons, both of efficiency and fairness, for rejecting this balancing-test implication of the single-constraint theory. First is the fact that there is no inherent limit on the taking power implied by this test. Whatever passes the test is all right. That the property has been taken from one private property owner at fair market value and conveyed to another at far below fair market value does not figure in the balancing test at all. But of course it should. Our presumption is and should be that when the parties to a transaction are private and the exchange concerns a private good, the most efficient method for determining relative valuation of that property is voluntary exchange. Only in circumstances that fall under the reasonably clear guidelines of "market failure" can a case be made for adopting some alternative method of determining relative value.

Suppose that General Motors had approached the residents of Poletown and had sought to purchase their property for the purpose of building a new assembly plant and that no voluntary exchange had taken place. What inference might we draw from that fact? Perhaps the value to the residents of staying in their neighborhood exceeded the present discounted value of GM's anticipated profits from the new plant. If so, then it was socially preferable that the property remain in the hands of the residents because they collectively valued that property more than did GM. We could even assume that the impediment to exchange here is the subjective value that the residents place on their neighborhood and that the sum of the fair market values of the residents' property is less than GM's valuation of the property. That does not change the fact that it is more efficient for the exchange not to occur.

What if the reason that the residents did not sell to GM was not their substantial subjective valuation on remaining where they were but the fact that the transaction costs of this multilateral transaction were extremely high? Under my theory that is not enough to justify the taking. My judgment is that it is better for society to forego a few of these multilateral transactions between private parties than to take a chance on extinguishing subjective value (which we do not really know ex ante), save in the case of the governmental provision of a public good.

A second reason for rejecting the balancing test justification for the taking power is that it is likely to create perverse incentive effects for the government and for private parties. Imagine the implications for the business community, the government, and private property owners of the *Poletown* decision. For the business community there is a strong incentive to attempt to get a deal from the State of Michigan that is as attractive as the one GM engineered. No doubt it would pay for a sizeable corporation to threaten to move to the Sunbelt unless the state and local governments could convey similar benefits. Moreover, why after *Poletown* should a private corporation ever bother to deal at arm's length with private property owners to acquire their party? Those dealings might well be perceived by all involved to be a sham. Private property owners might well infer from *Poletown* that there is not much point in resisting the overtures made by a private corporation for the purchase of one's property; eventually that corporation can appeal to the government to compel one to sell; why not cut one's losses and sell quickly without trying to protect one's subjective valuation? For the government's part it is difficult to see why after *Poletown* they would ever hesitate to take private property for *any* purpose.

A third reason for rejecting the balancing test is that it is grossly unfair. The beneficiaries of the taking from the members of the Poletown Neighborhood Council are the stockholders, employees, and customers of GM, and many of the taxpayers of Michigan. The costs have been largely but not exclusively imposed on the residents of Poletown, who have had to sacrifice the subjective value they attached to living in their ethnically cohesive neighborhood. I cannot imagine an argument that would justify placing a large share of the costs of retaining GM on that particular group.

The fourth and final reason that the *Poletown* holding is wrong is that there were other, far less intrusive policies available to the City of Detroit for retaining GM than taking the property of the Poletown residents. This is a vital point in my argument. Simply because the taking was not done to provide a public good does *not* mean that the goals that the Detroit Economic Development Corporation sought to achieve were illegitimate. There is absolutely no question that continued employment confers substantial social benefits, not least in the fact that the public fisc was not responsible for sizeable unemployment compensation. The relevant question is, however, the most efficient (and fairest) method for the government to achieve these legitimate goals. I have argued that it was inefficient and unfair for Detroit to reach its legitimate goal by means of exercising the taking power. If instead the City of Detroit had given GM a tax holiday for a term of years or had directly subsidized GM's production costs out of the public fisc or had issued bonds on GM's behalf or had stood as guarantor of loans for GM or had subsidized GM's (arm's length) purchase of land to build a new factory, there might have been objections, but the debate would probably have been conducted in an open forum and been adopted if the votes were there. One reason any of these alternatives would have been superior to the taking is that the costs of each of these alternative policies would have been spread among the same general citizenry that was the beneficiary of GM's staying in Detroit.

5. Recent Supreme Court Decisions and the Dual constraint Theory

The tension between the rights of the private property owner and the public use of his/her property regularly appears in actions before the U.S.

Supreme Court. While the courts have never enunciated the public-good constraint that I described above, there was at some point in the recent past a widespread but unarticulated consensus that taking should be confined to such clearly public goods as irrigation, drainage, reclamation of wetlands, highways, national, state, and local parks, and the like.[24] But this narrow range of acceptable takings expanded as the only meaningful constraint on taking was deemed to be the requirement to pay just compensation.

Predicting trends in the U.S. Supreme Court is notoriously risky. Nonetheless, I venture the view that the Rehnquist Court may represent the end of the period of expansion of the taking power and the beginning of an era in which something like the public-good constraint significantly limits the exercise of the power of eminent domain. Like any turning point the pattern is not entirely clear: there are simultaneous indications of both the era that is ending and the one that is beginning. In this section I shall first discuss one recent U.S. Supreme Court case that, like *Poletown*, seems to indicate that nearly any plausible governmental goal justifies exercise of the taking power. Then I turn to three important cases from the 1987 term of the Court that indicate a change of direction toward a much more constrained taking power.

In *Hawaii Housing Authority v. Midkiff* (1984) the U.S. Supreme Court reached a conclusion that implied that nearly any plausible government goal could justify a taking. The issue in *Midkiff* was the legitimacy of an action by the Hawaii state legislature to distribute land ownership more broadly. Because of Hawaii's early monarchy and consequent feudal land tenure system, land ownership rights in the state were concentrated in a few hands well into the late 20th century. The state and federal governments owned 49 percent of the land in Hawaii, and another 47 percent was in the hands of 72 private landowners. In the Hawaii Land Reform Act of 1967, the legislature allowed then current lessees of land to employ the Hawaii Housing Authority to take the land they rented in exchange for paying fair market value to the owners. Midkiff protested that this amounted to compelling the sale of private property not for public use but for *private* use. The Court held that the Hawaii state legislature's purpose of more broadly distributing land ownership was a valid public purpose for compelling the sale of private property.

This taking would have failed under the dual-constraint theory. There was no argument here that a multilateral transaction was required to put together a unified parcel, although it is possible that the taking could have been justified on the grounds that the private property owners were close to being a monopoly. Nor was there any attempt to argue that the purpose for which the property was taken was for the provision of a public good. The "broader ownership of land"—arguably a legitimate governmental goal—is not a public good. As in *Poletown*, if this goal justifies taking private property at fair market value, it is difficult to see what does not.

Let me reiterate the point that I made in my discussion of *Poletown*. The declared goal of the Hawaii Housing Authority and the state legislature was not an illegitimate governmental goal, although some would consider it ill-advised. There are policies other than taking that can more efficiently and less intrusively achieve that goal.

At the end of its 1987 term, the U.S. Supreme Court handed down three important decisions having to do with whether certain governmental regulations amounted to the taking of private property. The cases are important because they may mark a turning point: while the first of them seems to be a routine regulatory taking matter that breaks no new ground but rather establishes continuity with the past decisions in this area, the last two cases signal a turn away from the expansion of the public-use constraint on the rights of private property owners and a move toward the more efficient theory that I have called the dual-constraint theory.

The issue in *Keystone Bituminous Coal Association v. DeBenedictis* was whether a Pennsylvania act prohibiting coal mining that might cause subsidence damage to pre-existing buildings, dwellings, and cemeteries amounted to a taking of the private property of coal mine owners and should, therefore, be compensated. The owners contended that by requiring them to leave 50 percent of the coal beneath the threatened structures, the regulation so lowered the value of their subsurface mining rights as to amount to a taking. The Court held that the act was a legitimate regulation of public safety and that the loss of property value was not large enough to convert the regulation into a taking, principally because the act affected only 2 percent of the total holdings of the coal mine owners' association.

A different issue was at the heart of *First Evangelical Lutheran Church of Glendale v. County of Los Angeles*. The church had purchased land outside the City of Los Angeles in 1957 to operate as a camp for handicapped children and as a church retreat. In 1978 a flood destroyed the camp's building, and in response the County of Los Angeles adopted an ordinance prohibiting the construction or repair of any building in a flood protection area, which included the church's property. The church contended that this regulation denied it any use of its property and, therefore, amounted to a compensable taking. In the meantime the county rescinded the ordinance so that the issue presented to the court was whether the church was entitled to compensation for the temporary loss of the use of its property caused by the regulation. The U.S. Supreme Court held for the first time that the ordinance, though temporary, had been a compensable taking.

Finally, *Nollan v. California Coastal Commission* delivered one of the most important recent statements on the relationship between the private and public use of property. The Nollans owned property along the California coast, including the beachfront. On either side of their property was a public beach. Because the Nollans owned the beachfront, no one could pass between the public beaches without trespassing on their private property. As required by law, the Nollans applied to the California Coastal Commission for permission to build a much larger house on their property. The commission granted the permit on the condition that the Nollans allow the public an easement across their beachfront. The Nollans brought an action against the commission, contending that the easement in exchange for the building permit was a regulation that amounted to a compensable taking. The Supreme Court held that if the condition, the easement, had furthered the same legitimate regulatory purpose advanced by the requirement to seek a building permit, then it, too, would have been legitimate. Thus, for example, if the Nollans' new home would have blocked the public's view of the beach from the public highway, then the commission might legitimately have extracted from the Nollans an easement from the highway to the beach in order to allow the public to view the Nollans' beach. But the easement was not for that purpose; rather it was to allow easier access across the Nollans' property for the users of the public beaches, something completely independent of the building permit. In the Court's view this was not closely enough related to the detriment caused by the new home. The commission still remained free to advance its program of public use of the California coast by exercising its eminent domain power and paying for access easements.

The *Keystone Bituminous Coal Association* case represents the Court's bridge with the earlier era; indeed, it is striking how close the issues in that case are to those in *Mahon*. But the latter two cases break new ground. In both of them the government's restrictions on the use of private property are found, in a sense, to have gone too far. While it would be premature to proclaim these modest constraints in *First Evangelical Lutheran Church of Glendale* and in *Nollan* to be momentous, they are, I hope, the very small beginnings of a move toward the sort of constraint on the taking power for which I have here argued.

6. Summary and Conclusion

The purpose of this chapter has been to describe a theory of the taking power that both justifies the exercise of that power and prescribes its limits. Today there is only one constraint on government's power to compel a private property owner to sell his/her property: the requirement that the government pay the owner just compensation in the form of fair market value. This constraint is not enough to limit the taking power to circumstances in which the compulsory sale to the government creates net social benefits. Quite to the contrary, this single-constraint on the taking power is likely to generate net social costs and to be, therefore, inefficient. The single constraint of paying just compensation induces governmental bodies to resort to the taking power to achieve their legitimate goals when alternative public policies would be less intrusive, more efficient, and more just. To protect themselves against losses that they may suffer at the hands of these governmental bodies, private property owners may use their property in inefficient ways and may be induced to inefficiently expend considerable resources lobbying those governmental bodies not to take their property.

Efficiency in the exercise of the taking power can be restored by imposing a second, more binding constraint on its use: that a taking is justified only in circumstances in which the purpose of the taking is the provision of a public good and there are high transaction costs of acquiring the property to make that provision. If taking is limited by the dual constraints of just compensation and public-good provision, the government will exercise its power to take when there are net social benefits, and private property owners will use their property more efficiently.

Notes

1. Much of this section is drawn from Cooter and Ulen (1992, ch. 5).

2. In England there was no requirement that the private property owner be compensated if his property were taken. On the English background and constitutional debate on the takings clause of the Fifth Amendment to the U.S. Constitution, see Nowak, Rotunda, and Young (1983).

3. Most state governments have also from time to time delegated the taking power to private organizations that have a quasi-governmental function. For example, in the antebellum era state governments gave to canal and railroad companies the power to take private property as part of the grant of a corporate charter. Today nearly every public utility agency—water, natural gas, pipeline, telecommunication, sanitary sewage, and others—whether publicly or privately owned, has the power to exercise eminent domain. Later I shall discuss the efficiency aspects of the delegation of the taking power to private parties.

4. For a sample of important recent cases, see *Penn Central Transportation Co. v. City of New York* (1978), *Poletown Neighborhood Council v. City of Detroit* (1981), *San Diego Gas and Electric Co. v. City of San Diego* (1981), *Hawaii Housing Authority v. Midkiff* (1984), *First Evangelical Lutheran Church of Glendale v. County of Los Angeles* (1987), *Nollan v. California Coastal Commission* (1987), *Keystone Bituminous Coal Association v. DeBenedictis* (1987), *Hodel v. Irving* (1987), and *Pennell v. City of San Jose* (1988). I shall discuss some of these cases extensively later in the chapter. The recent scholarly literature on the taking power stems from Michelman (1967). Epstein (1985) is the most important and controversial addition. A particularly useful summary of the recent law and economics literature is contained in Farber (1990). For additional commentary see the references at the end of this chapter.

5. In this instance we may attribute the difference in value to Samson's subjective value, his sentimental attachment, to the property. Some noneconomists may have difficulty inferring the presence of subjective and possibly nonpecuniary values from the mere failure to transact, but what is the alternative explanation?

I doubt that anyone has deep qualms about accepting sentimental value arising from long family history as a likely and legitimate source of subjective value. However, there are other sources of subjective value that can and should give us pause. Suppose, for example, that Samson's failure to sell is attributable not to his family's long association with this property but rather to his detestation of the race, gender, ethnicity, sexual preference, age, or other characteristic of the potential buyer. We might be able to reach a fairly wide consensus on the fact that these are not legitimate sources of subjective value. But how, in practice, are we to distinguish between a value-enhancing failure to sell that is premised on a legitimate source of subjective value from one that is premised on an illegitimate source of subjective value? Much of the modern debate on the most appropriate antidiscrimination policy is, it seems to me, directed at finding plausible means for making this important distinction.

6. Among the other strong possibilities is that Samson attaches absolutely no subjective value to the property; he has simply made a strategic miscalculation about the price the government was prepared to pay. Perhaps the government was initially bargaining in good faith as if it were a private purchaser. (It had, by assumption, offered more than had a private real estate developer.) Possibly the government had no intention of compelling Samson to sell until he made an unreasonable demand. Perhaps at that point, considerations of time and litigation costs caused the government to conclude that it should stop negotiating in good faith and proceed to condemnation proceedings.

There can be no doubt that this sort of gaming characterizes the behavior of both the government and private property owners who are contemplating a transaction. What is not so obvious is who typically has the strategically superior position in this game. At first blush one might think that the government always has the better position in that if negotiation fails, it can always compel the private owner to sell at fair market value. But the individual owner is not so clearly outgunned. For example, the private property owner may, by such means as legal maneuvering, protracted negotiation, and appeal to powerful political friends, so delay the government's plans as to cause the government to offer a price that is considerably higher than fair market value. Many states, such as Illinois, have attempted to minimize the ability of private property owners to use these tactics by the passage of so-called "quick-take" statutes that greatly streamline the government's ability to condemn private property. I discuss the Illinois statute later in this chapter.

7. Below we shall see that there is yet another distortion in governmental behavior caused by the just-compensation constraint on the taking power: that governmental agents will be induced to use taking more than they ought by comparison to other governmental

policies for achieving similar objects. For example, suppose that the goal of the local government is to provide less congestion and more parking space downtown. This can be accomplished by the exclusive or simultaneous use of a variety of policies, for example, an ordinance requiring downtown merchants to set aside a certain fraction of their business space for parking spaces; creation of a special tax district on the downtown merchants with the new tax revenues to be used to provide more parking or increased public transport; using general tax revenues to increase public transportation; increasing parking rates downtown; or the government's taking a parcel of private property downtown for the purpose of building and operating a multiple-story parking garage. It is possible that in choosing which mix of these policies to apply that the taking option will appear more attractive than it should because the property for the parking garage can be purchased at too low a price.

8. The Uniform Relocation Assistance and Real Property Acquisition Policies Act of 1970 (42 U.S.C. §4601 *et seq.*) provides for the federal government's paying reasonable relocation costs occasioned by the federal government's taking. See also Executive Order 12630 (March 15, 1988). Most state statutes and common law interpretations also allow for relocation costs as part of just compensation.

9. By undercompensation I mean that these private property owners, unlike those in the previous paragraph, are not indifferent between having the enjoyment of their property and having the fair market value plus reasonable relocation costs. They prefer having the enjoyment of their property.

10. I discuss this possibility of partial or complete compensation for subjective losses from compulsory sales more fully below.

11. The upper limit on the amount that the final seller can command is slightly less than the purchaser's contemplated profit from the completed project and this in turn is closely related to the difference between the total revenues anticipated from selling the services of the completed project to consumers and the total amount that the purchaser has contracted to pay all the other sellers of the land parcels that must be assembled to complete the project.

12. Illinois Annotated Statutes, Chapter 110 §7–103 (1983).

13. There is an interesting question regarding the appropriate level of compensation to which the private property owner is entitled in a temporary taking of this sort. This issue of compensation for a temporary taking has not arisen in Illinois but was recently at the heart of a case before the U.S. Supreme Court, *First Evangelical Lutheran Church of Glendale v. County of Los Angeles* (1987), which I discuss below.

14. See Burrows (1989).

15. There are obviously lots of other sellers of real estate appropriate for the provision of a playground or public park but the immediate neighbors of the current school or park are situated in such a way as to be monopolists for the expansion of those *particular* public goods.

16. Recall that the Illinois quick-take statute allows public utilities regulated by the Illinois Commerce Commission to make use of the statute. More generally, the Illinois eminent domain statute as well as those of other states generally allow regulated public utilities to exercise the taking power upon application to the regulatory body.

17. Moral hazard and adverse selection are two central problems in insurance. Moral hazard refers to the inefficient behavior that makes an insurable loss more likely simply because someone has insurance. Consider someone who has just purchased a state-of-the-art car stereo system and has no insurance to cover herself against the loss of that system by theft. To the extent that her own actions can do so, she will minimize the probability of loss by always locking her car, parking it under a street light, installing a car alarm system,

avoiding parts of town where theft rates are high, and so on. After she purchases insurance against the loss of her stereo system through theft, her incentive to continue to take these precautionary measures is reduced. Why be so careful about where she parks or about arming her alarm system? Unfortunately, these actions by the insured make the insurable loss (theft of the stereo system) more likely. To reduce this perverse incentive, insurers typically require insured persons to maintain some exposure for loss by underwriting only a fraction of the loss.

18. Colwell (1990) finds the origins of the privatization proposal in the New Zealand Land and Income Tax of 1891 (dropped in 1896), self-assessment proposals made by Sun Yat-sen in early republican China, and in the work of Professor Arnold Harberger of the University of Chicago. The folk literature has it that a similar proposal was made many years ago by Professor William Vickrey. I say "folk literature" because I have never been able to find a reference to Vickrey's proposal.

19. An interesting question that I do not address in the text is what relationship there would be between the self-assessed value and compensatory damages in a private nuisance action.

20. It is worth noting here that most of the U.S. Supreme Court cases that have been examined by the other authors of this book and that I shall address below are cases about regulatory takings, not cases about takings per se.

21. See *Pennsylvania Coal Company v. Mahon* (1922) and Rose (1984).

22. This is the ambiguous rule enunciated in *Mahon* (1922). Despite the legal uncertainty that it creates, the rule is probably efficient. This is in part because it is not clear that a rule establishing a bright line reduction in value that would trigger compensation would be any better. If, for example, the rule were that a reduction in value of 35 percent attributable to a regulation was sufficient to trigger compensation up to the fair market value of the property, government actions would be focused on adopting regulations that imposed smaller costs, and private actions would be directed establishing that the loss in value was 36 percent. But there is no reason to have confidence that the 35 percent line efficiently allocates the risk of loss in property values between government and private owners. Thus, there is no reason to believe that it is an efficient use of the resources of government and private owners to try to stay within or prove violation of that line.

For alternative perspectives on the issue of regulatory takings, see Rubinfeld and Blume (1984) and Fischel and Shapiro (1989). On the historical assignment of the taking power to private parties, see Scheiber (1973).

23. The gist of my speculation here is that under the single-constraint on the taking power the relative price of taking *versus* regulation has the relative price of taking being too low, thus leading to an inefficiently high amount of taking and an inefficiently low amount of regulation. Adding the public-good constraint would raise the relative price of taking and thus lead to the same governmental goals being achieved by means of less taking and more regulation.

24. I suspect that the reason that the earlier constraint seemed more in line with the limited scope for the taking power that I outlined in the previous sections of this chapter is that there was also a consensus that the appropriate role of the government was fairly limited. With the expansion in the role of the government after the 1930s came the expansion in the instances in which the courts would allow the government to take private property.

References

Burrows, P. 1989. "Getting a Stranglehold with the Eminent Domain Clause." *International Review of Law and Economics* 9(2):129–48.

Colwell, P.F. 1990. "Privatization of Assessment, Zoning, and Eminent Domain." *ORER Letter* (University of Illinois, Office of Real Estate Research) 4(2):1–7.

Cooter, R.D., and Ulen, T.S. 1992. *Law and Economics*, 2nd ed. New York: HarperCollins.

Epstein, R. 1985. *Takings: Private Property and the Power of Eminent Domain*. Cambridge, MA: Harvard University Press.

Executive Order 12630 of March 15, 1988. "Governmental Actions and Interference with Constitutionally Protected Property Rights." *Federal Register* 53(53) (Friday, March 18, 1988):8859–8862.

Farber, D. 1990. "Economic Analysis and Just Compensation: Another View of the Cathedral?" Unpublished manuscript.

Fischel, W.A., and Shapiro, P. 1989. "A Constitutional Choice Model of Compensation for Takings." *International Review of Law and Economics* 9(2): 115–128.

Illinois Revised Statutes, Chapter 110, §7–103 (1983).

Knetsch, J. 1983. *Property Rights and Compensation: Compulsory Acquisition and Other Losses*. Toronto: Butterworth's.

Kreuger, S.J. 1989. "*Keystone Bituminous Coal Association v. DeBenedictis*: Toward Redefining Takings Law." *New York University Law Review* 64(4): 877–908.

Michelman, F. 1967. "Property, Utility, and Fairness: Comments on the Ethical Foundations of 'Just Compensation' Law." *Harvard Law Review* 80(6): 1165–1258.

Michelman, F. 1988. "Takings, 1987." *Columbia Law Review* 88(8):1600–1629.

Morosoff, N.V. 1989. "'Take' my beach, please!": *Nollan v. California Coastal Commission* and a Rational-Nexus Constitutional Analysis of Development Exactions." *Boston University Law Review* 69(4):823–876.

Nowak, J.E., Rotunda, R.D., and Young, J.N. 1983. *Constitutional Law*, 2nd ed. St. Paul: West Publishing Co.

Peterson, A.L. 1989. "The Takings Clause: In Search of Underlying Principles, Part I—A Critique of Current Takings Clause Doctrine." *California Law Review* 77(6):1299–1364.

———. 1990. "The Takings Clause: In Search of Underlying Principles, Part II—Takings as Intentional Deprivations of Property Without Moral Justification." *California Law Review* 78(1):53–162.

Rose, C.M. 1984. "*Mahon* Reconsidered: Why the Takings Issues Is Still a Muddle." *Southern California Law Review* 57(4):561–599.

Rose-Ackerman, S. 1988. "Against *Ad Hocery*: A Comment on Michelman." *Columbia Law Review* 88(8):1697–1711.

Rubinfeld, D., and Blume, L. 1984. "Compensation for Takings: An Economic Analysis." *California Law Review* 72(4):569–628.

Sax, J. 1964. "Takings and the Police Power." *Yale Law Journal* 74(1):36–76.

Scheiber, H.N. 1973. "Property Law, Expropriation, and Resource Allocation by Government: The United States, 1789–1910." *Journal of Economic History* 33(1):232–251.

Uniform Relocation Assistance and Real Property Acquisition Policies Act of 1970, 42 U.S.A. §4601 *et seq*.

CASES

First Evangelical Lutheran Church of Glendale v. County of Los Angeles, 482 U.S. 304, 107 S. Ct. 2378 (1987).

Hawaii Housing Authority v. Midkiff, 467 U.S. 229, 104 S. Ct. 2321 (1984).

Hodel v. Irving, 481 U.S. 704, 107 S. Ct. 2076 (1987).

Keystone Bituminous Coal Association v. DeBenedictis, 480 U.S. 470, 107 S. Ct. 1232 (1987).

Nollan v. California Coastal Commission, 483 U.S. 825, 107 S. Ct. 3141 (1987).

Penn Central Transportation Co. v. City of New York, 438 U.S. 104, 98 S. Ct. 2646 (1978).

Pennell v. City of San Jose, 485 U.S. 1, 108 S. Ct. 849 (1988).

Pennsylvania Coal Company v. Mahon, 260 U.S. 393, 43 S. Ct. 158 (1922).

Poletown Neighborhood Council v. City of Detroit, 304 N.W. 2d 455, 410 Mich. 616 (1981).

San Diego Gas and Electric Co. v. City of San Diego, 450 U.S. 621, 101 S. Ct 1287 (1981).

7 A CLASSICAL LIBERAL CRITIQUE OF TAKINGS LAW: A STRUGGLE BETWEEN INDIVIDUALIST AND COMMUNITARIAN NORMS

Robin Paul Malloy

1. Introduction

Law, like economics, is an evolutionary process of ongoing discourse in which new norms emerge from prior norms. It is a continuous process of dynamic change with conflict and competition between alternative conceptions of the "good," "fair," and "just" society. On this ever-changing landscape of legal evolution one needs to find a contextual foundation for critical commentary and interspection. Classical liberal theory forms the basis of my critique of law and in particular of the takings issue.

In this chapter, discussion will focus on the evolutionary trend in takings law jurisprudence. It will be argued that trends and developments in the takings law area are similar to evolutionary developments in the greater society (Malloy 1991a). In particular it will be argued that takings law jurisprudence reflects a trend toward a communitarian framework while rejecting individualist philosophy. Moreover, takings law embodies a strongly emerging trend toward statist ideology which is winning out over the classical liberal conception of natural rights. These trends and developments are important to everyone because the ideological struggles behind these trends reflect normative belief in how power and scarce resources should be allocated within society.

The first step in presenting this analysis will be to set out a definitional framework for understanding classical liberal theory as it affects both law and economics. Second, a critique of takings jurisprudence will be presented with special emphasis on a few leading cases. Finally, some concluding comments and observations will be made concerning the ideological drift toward an ever-increasing statist ideology in the legal economic discourse of American society.

2. Classical Liberal Theory—The Basic Framework

Classical liberal theory as used in this chapter refers to the philosophical tradition of Adam Smith.[1] It is a theoretical tradition that places high value on a capitalist socioeconomic organization and on the encouragement of decentralized and voluntary decisionmaking (Malloy 1988c, 1991a). The classical liberal tradition also makes the individual the key referential sign (Malloy 1990b, 1991b). This means that it is a tradition steeped in individualist philosophy. Modern-day classical liberal scholars include economist Frederich Hayek (Hayek 1952, 1960, 1973, 1976, 1979; Gray 1982) and Milton Friedman (Friedman 1962, 1983, 1984, 1987; Friedman and Friedman 1980); and I have undertaken the application of these views to law.[2]

It is important, at the outset, to understand classical liberalism as being neither a liberal or conservative political stance since those terms are frequently understood in the current American context. American liberals are basically communitarians who see a major and pervasive role for the state to play in the allocation of political power and scarce social resources. Liberals, as such, are frequently identified with the growth of the "welfare state" and typically take positions against the operation of the free marketplace, preferring that decisionmaking power be channeled through the political arena (Malloy 1990c, ch. 5). In contrast to liberals, conservatives are sometimes thought of as defenders of the marketplace and opponents of the welfare state (Malloy 1990c, ch. 4). To a classical liberal such a view of conservatives is erroneous. Conservatives in the United States tend to think very much like liberals, only they have a different set of constituents that they want to benefit by employing the power of the state in the aid of their "friends" (Malloy 1987). Conservatives tend to focus on the need for order and control whereas classical liberals understand that market theory is based on the absence of formal order and control (Malloy 1986, pp. 164–166; Malloy 1987, pp. 71–73). Classical liberals see as many problems with "conservative" government welfare programs for corporations and farmers as they do with "liberal" welfare programs for the urban poor. Classical liberals are neither liberal nor conservative in the American sense of these terms (Malloy 1986, pp. 164–166; 1987, pp. 71–73; 1990c, ch. 8).

Classical liberals share an affinity with libertarians (Malloy 1990c, chs. 7 and 8). Both philosophies share a commitment to the individual as the key referential point or baseline for analysis. Likewise, each shares a belief in the workings of the free market economy as a method of social organization. Both believe that the market economy is based on individualist philosophy and that it is the best method of social organization for the promotion of individual autonomy, liberty, and freedom. Unlike all of the other ideological approaches to legal economic analysis and discourse, only classical liberals and libertarians share a commitment to natural rights. This is a critical point to understand for natural rights discourse is the key to individualist philosophy and the rejection of statist ideology (Malloy 1990c, chs. 4–8; 1990d). Natural rights discourse involves a presumptive belief in the existence of certain individual rights that predate the emergence of the state (Epstein 1985). In other words, to believe in natural rights is to believe that there are some things which the state cannot (ought not) do to the individual. Not all rights are determined by proponents of the political process. This view, of course, has been openly rejected by proponents of critical legal studies (see Malloy 1990c, ch. 6), by liberals such as Bruce Ackerman (Malloy 1990c, ch. 5), and by conservatives such as Richard Posner (Malloy 1990c, ch. 4). The nonbelievers in natural rights all end up taking the position that the rights of an individual consist of only those rights obtained in and granted by the political process. This is of fundamental importance because it creates a presumption that the state can do whatever it wants against the individual unless the individual can carry the burden of persuading the state and the operators of state power not to act. In contrast to the anti-individualist presumption, classical liberals and libertarians employ natural rights discourse to create a presumption in favor of the individual. It is a presumption that acts as a rhetorical roadblock to the validation of state action and continually places the burden on the state to demonstrate the appropriateness of its action.

Classical liberalism and libertarianism, while similar in many respects, are nonetheless different schools of thought. Classical liberal theory, as I have explained elsewhere, is much more receptive to a broader role for government than that provided by the "minimal state" or "state of nature" rationales of libertarians (Malloy 1991a). Basically, classical liberals draw on the moral philosophy of Adam Smith to construct a notion of individual liberty that includes a conception of human dignity (Malloy 1988c, 1990a, 1990d, 1990e). By focusing on human dignity, classical liberals can advocate and justify certain limited wealth transfers that libertarians might not condone. Adam Smith first established this principle when he argued in the *Wealth of Nations* that everyone was entitled to at least a minimal education (Malloy 1988c, pp. 235–238; Smith 1976b, vol. II, pp. 302–309). He argued that a key negative consequence of industrialization was job specialization that alienated workers. In an effort to overcome this form of alienation, Smith argued that a free education was owed to all workers even if the total benefit would accrue only to the individual. Smith took this position because he felt that the mere fact that one was a human being was sufficient grounds for assuming that in a civilized society certain minimal benefits were available to everyone. Thus, a claim could be made against the wealth of others in the community so that certain minimal services could be provided to all people (Malloy 1990e).

Adam Smith did not, and the modern classical liberal does not, advocate the creation of an uncontrolled and discretionary state apparatus. To the contrary, classical liberal theory is a theory of limitations on the power and procedure by which the state should act. It does not provide an unfettered defense of laissez-faire capitalism nor does it allow arguments based on human dignity to validate the existence of an all-powerful and coercive state. Basically, as I have explained elsewhere, classical liberal theory imposes certain roadblocks on the actions of the state (Malloy 1991a). The key components of these theoretical roadblocks are (1) the state should act only when there is a market failure (example: the poor have no purchasing power by which to command the attention of private suppliers of essential services); (2) the state should only engage in activities that can be justified as related to or necessary for the protection or promotion of human dignity (example: a government subsidy to house homeless children as opposed to a subsidy to assist in the opening of a new Saks Fifth Avenue department store); and (3) the state must only act by general rules rather than by discretionary and outcome specific rules (example: establish an improved citywide infrastructure to encourage commercial activity rather than selecting a particular business for a specific and discretionary locational subsidy) (Malloy 1987, 1990e).

Understanding the basic contours of classical liberal theory is essential to appreciating the critique of takings law provided in this chapter. It is also important to comprehend economics as a symbolic and metaphorical device in the legal economic discourse of classical liberals (Malloy 1990b, 1990d, 1991b). This means that economics provides an ideal metaphor for understanding and talking about relationships in society. Economics is, after all, a discourse about the allocation of political power and scarce resources. In classical liberal theory the conversational focus is on the empowerment of the individual, spontaneous social order through decentralized decisionmaking, and the creation of wealth and promotion of liberty through the creative process of interpersonal (market) exchanges.

Classical liberal theory posits capitalism as the only form of social organization that can foster individual liberty (it is a necessary although not sufficient prerequisite) (Friedman 1962, pp. 1–22). This is because capitalism embodies the norms and values of the market metaphor and because capitalism is essential to a decentralized and counterbalancing system of power. That is, capitalism permits private control and ownership of vast amounts of power and wealth—power and wealth that are available to private individuals and groups to use as a counterbalance to the emergence of an all-too-powerful state apparatus. At the same time, classical liberalism envisions a meaningful role for government so that the state can protect individuals from the emergence of powerful monopolists, dictators, or oligopolies of power in the private sector. In this metaphorical form of social organizations the various levels and branches of government continuously interact with a variety of private parties and create a symbolic market for competing and counterbalancing power sources. And, just as this tension and competition creates benefits for consumers in consumer markets, so too do these counterbalancing power sources protect individuals in the "marketplace" of social interaction (Malloy 1988b, 1991a).

It is from this complex ideological framework that I will critique the evolution of American takings law. It is an approach that presumes that alternative ideological beliefs about political and economic organizations are important. They are important because one's ideological beliefs on these matters, be they Marxist or free market capitalist beliefs, will shape one's view of law and legal institutions. Furthermore, these beliefs will shape the structure and ultimately the content of our socially validated discourse and evolution. Because I will be focusing on the way in which law affects the allocation of power and resources in American society, I will be engaging in a legal economic discourse; and it is within the context of a classical liberal tradition that I will critique current trends in the evolution of American takings law jurisprudence.

3. Takings Law—The Leading Cases and the Evolution of Statist Ideology

In approaching the evolution of case law in this area, one must have a framework in mind for the critical evaluation of takings law jurisprudence. I have devised a three-stage framework for considering the evolution of both takings law and the development of zoning and planning law in United States. These three stages correspond to approaches I call (1) laissez-faire, (2) general rules, and (3) discretionary (Malloy 1991a, part II).

The laissez-faire stage of takings law is an approach that dominated American jurisprudence before the 20th century. I refer to it as laissez-faire because it represented a period in which preeminence was given to the protection of individual private property rights. Attitudes in this area were revealed in the stringent construction given to the takings clause provision of the Constitution. In the laissez-faire period the emphasis was on dramatically limiting the government's ability to take property from the citizenry.

In this first stage of takings law jurisprudence the restraint on government action was strong in character. In many respects this laissez-faire approach to takings law was reflective of libertarian philosophy. An example of the attempt to revise the strongly individualist norms of the laissez-faire era can be seen in the recent work of libertarian legal economist Richard Epstein of the University of Chicago Law School. Epstein's book on *Takings* is an excellent attempt to revive a libertarian conception of limited government by severely restricting government action under the takings clause (Epstein 1985). In general, by requiring compensation in most cases of government action the takings clause, under Epstein's theory, becomes a means of severely limiting government activity by making such activity too costly. Thus, like libertarian philosophy in general, the laissez-faire approach to takings law is extremely protective of the individual property rights of those that have already acquired private property (Nozik 1968; Nock 1983; Lane 1943). The acquisition of private property is seen, in libertarian theory, as the legitimate return to the output of one's labor and ability, and thus the government's uncompensated transfer of this "wealth" is by its very nature destructive of individual liberty.

Epstein's book *Takings* is an excellent example of an advocate's "brief." It advocates stringent requirements for the exercise of the police power in an effort to limit severely the ability to engage in such action. The structure of his legal economic discourse affects both the content and substance of the legal environment by placing severe burdens upon the exercise and expansion of state power. His form of discourse, therefore, provides a wide scope of protection for individuals already possessed of wealth and power. Such an approach favors the present and future validation of prior methods of acquisition and distribution of power and property. Obviously, some groups will be able to object to the validation of rules that favored prior distributions of property rights. Such groups may include women or minorities who feel that prior rules for acquisition and distribution unfairly excluded or underrepresented them. Consequently, they might reject Epstein's form of legal economic conversation and argue that present and future allocations of power and wealth should not be validated on the basis of possibly "tainted" or exploitive historical rules.

The second stage of takings law jurisprudence involves what I call the general rules approach. This approach dominated our recent past. It is an approach that attempts to strike a balance between the protection of private property rights and the needs of the community in recognition of the fact that although the key referential sign is the individual, individuals do not exist alone and isolated; they exist in community with others. Consequently, a number of wealth transfers can be undertaken by the state even though the taking diminishes the private property of particular individuals for the benefit of others (Malloy 1990e; 1991a, part I).

This general rules approach is consistent with classical liberal theory and justifies a broader scope for the exercise of the takings power than that permitted by laissez-faire or libertarian approaches. Richard Epstein in his book argues, for instance, that most wealth transfer programs employed in the United States since the New Deal are unconstitutional as impermissible takings (Epstein 1985). This conclusion is consistent with a libertarian construction of an interpretation of the takings clause. It is, however, an interpretation anchored in the ideological context of Epstein's own libertarian philosophy. A broader interpretation of the takings power can be permitted under the general rules approach of classical liberal theory. The broader interpretation can still be consistent with a concern for individual empowerment, spontaneous social order, market capitalism, and inalienable or natural rights discourse.

A general rules approach focuses on the need for counterbalancing power sources. As I explain in my book *Planning for Serfdom*, a delicate balance between the public (state) sphere and the private (capitalist/individualist) sphere is essential to the protection of individual liberty (Malloy 1991a, part I). A situation of disequilibrium between the public and private spheres of modern social organization can lead to abuse and coercive undermining of individual freedom. The theory posits a need for a strong private or capitalist sphere so that effective power exists outside the control of the state. At the same time, the state must perform the role of counterbalancing the potential abuse of power by private people or groups. Thus, the counterbalancing interplay between the public and private spheres performs the metaphorical market function of protecting individuals as a result of meaningful competition and consequently results in the greatest sphere of personal autonomy through no design or intention of any particular participant.

Important in understanding the justification of this view, in contrast to the libertarian view, is the fundamental role of human dignity in defining individual liberty. A libertarian, for instance, may argue that the homeless have no legally recognizable claim to shelter although wealthy individuals ought to be charitable and try to help the less fortunate. In contrast, the classical liberal, in the humanistic tradition of Adam Smith, might argue that there is a legally recognizable right to housing. This is because certain fundamental matters such as shelter, food, and education are essential to individual liberty and form the basis of legal economic discourse in any social organization worthy of validation (Malloy 1986, 1990a, 1991b). That is, one cannot speak of "individual liberty" in a meaningful way in the absence of assuming some minimal safeguards for human dignity. To speak of individual liberty as the mere protection of the private property rights of those that already have wealth is to validate prior distributions. These distributions may have been acquired by unfair or biased legal rules which systematically excluded or underrepresented particular individuals.

The general rules approach and classical liberal theory posit the protection of individual liberty and human dignity over the mere protection of wealth, private property, or capitalism for *their own sake*. In other words, the end-state objective of classical liberal theory is to promote individual liberty and not a particular distribution of wealth or market structure. To the extent that certain general structures seem to promote individual liberty and human dignity, then they are worthy means, but they are not ends in themselves.

The general rules approach is consistent with the philosophy of Adam Smith, Fredrich Hayek, and Milton Friedman. It basically requires government to refrain from acting by specific outcome-oriented legislation (Malloy 1987, pp. 254–258; 1991a, part I). It does not prevent government from acting but rather places restraints on the contours of acceptable action so as to prevent an all-pervasive state from becoming a powerful and coercive bully that defines all rights as merely the product of the exercise of political power. The use of general rules involves a process similar to setting up a market. Consider the stock market as an analogy. There are many rules that govern the creation of this market and the parameter by which "play" in the market occurs. However, once established by general rules applicable to all participants, it is the individual who decides whether to enter or exit and how to interact in this marketplace. The rules are established in advance and provide guidance on the generally accepted norms applicable to the activity. This conception of the general rules approach will be made more clear as I now turn to the contrasting approach of discretionary and outcome-specific state action embodied in the third and present stage of takings law jurisprudence.

The third and present stage of the takings law evolution involves a framework that I identify as the discretionary approach (Malloy 1991a, part II). This stage is dominated by a highly statist ideological conception of the community. Legal economic conversation by leading conservative, liberal, and critical voices all concur on the nonexistence of natural and inalienable rights. Rather, the rights of individuals are reconstructed as the rights of the community, thereby shifting the key referential sigh of discourse away from the individual and on to the community or group. Under the discretionary approach there are no individual rights that predate the creation or existence of the state. All rights are the product of the political process. This means that as a matter of presumption the state is always free to act against the individual unless a convincing counter-challenge can be raised. This presumption itself dramatically changes the structure of acceptable legal discourse and consequently changes the content and substance of the law.

The discretionary approach validates pervasive state action provided only that the political process confirm the necessity of action. This approach allows the state to take property subject only to rather minimal requirements that findings be made by public officials that the taking is for a public purpose. In the context of urban revitalization such an approach to takings law has been used to validate takings of private property for the use and benefit of other, more politically connected, private parties. By merely declaring that a particular private use favored by local politicians will advance vague public goals or market efficiency, the discretionary approach allows a permissive exercise of takings power (Malloy 1987).

While takings law is currently in a state of flux, the law of zoning and planning provides an easy illustration of the three stage evolutionary process just outlined (Malloy 1991a). Reviewing the evolutionary process in zoning and planning will make it easier to understand the detailed discussion of takings law cases that follows. During the early years of the country there were minimal zoning and land-use restrictions. Basically a laissez-faire attitude prevailed as people continually moved westward and exercised considerable control over the way in which they used their property. By the middle 1900s, however, a general rules approach began to dominate zoning and land-use planning. It was a process whereby planning officials made general zone categories applicable to a given community in advance of particular project requests. There were typically industrial, commercial, multifamily residential, single-family residential, and other types of general zones classifications. Having designated the general zones and elaborating on the types of permitted uses in each zone, an individual could enter, exit, or participate in the zoned marketplace as a matter of right. Recently, this general rules approach has given way to a discretionary approach. Now, modern zoning and land-use planning focuses on obtaining discretionary permission from the "state" for individuals to enter a zoning marketplace. This is accomplished through an array of special zoning districts, planned and mixed unit development guidelines, and a contractual zoning approach. Rather than being able to enter a particular zone of a community as a matter of right, discretionary zoning requires one-on-one negotiation between the "state" and the party seeking to act. The one-on-one interaction is personal, heavily discretionary, and contrary to the impersonal nature of the metaphorical marketplace. It is a statist approach that allows "expert planners" to exercise the power of the state in pursuit of specific outcome-oriented political objectives. Consistent with a disbelief in natural rights discourse, it validates the principle that no one has "as of right," or independent of the political process, the ability to pursue particular uses of private property. As I argued in *Planning for Serfdom*, this approach is destructive of the delicate balance needed between the public and private sphere and can ultimately lead to the destruction of an environment suitable for the promotion and protection of individual liberty.

With these three frameworks in mind I will now consider several leading cases on takings law. An effort will be made to critique these cases from the standpoint of an evolutionary baseline measured in terms of the three-stage approach just outlined. It is not my assertion that a cohesive and unifying theory of takings law can be constructed within this three-stage framework. Rather, may objective is to examine the degree to which takings law reflects an evolutionary drift, similar to that found in zoning and planning law, by embracing a major ideological transition in underlying norms concerning the individual, natural rights, and the marketplace.

At the outset it should be understood that my approach to constitutional law interpretation is guided by an underlying rejection of social contract theory. Unlike Richard Epstein's reliance on John Locke, I look to the philosophical work of Adam Smith (Epstein 1985, pp. vii–18; Malloy 1988c, pp. 238–240). In his work Smith rejected the notion of a social contract and argued instead for the recognition of the need for some *authority* to be in place for the resolution of conflicts and that the existence of such a referential authority and process provided special *utility* for the organization and operation of society (Malloy 1988c, pp. 238–240). This different premise is important. For, if one holds to a social contract theory, then one should feel more constrained in determining the context, intent, and meaning of that contract. Under a Smithian interpretation, however, the restraint is far less limiting. Changing norms and circumstances allow us to revise continually the original arrangement in a more generous fashion than if we were constrained by a desire to perpetuate an earlier or an "original" intention.

Against this background, we turn now to an examination of some principle "artifacts" of takings law discourse. Specifically, we consider the judicial opinions and the Executive Order described in the introductory chapter to this book. It is interesting to note at the outset that the legal artifacts included in this work are all relatively contemporary—the oldest opinion is from 1978. Likewise, none of the opinions reflects an assertion of a federal government taking other than the somewhat unique instance in *Hodel* concerning Native American peoples (*Hodel v. Irving* 1987). Rather, all the disputes gathered here are focused on state and local actions that are alleged to be takings.

As artifacts of legal culture it is important to think of Supreme Court opinions as more than just decisions rendered in the resolution of a particular dispute. These opinions map out the landscape of our collective legal memory. They are symbolic repositories of contextually related disputes, combatants, norms, values, and ideological struggles for control of the structure and consequently the content of legal economic discourse. The idea that judicial opinions serve a function as a validated form of social memory is important. The written legal memory is a much longer memory than that of political expediency. Thus, conflicts in judicial decisionmaking can move in considerably different cycles than that witnessed in the exercise of legislative, administrative, and regulatory decisionmaking. The common law's convention of following precedent means that legal discourse is often burdened with the continuation or resurrection of old ideas and norms in unrelated contexts.

The difference in "memory" in part explains why a study of zoning and planning activities by state and local governments can be critiqued on a more clear evolutionary timeline or baseline than can takings law considered by reference to judicial opinion. The judicial opinions embody the memorialization of the state and local government activity that is alleged to be a taking in violation of the U.S. Constitution. Each of the case opinions included here indicates that state and local governments are becoming increasingly bold in their efforts to assert a public right to engage in a wide scope of activity directed against the private property claims of particular individuals. Examination of the underlying state actions at issue in these cases reveals a great deal about the ideological status of private property and takings law. In the short-term memory of legislative, administrative, and regulatory action, it appears that popular trends and legal culture have shifted dramatically away from internalized restraints on state action.

When contemporary judicial opinions on takings law are considered for their legal economic value, they seem to make up a hopelessly messy web of confusing and sometimes contradictory conversation. Thus, one very clear observation about the opinions considered here is that they represent ad hoc and after-the-fact decisionmaking at its best. I say "at its best" because they are not only ad hoc and after the fact but they provide almost no clear indication of any guidelines for future application. This in itself has very serious legal and economic consequences. It makes the law less predictable and therefore more discretionary. This discretionary status of law leaves the people charged with applying the law and those charged with obeying the law with little information on how to conform their conduct. In the not-so-long run, such a state of affairs destroys the legitimacy of the law and of legal institutions operating within a given culture. Economically such a state of affairs is devastating. One of the primary functions of law is to provide a forum in which exchange, transactions, and planning can be accomplished. Such activities can only be encouraged and effectively carried out within a framework where expectations can be established and reasonably fulfilled. Destruction of this framework forces interaction to be more focused on the short term rather than long term and makes interaction less stable, more risky, and less viable.

Takings law is no exception. For instance, when I was in practice in Florida I worked in the area of commercial real estate development. Our firm always advised investors that buying vacant land and holding it for a long period of time was risky as was the purchase of older, unique, or waterfront property. There was added risk because one never knew what state and local governments would do that might substantially reduce the expected value of an investment. Not only was it difficult to predict what actions might be taken but it was also difficult to know if the action would be validated in a formal legal dispute. It soon became clear that the heart of a real estate practice was not in studying court opinions but in getting "connected" with state and local zoning and planning officials. The practice of law by personal political contact was clearly more important than reliance on impersonal market forces and appeal to mythical neutral principles of law. The shift from impersonal decisionmaking to politically personal, ad hoc, and discretionary decisionmaking is exactly the ideological shift embodied in the rejection of individualist market metaphors in the broader legal economic context.

Another theme that emerges from the particular artifacts collected for this book is one that seemingly relates to the nature of the parties involved in the dispute. In each of the included judicial opinions the majority decision, whether joined in by "conservative" or "liberal" members of the Court, reflects a distinct bias against "market players." In *Penn Central Transpotation Co. v. City of New York* (1987), *San Diego Gas and Electric Co. v. San Diego* (1981) and *Keystone Bituminous Coal Association v. DeBenedicts* (1987), and *Pennell v. San Jose* (1988), the Court rejects the claims of the aggrieved party. Not all of the cases reach this result by the same method. In *Pennell*, for example, the majority simply avoids the ultimate issue by saying the entire matter is premature for decision on the merits (*Pennell* 1988, p. 859). They seem to indicate, however, that on the merits *Pennell* would probably not fare well. As a consequence *Pennell* is left being subject to the regulation at issue and as a practical matter it is as if the Court had simply ruled against him.

Now, when I say that each of the above cases comes out against a "market player" I am referring to the fact that each plaintiff was either a major corporate actor or a representative of a group or association identified with major market power. In *Pennell* it was a tricounty association of *Landlords* that were involved in the dispute against the City of San Jose. Each of the above referenced cases focuses on the alternatives that these market players have. In *Penn Central*, for instance, the court took pains to point out that the company owned other major properties nearby that could be benefitted by the ability to transfer development rights from the Grand Central Station location (*Penn Central* 1987, pp. 2654–2655). Likewise, in *Keystone* the court seemingly dances around the fact that coal owners will lose 50 percent of their coal assets as a result of the regulation in question. The Court concludes that, as market players, these coal producers still have ample opportunities to profit from their market activity.

Similarly, *San Diego Gas* comes out against the market player. It reveals in its clearest form a major reason for the extent of regulatory-taking activity by state and local governments. In this case the City of San Diego passed an ordinance that required the Gas company to maintain a significant parcel of land as open space for public park purposes (*San Diego Gas* 1981, pp. 1289–1290).[3] In the initial undertaking the city proposed floating a bond to provide the revenue to compensate the company for the land. The bond issue was rejected by voters, but the city retained its ordinance. This case demonstrates what people active in the business have long known—government officials like to regulate away private wealth because then they don't have to justify *their* notion of the "public" good by persuading taxpayers to finance their activities. Instead, when a city like San Diego decides to go to the voters—to submit *their* idea of the public good to the public, if the outcome doesn't validate the prior determination of "expert" planners then city officials look for a way around the voters. In short, such planners reject the economic marketplace because they believe self-interested private actors don't undertake to protect enough public value. Likewise, they end up rejecting the political process, as an alternative to the market, when it too rejects *their* "expert" guidance on the determination of the public good.

In each of the above-cited cases the market players involved seem to be cloaked by the legal discourse with an implicit power to take charge of the new legal economic environment and come up with alternatives that preserve ample value despite the regulation in question. Maybe there is something lurking in the background, an unspoken view reflected in much of the American popular culture, that corporate or market players are "evil." The unexpressed assumption seems to be that they are always looking for a profit, never want to help the public, and can always and everywhere either pass additional costs on to customers or merely absorb them out of their "excess" or "windfall" profits.

In contrast to these cases, the opinions in *Hodel*, *First English*, and *Nollan*, are all favorable to the party claiming injury. The *Hodel* case involves the elimination of the power to devise private property on the part of certain Native American peoples governed by the Bureau of Indian Affairs. Native Americans, of course, have always been victimized by the descendants of white Europeans, white Europeans having based their original position of power upon their having been fortunate enough to be the first people (white people) to "discover" the new world. Consequently, any study of Native Americans will reveal that they have never really been in the "loop," so to speak, when it comes to being a market player. Even their initial ability ("permission") to own private property was restricted by limitations on their power to sell and transfer the property in an open marketplace (*Hodel* 1987, pp. 2078–2079). In contrast, whites have always enjoyed access to the marketplace. Presumably, if Native Americans had been permitted to participate in an open marketplace they would have moved toward an efficient form of property ownership. Instead of the highly fragmented ownership of property illustrated by this case, they would have consolidated the ownership in the interest of efficiency. To presume that they would not do this on their own would be to suppose that Native Americans were unlike all other people in terms of their ability to act rationally in their own self-interest. Of course, their values may lead them to take rational self-interested action that would be different from that fostered by the values of white culture. Thus, Native Americans are clearly nonmarket players, and the Court, for whatever reason, rules in favor of them by declaring that the *total elimination* of a power to devise private property (a right enjoyed for centuries by white Europeans) would be an unlawful taking (*Hodel* 1987, p. 2084).[4]

Likewise, the First English Evangelical Lutheran Church of Glendale is successful in its case. The church in *First English* is, after all, running a retreat and a recreational camp for handicapped children (*First English* 1987, p. 2381). This is certainly not the profit-seeking and self-centered activity of a major market player. In holding for the church, the Court in *First English* takes the bold step of declaring that even a temporary taking can require compensation under the Constitution (*First English* 1987, pp. 2388–2389). This move is of great significance. The Court focused on the temporary period between passing the regulation in question and the period for determining if it was in violation of the takings clause. The Court stated that it was not enough to merely rescind the regulation at a later date but that compensation for that interim or temporary taking was due. This is a powerful position because it creates a "chilling" effect on legislative, administrative, and regulatory action by telling governmental actors that their actions are not going to be costless. The dissent seemingly recognizes this chilling effect and rejects the majority view because it interferes with the liberal ideology of letting the legislative branch have a maximum degree of low-cost discretion.

Finally, in *Nollan*, the Court invalidates a local requirement that as a condition to obtaining a building permit a property owner must give an easement for beach access to the public. As in the other similar cases, the

Nollans are not market players. The majority in *Nollan* tries to return substance to the requirement that there be a nexus between a stated public purpose for a regulatory taking and the *merits* of the state assertion (*Nollan* 1987, pp. 3147–3150). In other words, the mere statement that a public purpose is being served by a particular regulation is not enough. This nexus must at least be arguably persuasive, and in *Nollan* the Court found it lacking in persuasiveness because the access easement did not assure the uninterrupted view and other objectives asserted for support of the regulation.

Having briefly touched on each of the selected cases, I now turn to an examination of Executive Order 12630 of March 15, 1988, issued by then President Ronald Reagan (Executive Order 1988). The order is of greatest value for what it represents or reflects of the Reagan presidency. A document of rhetorical power and very little substance, it has no binding effect in Court; it states that it creates no rights in any individual (§6). Furthermore, it is a document that rejects the libertarian and classical liberal concept of private property by failing to recognize any inalienable or natural rights concerning private property. Instead it defines private property as "all property protected by the Just Compensation Clauses of the Fifth Amendment" (§26). Thus, by its very terms it submits all property to the circular arena of definition worked out by the political process. In addition, the document instructs federal officials to follow the guidelines of takings law in their efforts to "paper the files" with all the appropriate materials deemed necessary to avoid an adjudication of an unlawful takings. This is classic Reagan. Long on rhetoric and short on substance the Reagan presidency was always, as Milton Friedman argued, trapped in the tyranny of the status quo (Friedman 1984). The Reagan rhetoric was for change, private enterprise, and individualist market philosophy. The Reagan substance was not much different than that of any other political leader of our time.[5]

The Reagan presidential order is important. It places on record a nonjudicial opinion seemingly meant to give support to the efforts by some of the "conservative" members of the Supreme Court that have been trying to revise the takings clause as a tool for limiting the power of government. There is a difference, however, between this presidential order and a court opinion. The order is in the sphere of political expediency and short-term collective memory. It represents a temporary rhetorical effort to strike out a theme identified with the president—a theme of freeing the "little guy" from the clutches of the state. Reagan never really accomplished this goal and perhaps never even believed in it. What counted was the thematic importance of the image for the moment.

In contrast to the Reagan order, recent Supreme Court opinions reveal real underlying ideological conflicts between the justices. These ideological conflicts are linked to the nature of long-term memory in the law. Out of context, in a changing context, sometimes abstracted from all context, the various justices seem to sift through the landscape of prior artifacts in an effort to resurrect or deconstruct any variety of argument. This intellectual struggle reflects a much deeper social conflict than any represented by a nonbinding presidential order. These judicial opinions make us confront the long evolutionary history of our cultural norms and values. They constantly force us to reexamine our social history and our communal memory, and this can cause social dissonance and unease. I believe that this unease is a symptom or symbol of our transition to a highly statist society with little regard for individualist philosophy, natural rights, or free market capitalism.

Our legislative, administrative, and regulatory actors have been very much on course with an expansive program for a more discretionary, personal, and political society centered around communitarian values and the denial of natural and inalienable rights (Malloy 1991a). The Court, on the other hand, with its institutionalized long-term memory seems to be lagging behind in the transformation of values. The Court seems to be playing out the last stages of a struggle over the ascendancy of a new set of social norms. This struggle, while providing little guidance on the takings issue, may be valuable in buying time for a resurgence of belief in competing values that support the individualist and market players. Conflict between the justices is focused on nonmarket players. This reveals a lack of judicial understanding concerning the importance of private capital in maintaining a free society based on a system of counterbalancing sources of private and public powers. These opinions accept a statist notion that the important focal point for checks and balances is *within* the branches of government. Thus, they fail to perceive that the most important check in our system of checks and balances is our capitalist system of private property and market activity (Malloy 1991a, part I).

4. Conclusion

Economics is a form of discourse, a way of talking about relationships. Law and economics is a method of addressing the division and allocation of political and economic power by means of law, legal institutions, and legal culture. In this chapter I have attempted to provide the reader with the general framework from which a classical liberal might approach the legal economic discourse of takings law jurisprudence. While I am by no means satisfied that I resolved any pressing social problems by my work in this chapter, I am nonetheless confident that a number of important insights work their way in and out of my discussion. It is my hope that some of these insights will strike readers as creatively interesting and that they might invoke some new and creative response in the reader.

In the end, however, it is clear that cases under discussion in this work concern themselves with more than the interpretation of a particular provision of the U.S. Constitution. These cases reflect a broader ideological struggle over the ascendancy of competing and often times conflicting views of the good and just society. They discuss certain actors and certain activities in a particular conversational form. And form is important because *form is substance* in that alternative forms of conversation result in the promotion of different values. Consequently, as microcosmic illustrations of much grander problems, these cases serve as silhouettes of the struggle over competing *legal and economic* forms of discourse. This competition between forms of discourse, like competition in the commercial marketplace, is a spontaneous and dynamic process fueling the evolutionary development of law and society.

Notes

1. For a discussion of this tradition, see (Malloy 1988a; Smith 1976a, 1976b, 1978, 1980). See also (Malloy 1990e; Malloy and Evensky, forthcoming).
2. See Malloy and Evensky (forthcoming) and Malloy (1986, 1987, 1988b, 1988c, 1990a, 1990c, 1990d, 1990e, 1991a, 1991b).
3. In this case the Court avoids a decision by holding that the matter appealed was not a final judgment (*San Diego Gas* 1981, p. 1294).
4. As the Court states: "In one form or another, the right to pass on property—to one's family in particular—has been part of the Anglo-American legal system since feudal times" (*Hodel* 1987, p. 2083).
5. See also Malloy (1987, pp. 104–108), arguing that the statist idealogy of New Federalism is little different than that of the New Deal. New Federalism seeks to shift power from one constituency (liberal Democratic politics) to another (conservative Republican politics), but neither program really focuses on reducing the coercive power of the state viz-a-viz the individual.

References

Epstein, R. 1985. *Takings: Private Property and the Power of Eminent Domain.* Cambridge, MA: Harvard University Press.

Friedman, M. 1983. *Bright Promises, Dismal Performance*, ed. W. Allen. New York: Harcourt Brace Jovanovich.

———. 1984. *Tyranny of the Status Quo*. New York: Harcourt Brace Jovanovich.

———. 1987. "Free Markets and Free Speech." *Harvard Journal of Law and Public Policy* 10(1):1–9.

Friedman, M., and Friedman, R. 1962. *Capitalism and Freedom*. Chicago: University of Chicago Press.

———. 1980. *Free to Choose*. New York: Harcourt Brace Jovanovich.

Gray, John N, Gray. 1982. "F.A. Hayek and the Rebirth of Classical Liberalism." *Literature of Liberty* 5:19–68.

Hayek, F. 1944. *The Road to Serfdom*. Chicago: University of Chicago Press.

———. 1952. *The Counter-Revolutions of Science—Studies on the Abuse of Reason*. Indianapolis: Liberty Press.

———. 1960. *The Constitution of Liberty*. Chicago: University of Chicago Press.

———. 1973. *Law, Legislation and Liberty: Rules and Order*. Chicago: University of Chicago Press.

———. 1976. *The Mirage of Social Justice*. Chicago: University of Chicago Press.

———. 1979. *The Political Order of a Free People*. Chicago: University of Chicago Press.

Lane, R. 1943. *The Discovery Of Freedom—Man's Struggle Against Authority*. New York: Laissez Fair Books, The John Day Co.

Malloy, R. 1986. "Equating Human Rights and Property Rights—The Need for Moral Judgment in an Economic Analysis of Law and Social Policy. *Ohio State Law Journal* 47(1): 163–177.

———. 1987. "The Political Economy of Co-financing America's Urban Renaissance." *Vanderbilt Law Review* 40(1):67–134.

———. 1988a. "The Merits of the Smithian Critique: A Final Word on Smith and Posner." *Kansas Law Review* 36(2):267–274.

———. 1988b. "Market Philosophy in the Legal Tension Between Children's Autonomy and Parental Authority." *Indiana Law Review* 21(4):889–900.

———. 1988c. "Invisible Hand or Sleight of Hand? Adam Smith, Richard Posner and the Philosophy of Law and Economics." *Kansas Law Review* 36(2):209–259.

———. 1990a. "Is Law and Economics Moral? Humanistic Economics and a Classical Liberal Critique of Posner's Economic Analysis. *Valparaiso University Law Review* 24(2):147–161.

———. 1990b. "A Sign of the Times—Law and Semiotics." *Tulane Law Review* 65(1):211–219.

———. 1990c. *Law and Economics: A Comparative Approach to Theory and Practice*. St. Paul, MN: West.

———. 1990d. "The Limits of "Science" in Legal Discourse." *Valparaiso University Law Review* 24(2):175–184.

———. 1990e. "Of Icons, Metaphors and Private Property—the Recognition of "Welfare" Claims in the Philosophy of Adam Smith." In *Law and Semiotics*, vol. III, ed. R. Kevelson. New York: Plenum.

———. 1991a. *Planning for Serfdom: Legal Economic Discourse and Downtown Development*. Philadelphia: University of Pennsylvania Press.

———. 1991b. "Towards a New Discourse of Law and Economics." *Syracuse Law Review* 42:27–73.

Malloy, R., and Evensky, J. Forthcoming. *Adam Smith and the Philosophy of Law and Economics*. Boston: Kluwer Academic Publishers.

Nock, A. 1983. *Our Enemy, the State*. Delevan, WI: Hallberg Publishing.

Nozik, R. 1968. *Anarchy, State and Utopia*. New York: Basic Books.

Smith, A. 1976a. *The Theory of Moral Sentiments*, ed. E. West. Indianapolis: Liberty Press.

———. 1976b. *The Wealth of Nations*, ed. E. Cannon. Chicago: University of Chicago Press.

———. 1978. *Lectures on Jurisprudence*, eds. R. Meek, D. Raphael, and L. Stein. Indianapolis: Liberty Press.

———. 1980. *Essays and Philosophical Subjects*, ed. W.P.D. Wightman. Indianapolis: Liberty Press.

U.S. Executive Office of the President. 1988. Exec. Order No. 12632, "Government Actions and Interference with Constitutionally Protected Property Rights." *Federal Register* 53 (March):8859–8862.

CASES

First English Evangelical Lutheran Church of Glendale V. City of Los Angeles, 107 S. Ct. 2378 (1987).

Hodel v. Irving, 107 S. Ct. 2076 (1987).

Keystone Bituminous Coal Association v. DeBenedictis, 107 S. Ct. 1232 (1987).

Nollan v. California Coastal Commission, 107 S. Ct. 3141 (1987).

Penn Central Transpartation Co. v. City l New York, 90 S. Ct. 2646 (1987).

Pennell v. San Jose, 108 S. Ct. 849 (1988).

San Diego Gas and Electric Co. v. San Diego, 101 S. Ct. 1287 (1981).

Index